Guide to
International Human Rights Practice

Guide to International Human Rights Practice

edited for
The International Human Rights
Law Group
by

Hurst Hannum

MACMILLAN PRESS
LONDON

Published by
THE MACMILLAN PRESS LTD
London and Basingstoke
Companies and representatives
throughout the world

ISBN 0-333-37076-7

Printed in the United States of America
by Edwards Brothers, Inc., Ann Arbor, Michigan.

Someone must have traduced Joseph K., for without having done any-thing wrong he was arrested one fine morning. . . .

Who could these men be? What were they talking about? What authority could they represent? K. lived in a country with a legal constitution, there was universal peace, all the laws were in force; who dared seize him in his own dwelling?

. . . "What are your papers to us?" cried the tall warder. . . . "We are humble subordinates who can scarcely find our way through a legal doc-ument and have nothing to do with your case except to stand guard over you for ten hours a day and draw our pay for it. That's all we are, but we're quite capable of grasping the fact that the high authorities we serve, before they would order such an arrest as this, must be quite well in-formed about the reasons for the arrest and the person of the prisoner. There can be no mistake about that. Our officials, so far as I know them, and I know only the lowest grades among them, never go hunting for crime in the populace, but, as the Law decrees, are drawn toward the guilty and must then send out us warders. That is the Law. How could there be a mistake in that?"

Franz Kafka, The Trial

It is essential, if man is not to be compelled to have recourse, as a last resort, to rebellion against tyranny and oppression, that human rights should be protected by the rule of law. . . .

Universal Declaration of Human Rights

Contents

PART IV
Domestic or National Remedies

APPENDIXES

Foreword

The International Human Rights Law Group was established in September 1978 by the Procedural Aspects of International Law Institute, an organization of distinguished lawyers and scholars that has consultative status with the United Nations (Economic and Social Council—ECOSOC). With the assistance of funding from the Ford Foundation and the Rockefeller Brothers Fund and through membership contributions, the Law Group has become a legal resource center providing information and professional assistance to help remedy human rights violations. This expertise is provided on a *pro bono* basis to nongovernmental organizations and to individuals. In addition to its own professional staff, the Law Group is assisted by attorneys who volunteer their services on particular cases and projects.

The Law Group has assisted numerous organizations and individuals in filing petitions before international and regional bodies concerned with the protection of human rights. In the course of this work, and especially in preparing materials for a Law Group seminar series, "The Nuts and Bolts of Practicing International Human Rights Law," we realized that there is a critical need for a publication which describes all the major human rights procedures in one understandable, comprehensive, and practice-oriented package. This book is designed to respond to that need and to assist lawyers, nongovernmental organizations, and individuals in identifying, selecting, and effectively using the growing number of procedures available to redress violations of human rights.

We are deeply indebted to a man of great vision and perseverance, Sidney Liskofsky, who assisted the Law Group in obtaining initial funding for this guide from the Jacob Blaustein Institute for Human Rights. Without his encouragement and the generosity of the Institute, the guide would still be in the planning stage. Special thanks go as well to Shepard Forman for the very generous contribution of the Ford Foundation, which sustained the project and enabled us to complete the manuscript.

The numerous experts who contributed to the guide deserve special praise for their faith in the project, their patience (those with timely submissions), and their persistence (those with tardy submissions). We are grateful for the factual information, insight, and years of expertise they so willingly shared with us. Their labors, of course, would have come to nothing without the support of Amy Novick, my assistant at the Law Group, Rosamund Timberg, Lesley Turner, and others who worked closely with the editor in transforming drafts to typed manuscripts.

A special debt of gratitude is owed to Hurst Hannum, the quintessential international human rights advocate, for the liberal use of his very special talents in editing an unwieldy and difficult manuscript. And finally, the creator of the guide and the Law Group deserves special mention, as without Richard B. Lillich's creativity, persistence, and support, the Law Group would not have been able to make this contribution to the promotion of human rights law.

AMY YOUNG-ANAWATY
Executive Director
International Human Rights Law Group

Introduction

To say that human rights have come of age is perhaps to underestimate the maturity of such institutions as the International Labor Organization (ILO), International Committee of the Red Cross, and European Commission of Human Rights, all of which became active and successful well before the surge of interest in international human rights that became noticeable in the mid-1970s. Nevertheless, the past decade has witnessed a marked increase in both nongovernmental and, more importantly, governmental interest in and concern for the promotion and protection of human rights.

Following the debut of ECOSOC's "1503 procedure" in 1971, the agreement on Basket Three of the Helsinki Accord in 1975, the coming into force of the two International Covenants in 1976, adoption of the UNESCO individual complaint procedure and the coming into force of the American Convention on Human Rights in 1978, and the adoption by the Organization of African States of the African Charter on Human and Peoples' Rights in 1981, one can state with some assurance that we have passed from an era of international standard-setting to an era when real implementation of international procedures will become the focus of nongovernmental organizations (NGOs), individuals, and (one hopes) governments.

The purpose of this book is to encourage and to assist in this process of implementation. Its design is not merely to expose existing procedures to an interested public, but rather to analyze these procedures and to suggest practical steps that practitioners might take to utilize them successfully. Indeed, one important issue is to determine what constitutes success, and the answer to that question will influence the procedure chosen.

The majority of the contributors to this guide are lawyers, and the material has been organized and edited from an avowedly legal perspective. Law and "merely" legal victories do not guarantee respect for human rights (although in the European context, for example, decisions of the European Commission and Court on individual cases certainly carry sufficient political clout to ensure their effective implementation by the states concerned).

Yet if the goal of the human rights advocate is to advance the cause of human rights, actually to improve the situation of real people, then effective use of the rules and procedures outlined in this guide—international "laws" in a broad sense—is essential. The key is "advocacy," and within the context of existing international human rights machinery the logical, well-substantiated, procedurally correct approach utilized by able lawyers is the one most likely to lead to success.

Put simply, one needs to know the rules of the game in order to decide whether or not to play. Knowing the rules also implies an ability to gauge the prospects of success, the outlay of resources required, and the response of the government if a favorable result is achieved. One should also be able to integrate the use of international procedures with other techniques of promoting human rights, such as political pressure, education, and publicity.

Although the fact that one has engaged international procedures in a relatively formal attempt to prevent human rights violations can and should be exploited where appropriate as part of a wider campaign against such violations, the time is passed when merely filing a complaint constituted a sufficiently unusual event to receive publicity and support other activities. The procedures themselves need to be developed through the presentation of well-documented cases that will enable the various human rights bodies to make decisions based, insofar as possible, on sound legal arguments and at least relatively certain facts.

Of course, this emphasis on good "lawyering" assumes that the procedures *do* make a difference, that they do contribute to the promotion and protection of human rights. While this is not a premise that should be accepted blindly, a sort of skeptical faith in the potential of international mechanisms is necessary.

It is often impossible to establish a direct causal relationship between most human rights procedures and specific improvement in the human rights situation in any country. Most allegations of large-scale human rights violations are accompanied by other political initiatives that seek to improve the situation, whereas individual complaints may lead to informal negotiations with a government in order to resolve the issue in a way that will not directly involve an international decision. In most cases, the procedures described in this guide are only an adjunct to many other forms of pressure on a violating government; unlike such other pressures, however, international investigations may be set in a relatively neutral context, thus enabling a government to respond to the findings or opinions of an international body without appearing to bow under political pressure.

Did the rate of disappearances in Argentina decline in the early 1980s because of the continuing publicity directed against the Argentine government, or does the decline merely signify that repression need not continue forever at the same rate in order to be effective? Did the British government finally institute reforms in the late 1970s for the protection of detainees during interrogation in Northern Ireland as a result of cases brought before the European Commission of Human Rights or because of unrelated political developments? While no answer can be definitive, it is reasonable to suggest that the "legal" issues raised and battles fought in UN, Organization of American States (OAS), and Council of Europe forums did contribute to pressures on Argentina and the United Kingdom, respectively, to end violations that were egregious and clearly within the government's control. There also can be no doubt that the increasing political importance of human rights concerns (at both the governmental and nongovernmental levels) made it easier for those who eventually toppled repressive regimes in, for example, Iran, Nicaragua, and Uganda and provided an added impetus to strengthen or reestablish democratic traditions in the Dominican Republic, Nigeria, and Peru.

With these last examples, we touch on an important factor that is too often overlooked by those who denigrate international solutions to human rights problems: the encouragement and support provided by international initiatives to purely domestic movements for greater and more equitable participation in the political and economic life of a country. Questions are often raised as to whether focusing on human rights violations helps or hurts such human rights monitors as the members of Charter 77 and the Moscow Helsinki Watch Committee, but the message that is almost always received from such activists is to continue international efforts to bring attention to violations.

Use of the procedures described in this book certainly will not guarantee an amelioration of human rights in any country. Assessing the value of these procedures in a given context should be based on realistic expectations and not on a misplaced belief that law will always (or often) succeed where politics have failed. At the same time, however, governments must be held accountable for their words as well as their actions, and hypocritical mouthing of human rights principles while no effort is made to end violations should be highlighted by the human rights activist.

Although one can legitimately question the motives or sincerity of some countries' human rights initiatives, this does not obscure the fact that human rights are now generally accepted as a legitimate subject of international concern. Governments still occasionally raise the hoary specter of nonintervention in internal affairs as a weak defense to outside criticism of human rights violations, but the broad scope of international institutions and instruments that now deal with human rights in a country-specific manner have effectively demolished the "domestic jurisdiction" argument. Countries of all political blocs have participated in investigations and public debates concerning South Africa, the occupied territories in the Middle East, Chile, Afghanistan, and Kampuchea, to note only some of the most obvious and formal objects of UN concern. These precedents cannot be easily dismissed by a country which seeks to avoid examination of its own human rights practices.

There is much academic debate among legal and other scholars as to whether human rights advocates are sufficiently realistic or sufficiently aware of Third World and/or socialist objections to certain "universal" human rights, such as the right to property or the extent of freedom of expression. Quite simply, those who are likely to be using this guide are not likely to be concerned with the philosophical underpinnings of their efforts to free prisoners, end torture, or participate in political and economic life. Insofar as "realism" requires acceptance of the world as it is, then we have sought to deal with the existing human rights machinery as we find it, with all its weaknesses.

Realism does require, however, a recognition that many of the procedures and techniques outlined in the present volume are innovative, and their real value in promoting human rights cannot reasonably be judged for several years. The ten years' experience under the 1503 procedure, for example, has been more disillusioning than encouraging, though few are ready to abandon it totally. The activity of the Human Rights Committee established under the International Covenant on Civil and Political Rights, on the other hand, has generally exceeded expectations, and it is possible that examination of country reports under article 40 of the Covenant will provide a meaningful forum for criticism of and assistance to countries with human rights problems.

Of course, assisting a country in resolving its human rights problems requires a willingness on the part of the state concerned to admit that its human rights record is less than perfect and to accept the legitimacy of international concern with the problems. It is clear that no country will dismantle itself—replace its single-party system or military junta, for example, or alter fundamental perceptions as to the extent of permissible public disagreement with the government—on the basis of cases or complaints brought under the procedures outlined herein. To this extent, the complaint of some Western countries that there is a double standard of human rights is justified: pressure is more likely to be brought to bear on relatively responsive governments than on those where violations are so pervasive as to render substantial change impossible.

Several responses to this imbalance are possible. First, it can never be an excuse for inaction or inattention to any human rights violation that there are worse violations elsewhere. Second, complaints to international forums that concern major or systematic violations *do* contribute to the cumulative impact of other political actions whose goal is to improve the lot of, for example, Jewish emigrants from the Soviet Union or Baha'is in Iran. Third, individuals may, in fact, be helped through these international efforts, even though the machinery utilized cannot address the larger issues that have resulted in the individual violation, as in the case of an Uruguayan citizen's being granted a passport or an East African Asian's being granted a visa to rejoin family members in the United Kingdom.

Finally, as noted above, there may be a certain legitimacy or credibility to the condemnation of a government on human rights grounds rather than on purely geopolitical grounds, which may lend support to other, more direct means of establishing a more democratic, equitable society. For instance, widespread publicity of human rights violations and support for "fundamental freedoms" may have contributed (in a minor way, to be sure) to acceptance by the international community of the overthrow of Idi Amin in Uganda, the Greek colonels, General Somoza in Nicaragua, and the Shah of Iran. It is not coincidental that criticisms of the current regimes in both Nicaragua and Iran are, in large part, based on human rights rather than on ideological grounds.

The limits on the effectiveness of international human rights law and procedures are too evident to those directly involved to require further elaboration here. Human rights cannot be guaranteed in any real sense without a resolution of major political and economic structural imbalances, both internal and international, or without answers to the problems posed by nuclear proliferation and environmental degradation that affect the entire world. International law is but one means of attacking one set of problems; we hope this book will help to make that attack more effective.

A few comments on the organization and style of this collection may be helpful. As indicated by the title, the book has been conceived as a practical guide to international human rights practice. Every attempt has been made to avoid merely presenting a disparate compilation of vaguely connected articles. While a certain amount of detail and comprehensiveness is necessary to a proper understanding of the procedures and forums discussed, there has also been a deliberate effort to avoid the heavily footnoted style of most law-review and academic-journal articles.

Given the great knowledge and conscientiousness with which the contributors approached their tasks, the editor's (only partially successful) efforts to simplify and, insofar as possible, to coordinate the various chapters inevitably resulted in the deletion of some material that, in other contexts, would certainly be relevant. Thus, the occasional omission of references and the summary nature of most of the historical material should be attributed to the editor's blue pencil rather than to any lack of completeness on the part of a contributor. Similarly, the overall style and arrangement of some chapters has been altered to give as much continuity to the works as possible, at times at the price of sacrificing an original organizational format that might have been preferable in isolation.

This being said, the opinions expressed in each contributor's chapter are his or her own, except for editorial notes clearly designated as such.

As the texts of many of the major international instruments are available elsewhere, we have decided *not* to include any documents in the present volume. A separate Documents Supplement to this guide has been prepared and is available from the International Human Rights Law Group. It includes all the major European, American, and African regional treaties; the major instruments adopted under UN auspices; and many of the less readily available UN and UNESCO resolutions and procedural texts.

Without repeating the prefatory acknowledgments by the Executive Director of the International Human Rights Law Group, let me simply add my thanks to the foresight and perseverance of Amy Young-Anawaty, Richard B. Lillich, and Sidney Liskofsky for developing the concept of this book; to the Ford Foundation for making the editing of the book possible; and, most of all, to the contributors, who gave not only of their knowledge, but also of their good humor and understanding in sacrificing more than a few well-turned phrases and painfully researched paragraphs in the interests of the project as a whole.

Washington, D.C.   HURST HANNUM
November 1981

PART I

Preliminary Considerations

1
An Overview
of International Human Rights Law

RICHARD B. BILDER

The international human rights movement is based on the concept that every nation has an obligation to respect the human rights of its citizens, and that other nations and the international community have a right, and responsibility, to protest if this obligation is not lived up to. International human rights law consists of the body of international rules, procedures, and institutions developed to implement this concept and to promote respect for human rights in all countries on a worldwide basis.

While international human rights law focuses on international rules, procedures, and institutions, it typically also requires at least some knowledge of and sensitivity to the relevant domestic law of countries with which the practitioner is concerned—in particular, national laws regarding the implementation of treaties and other international obligations, the conduct of foreign relations, and the protection accorded by domestic law to human rights. Indeed, since international law is generally applicable only to states and does not normally create rights directly enforceable by individuals in national courts, international human rights law can in practice be made effective only if each nation makes these rules part of its own domestic legal system. Many international human rights activities are directed at encouraging nations to incorporate international human rights standards into their own internal legal order in this way.

Thus, the work of international human rights lawyers and national human rights (or "civil rights") lawyers is closely related and often overlaps.

The international human rights lawyer will often become involved in domestic human rights law and issues, and civil rights lawyers will often find that international human rights law can be an important tool in advancing domestic objectives. A major objective in international human rights law teaching has been to make civil rights law practitioners more aware of the relevance of international human rights. In practice, the differences between international human rights and national civil rights often lie more in emphasis than substance. Concern for human rights rarely begins or ends at any single nation's boundaries, and effective action to protect and promote human rights, whether at home or abroad, can be furthered by the imaginative use of both national and international techniques.

It is not necessary to be an expert in international human rights law to be able to make a significant contribution to the promotion of human rights. However, a knowledge of this body of law may suggest ways in which such efforts can be pursued more effectively. The purpose of this introductory chapter is to present at least a broad overview of the field.

A Brief Historical Note

Although the idea that human beings are inherently entitled to certain fundamental rights and freedoms has roots early in human thinking, the concept that human rights are an appropriate subject for international regulation is very new. Throughout most of human history, the way one government treated its own citizens was considered solely its own business and not a proper concern of any other nation. From an international legal standpoint, human rights questions were regarded as matters entirely within each nation's own domestic jurisdiction and wholly inappropriate for regulation by international law. The United States, for example, could properly complain to France if France mistreated *American* citizens living in France; international law had early established rules as to how each nation had to behave regarding nationals of another state ("aliens") present within its territory, and a state could protest or extend its diplomatic protection to its own nationals if their rights were violated. But, traditionally, the United States could *not* legitimately complain solely because France mistreated its own *French* citizens; if the United States tried to interfere in such matters, France could claim that the United States was violating French sovereignty by illegally intervening in its domestic affairs.

While this attitude that human rights questions were generally outside the purview of international concern or regulation was broadly accepted until World War II, several developments before then suggested at least limited exceptions to the rule that human rights questions were wholly internal. These included the antislavery movement of the nineteenth and early twentieth centuries, which culminated in adoption of the Slavery Convention of 1926; early international expressions of concern over the treatment of Jews in Russia and Armenians in the Turkish empire; the inclusion in certain post–World War I treaties establishing new states in Eastern Europe of provisions and procedures to protect minorities within those new countries; certain provisions of the League of Nations mandates system; and the establishment in 1919 of the International Labor Organization (ILO) and the subsequent activities of that organization.

However, most of what we now regard as "international human rights law" has emerged only since 1945, when, with the implications of the holocaust and other Nazi denials of human rights very much in mind, the nations of the world decided that the promotion of human rights and fundamental freedoms should be one of the principal purposes of the new United Nations organization. To implement this purpose, the UN Charter established general obligations requiring UN member states to respect human rights and provided for the creation of a Human Rights Commission to protect and advance those rights.

UN concern with and involvement in human rights has expanded dramatically since 1945.[1] Numerous international instruments have been adopted, including the Universal Declaration of Human Rights and the Genocide Convention in 1948; the Convention on the Political Rights of Women in 1952; the Standard Minimum Rules for the Treatment of Prisoners in 1957; the Convention on the Elimination of All Forms of Racial Discrimination in 1965; and the International Covenant on Civil and Political Rights and International Covenant on Economic, Social and Cultural Rights in 1966. More specific actions concerning particular human rights questions also have been taken. Increased UN involvement in human rights matters during this period was mirrored by growing regional interest in human rights questions, as illustrated by the entry into force in 1953 and subsequent evolution of the European Convention on Human Rights, the formation of the Inter-American Commission on Human Rights in 1960, and the entry into force of the American Convention on Human Rights in 1978.

By the late 1950s these developments had firmly established human rights on the international agenda, but only fairly recently have human rights issues achieved real political recognition and importance. Before 1960, human rights questions were regularly discussed in UN debates, but few nations paid them much attention. The rapid growth of UN membership in the early 1960s to include a significant number of African and other developing nations deeply concerned with problems of self-determination and racial discrimination, particularly in southern Africa, and the growing emphasis by Arab countries on human rights aspects of the Palestine question resulted in these specific human rights issues assuming a leading role in UN politics. U.S. congressional action beginning in 1973, based on international human rights principles, and President Jimmy Carter's position that international human rights should play a leading role in U.S. foreign policy raised interest in human rights, not only in the United States, but around the world. The international human rights movement received further world attention when the Nobel Prize for Peace was awarded in 1977 to Amnesty International for its human rights work for "prisoners of conscience," and, in 1980, to the Argentine human rights activist Adolfo Perez Esquivel.

Considering the recent emergence of much international human rights law, it is not surprising that the field is one in which relevant rules are still imprecise, fragmentary, and sometimes overlapping, and in which institutions and procedures are still evolving. There seems little doubt, however, that the basic concept of international human rights has become firmly established in international law and practice, and that international human rights law is now recognized as an important and distinctive subject.[2]

What Is the Content of International Human Rights Law?

International human rights law is derived from a variety of sources and involves many kinds of materials, both international and national. The details of international legal and other procedures to protect human rights are examined in the remainder of the present volume. However, a few examples may illustrate the many different types of materials with which lawyers and others concerned with international human rights can expect to deal.

First, there are now over twenty important multilateral treaties in force in the field of human rights, which create legally binding obligations for the nations that are parties to those treaties.[3] The most important of these is the UN Charter itself. The Charter is binding on almost every country in the world and establishes at least general obligations on UN members to respect and promote human rights. More specific international human rights obligations are established in a series of UN-sponsored international human rights agreements (such as the International Covenant on Civil and Political Rights, International Covenant on Economic, Social and Cultural Rights, and Convention on the Elimination of All Forms of Racial Discrimination) and the two important regional European and American human rights conventions now in force. Other relevant and important treaties have been concluded under the auspices of the ILO, UNESCO, and other UN specialized agencies.

Second, there are a great number of international declarations, resolutions, and recommendations relevant to international human rights that have been adopted by the UN or by other international organizations or conferences. While these instruments are not directly binding in a legal sense, they establish broadly recognized standards and are frequently invoked in connection with human rights issues. The most important of these is the Universal Declaration of Human Rights, adopted without a dissenting vote by the UN General Assembly in 1948, which has provided a framework for much subsequent work. Another important instrument is the 1975 Final Act of the Conference on Security and Cooperation in Europe (the Helsinki Accord), which has quickly acquired major political significance in international human rights efforts. Other examples include such instruments as the UN Declaration on the Protection of All Persons from Being Subjected to Torture and Other Cruel, Inhuman, or Degrading Treatment or Punishment; the Declaration on the Rights of the Child; and the Standard Minimum Rules for the Treatment of Prisoners.

Third, a variety of decisions and actions by UN organs or other international bodies support specific efforts to protect human rights. Examples include the International Court of Justice's 1971 Advisory Opinion on the Continued Presence of South Africa in Namibia (South West Africa); Security Council resolutions imposing mandatory sanctions on Rhodesia in 1968 and on South Africa in 1977; General Assembly resolutions dealing with human rights issues in Southern Africa, Chile, and the Middle East; resolutions and other actions by the UN Commission on Human Rights, the Human Rights Committee established under the Covenant on Civil and Political Rights, and the Committee of Experts functioning under the International Convention on the Elimination of All Forms of Racial Discrimination; an extensive body of decisions by the European Commission and European Court of Human Rights; and reports and investigations by the Inter-American Commission on Human Rights.

Fourth, there are a great many national laws, regulations, court and administrative decisions, and policy pronouncements in various countries relevant to the implementation of international human rights objectives, both within each country and in its relations with other countries. In the case of the United States, for example, these domestic tools include provisions of the U.S. Constitution and Bill of Rights; legislation prohibiting discrimination and slavery and ensuring the political rights of women; legislation and regulations implementing UN sanctions against South Africa;[4] legislation denying security assistance to any country whose government engages in a consistent pattern of gross violations of internationally recognized human rights;[5] judicial decisions dealing with aspects of international human rights law;[6] and state or municipal judicial and administrative decisions dealing with aspects of American corporate operations in South Africa.[7] Similarly, many other countries, particularly those that are parties to the European Convention on Human Rights, have extensive bodies of internal law and precedent relevant to international human rights.

Finally, there are a variety of international and national institutions relevant to the international protection of human rights, many of which are discussed in subsequent chapters. In addition to those specifically concerned with human rights, international organs or agencies such as the UN General Assembly, Security Council, Economic and Social Council, and specialized agencies; the International Court of Justice; the Organization of American States (OAS); the Council of Europe; the European Court of Justice; and the Organization of African Unity may become concerned with human rights issues. At the domestic level, legislative bodies; executive branches dealing with foreign relations, trade, and defense; and courts at all levels may on occasion become involved in human rights questions or serve as arenas for promoting human rights objectives.

Obtaining documents, other materials, or information relevant to international human rights law is not always easy. While the most important materials are indicated in the bibliographical note at the end of this book, one should be aware of the basic sources for both legal and factual information on international human rights:

— compilations of basic human rights documents, contained in UN and other reference works;
— legal-oriented case books or course books, primarily utilized in law schools, and other teaching materials;

— regular reports of intergovernmental organizations, such as the UN, Council of Europe, and OAS;

— periodic reports of specialized human rights bodies, such as the Human Rights Committee established under the International Covenant on Civil and Political Rights or the European Commission of Human Rights;

— periodicals and reports of NGOs, including such helpful publications as those of Amnesty International and the Minority Rights Group (both based in London) and the International Commission of Jurists (based in Geneva);

— human rights periodicals, including reporting services like the *Human Rights Internet Reporter* (published in Washington, D.C.) and more academic journals such as *Human Rights Quarterly* (Baltimore, Md.), and *Human Rights Law Journal* (Arlington, Va.; Kehl am Rhein, Germany; Strasbourg, France).

— bibliographies, both general and those which specialize in human rights, e.g., *Checklist of Human Rights Documents* (University of Texas Law School, Austin);

— official government documents, which often spell out government policy in the human rights area; and

— news media reports, which often provide factual information on a particular human rights situation.

Who Is Bound by International Human Rights Law?

Unlike national states, the community of nations has no international legislature empowered to enact laws directly and uniformly binding on all countries. (Resolutions adopted by the UN General Assembly are considered only recommendations, not legally binding on UN members.) Instead, nations establish legally binding obligations among themselves in other ways, principally by either expressly consenting to a rule by ratifying a specific treaty or other international agreement or through wide acceptance in state practice of a rule as binding customary international law.

Moreover, international law, including human rights law, is primarily applicable to nation states rather than to individuals. Consequently, these international rules generally can become a source of domestic legal obligation to a state's officials and of domestic rights for that nation's citizens only through their incorporation in some manner into that nation's own internal law.

Since these principles can affect the usefulness of particular rules of international human rights law to lawyers or other persons pursuing human rights objectives, a brief discussion of them may be helpful.

In practice, the most important and useful source of international human rights law is likely to be international treaties, which clearly and directly create international obligations for the parties. But treaties are binding only when they are in force and only with respect to the nations that have expressly agreed to become parties to them. Thus, in determining whether a treaty is legally relevant to a particular human rights situation in a particular country, it is important to ascertain: (1) whether the treaty contains express language requiring the parties to respect the particular human rights at issue; (2) whether the treaty is in force, since multilateral treaties typically do not take effect until a certain minimum number of nations have deposited their ratifications (formal instruments indicating their intent to be bound); (3) whether the nation involved has in fact ratified the treaty, since signature alone may not legally bind a nation to the obligations of a multilateral treaty; and (4) whether the nation in question has filed any reservations that expressly modify the relevant treaty obligation.

As indicated, there are a substantial number of human rights treaties in force, which together establish a widespread network of human rights obligations.[8] Almost all nations in the world are now parties to the UN Charter. While the human rights provisions of the Charter are broadly stated, it seems now generally accepted that at least gross and systematic government-imposed or endorsed denials of human rights, such as the imposition of apartheid or governmentally sanctioned genocide, may directly violate Charter obligations. Many of the more specific human rights conventions have been widely ratified. For example, as of 1 July 1982, 70 countries were parties to the Covenant on Civil and Political rights, 115 countries were parties to the Convention on the Elimination of All Forms of Racial Discrimination, and 89 countries were parties to the Genocide Convention.

It should be noted the United States has thus far ratified very few of these human rights treaties.[9] Specifically, the United States is now a party to and legally bound by only the following treaties (in addition to the UN and OAS Charters): the Slavery Convention of 1926 and the Protocol amending that Convention; the Supplementary Convention on the Abolition of Slavery, the Slave Trade and Institutions and Practices Similar to Slavery; the four Geneva Conventions of 1949 relating to armed conflict;

the Protocol Relating to the Status of Refugees; the UN Convention on Political Rights of Women; and the Inter-American Convention on the Granting of Political Rights to Women. The United States has signed, but not yet ratified, the Genocide Convention, the two International Covenants on Human Rights, the Convention on the Elimination of All Forms of Racial Discrimination, and the American Convention on Human Rights, all of which are pending before the U.S. Senate.

A second source of international human rights law is international custom. In order to establish the existence of a rule of customary international law, it is necessary to show a widespread practice by states conforming to the alleged rule, together with evidence that they have followed this practice because they believe that they are under a normative obligation to comply with that rule. If a particular human rights rule has become part of customary international law, this can be especially useful to practitioners seeking to advance human rights objectives, since customary international law is generally binding upon *all* nations, without regard to whether they have expressly consented to a treaty. However, the concept of customary law is somewhat technical, and proving the existence of a customary rule can be difficult.

Questions relating to the utilization of customary international law in U.S. courts are discussed in chapter 13. One oft-stated argument is that at least some standards set by the Universal Declaration of Human Rights, although initially only recommendatory and nonbinding, have now become legally binding as customary law through their wide acceptance by nations as having normative effect. Alternatively, it has been suggested that the Declaration is legally binding on all UN members as an authoritative interpretation of the general human rights commitments contained in the Charter. In any event, the Declaration is frequently invoked as if it were legally binding, both by nations and by private individuals and groups.

One could argue similarly that widely ratified treaties, such as the Genocide Convention or Racial Discrimination Convention, or other universally supported declarations or resolutions, such as the UN General Assembly's resolution recognizing the Nuremberg principles as international law[10] or its Declaration on Torture,[11] have also now assumed the status of customary international law.

Even if particular international human rights instruments such as treaties or declarations are not *legally* binding on a particular nation (either because it has not ratified the treaty or because the particular rule is not recognized as customary law), such instruments are likely to possess a moral or political force that may be useful in persuading government officials to observe particular human rights standards. For example, signatories to the Helsinki Accord have regularly condemned each other's violations of human rights despite the fact that the Accord is not a legally binding treaty. Moreover, national courts may be responsive to arguments that domestic laws should be interpreted consistently with international human rights standards, particularly in cases where an inconsistent interpretation, even if not technically a breach of international law, might nevertheless be politically embarassing.

While international law has traditionally been concerned primarily with relations among states, it is becoming widely recognized that individuals are the real subjects and beneficiaries of international human rights law. Individuals may have access to assert the rights granted to them under international law in different ways.

First and most important, nations may incorporate the international obligations expressed in human rights treaties into their domestic law; the rights provided can then be invoked directly by individuals as part of that nation's internal law. Whether and how such incorporation takes place depends on each nation's own law, and nations differ in this respect. Under the basic law of some countries, a ratified treaty automatically becomes a part of domestic law; in others, specific implementing legislation is required to create any domestic effect.

In the United States, the domestic effect of a treaty turns on whether the terms of the treaty are "self-executing" and are thereby directly applicable in national courts without implementing legislation. This issue is described by the courts as a question of treaty intention and interpretation and is discussed more fully in chapter 13. Human rights standards reflected in customary international law can also become incorporated into national law (at least in the absence of conflicting legislation or government policy) as part of "the law of the land."

Second, some human rights treaties establish standing for individuals and/or NGOs to bring complaints directly before international bodies. This is the case, for example, if a nation has acceded to article 25 of the European Convention on Human Rights, the Optional Protocol to the International Covenant on Civil and Political Rights, or the American Convention on Human Rights.

Finally, a few treaties, such as the Genocide Convention and the Convention on the Suppression and Punishment of the Crime of Apartheid, impose individual responsibility on government officials for implementation of the human rights protected by these Conventions. They also create procedures under which these responsibilites can be directly enforced by the state parties against such individuals.

How Can International Human Rights Obligations Be Enforced?

Implementation is a key problem in making the system of international protection of human rights effective, and it has proved a difficult and troublesome one. The jurisdiction of international courts depends upon the consent of nations involved, and few states have given such consent with respect to disputes involving human rights. (The European Convention, under which a number of European states have consented to the jurisdiction of the European Court of Human Rights, is a notable exception; the Inter-American Court of Human Rights, on the other hand, languishes with only four consents to jurisdiction as of January 1983.) Moreover, international courts are generally open only to nations and not to individuals. Finally, even if international courts are in some cases given jurisdiction to render judgments against nations violating human rights obligations, there is no international police force to enforce such orders. Consequently, international human rights law, like all international law, must rely heavily on voluntary compliance by states, buttressed by such moral and other influence as other nations are prepared to exert.

One way of examining enforcement or implementation options is in terms of the "level" at which enforcement or implementation occurs. Thus, international human rights obligations can be implemented through action: (1) within the national system of the state concerned; (2) by other states in the course of international relations; or (3) by international bodies.

Once again, the easiest and most effective way to implement human rights is through action within each nation's own legal system. If domestic law provides an effective system of remedies for violations of international human rights obligations, the authority and weight of a nation's own legal system can be mobilized in support of compliance with international norms. Most human rights treaties require that the states parties incorporate relevant obligations into their domestic law and that they provide appropriate local remedies. This, in turn, provides the rationale for the common requirement that domestic remedies be exhausted before an international body will investigate a complaint of human rights violations. Human rights treaties and procedures also frequently require that nations periodically make reports to other parties or international institutions overseeing the treaties on their compliance with human rights obligations, including the incorporation of these obligations into domestic law.

Enforcement can also occur at the interstate level. Thus, one nation may complain directly to another nation concerning that nation's alleged breach of human rights obligations and can bring formal and informal diplomatic pressure to bear in an attempt to influence the other nation to cease such violations. The United States, for example, has employed "quiet diplomacy," public criticism, and denial of military and economic assistance in attempts to persuade other nations to conform to their international human rights obligations.

Enforcement can also occur at the level of international organizations. There are now a variety of international forums in which complaints of human rights violations can be raised, either by states or, in some cases, by individuals. These include the regional procedures under the European and American human rights conventions and state complaints under article 41 of the International Covenant on Civil and Political Rights. Within the European system, for example, Austria, France, Greece, the Netherlands, Denmark, Norway, Sweden, Ireland, and Cyprus have all filed formal complaints against other states. Some international institutions—e.g., UN bodies such as the General Assembly, Security Council, Human Rights Commission, or Council for Namibia; the Inter-American Commission on Human Rights; and the review conference held periodically under the provisions of the Helsinki Accord—consider human rights matters on their own initiative without any formal state-to-state complaint.

Another way of looking at enforcement and implementation options is in terms of the nature of the party instituting the complaint. Thus, the complaining party may be either; (1) a state; (2) an international organization or agency; or (3) a private individual or group.

As is the case with the system of international law in general, an effective system of international human rights law rests primarily on the concept of enforcement by states. In theory, when a state violates its international human rights obligations, it will be called to account by other states. In practice, however, this has rarely occurred. States have generally been reluctant to antagonize friendly nations by criticizing their human rights behavior; they have typically been willing to raise human rights issues only with respect to either their enemies or certain politically unpopular states, such as South Africa and Israel. Even gross violations of human rights by other states—such as Uganda under Idi Amin—have often been ignored. Many have argued that, in view of the highly political factors which affect the willingness of states to criticize each other's human rights conduct, any system that places heavy reliance on state-to-state complaints as the means of enforcement is almost certain to be illusory and ineffective.

One possible alternative is to rely on an international organization or institution, such as the UN Human Rights Commission, to raise human rights issues. Of course, the issue must somehow be brought to the attention of the international organization, and this frequently requires that the matter be raised by some state or group of states (although it may in some cases be raised by a NGO or individual petition). Once having jurisdiction over the matter, the agency may in some cases be empowered to pursue it through fact-finding, investigation, or initiatives to promote a settlement of the dispute. However, since international organizations are comprised of states, political considerations will continue to have a strong influence, and an influential country or bloc of countries can often block any effective action. Certain proposals aimed at giving the UN and other international organizations more independence and initiative, such as establishing a UN High Commissioner for Human Rights, have been blocked by countries fearful of the potential scope of more independent international action.

Another alternative is to permit human rights issues to be raised by private individuals or groups. Where human rights obligations are incorporated in domestic law, or where domestic law links foreign policy to human rights performance, individuals or groups may raise relevant human rights issues directly in national courts or agencies. They may also, of course, bring influence to bear on national legislatures, foreign relations offices, or other agencies that either implement human rights obligations internally or implement national policies to encourage compliance by other countries. Institutions within the government apparatus with special concerns and responsibilities regarding human rights, such as the U.S. House of Representatives Subcommittee on Human Rights and International Organizations, and the Bureau of Human Rights and Humanitarian Affairs in the U.S. State Department, can be helpful in providing a focus and accessible forum for such efforts. Of course, certain treaties establish procedures under which individuals or groups may file complaints directly.

A third way of looking at enforcement options is in terms of the types of enforcement techniques that can be employed in an attempt to secure compliance with human rights obligations. For example, a private individual or group may seek a judgment or decision by a national court or administrative agency, an international judgment, or the establishment of an international fact-finding body. A state may employ techniques ranging from "quiet diplomacy" to public condemnation, trade embargoes, cessation of diplomatic relations, or perhaps even the use of force through so-called "humanitarian intervention." International organizations may similarly employ a wide range of enforcement devices including the use of "good offices," diplomatic persuasion, public exposure and criticism,

expulsion of the offending state from the international organization, imposition of the trade and diplomatic sanctions, or, conceivably, even the collective use of armed force.

Problems and Prospects

Despite the rapid growth of international human rights law during the
last thirty-five years, massive and shocking violations of fundamental human rights continue to occur in many countries, and progress in achieving
greater respect for these rights has been sporadic and slow. Some commentators are skeptical as to the potential effectiveness of international
law and institutions in promoting human rights objectives, and a number
of basic questions remain unanswered.[12]

First, what is meant by human rights? Can over 150 different nations
with different cultures, political systems, and ideologies, and at different
stages of economic development, really hope to agree on the content of
fundamental human rights that ought to be protected through international
rules and institutions, or on the priorities among them when these rights
conflict with one another? Differences in perspective have emerged in the
past, for example, between Western developed nations, which have generally emphasized the importance of civil and political rights, and the
developing and socialist nations, which have generally emphasized the
importance of economic and social rights. More recently, however, there
has been growing agreement that human rights must be considered in their
entirety and that civil, political, economic, social, and cultural rights are
closely intertwined. Some nations have pressed for greater recognition for
"collective" human rights, such as the right of self-determination, right to
development, and right to peace; others believe "collective rights" are ill
defined and inconsistent with the concept of individual human rights. More
generally, there is concern that international organizations have tended to
label too many aspirations as "human rights," and that this process of
proliferation may diminish the concept of human rights as a claim of individual freedom and dignity against the authority of the state.

Second, can one expect government officials to support human rights
objectives and efforts impartially even if this poses foreign policy risks,
or will they in practice only give such support selectively, hypocritically,
and when it serves their nation's pragmatic foreign policy interests? As
indicated, it is apparent that many nations apply a "double standard" in

their attitudes toward human rights, harshly condemning violations by political enemies but ignoring equally serious violations on the part of nations with whom they wish to maintain good relations. For example, critics have attacked the Reagan administration's attempt to distinguish for purposes of U.S. human rights policy between so-called "authoritarian" and "totalitarian" regimes as, in effect, the use of such a "double standard." Similarly, the United Nations has focused its human rights efforts principally on problems involving South Africa and Israel, while paying little or no attention to equally or more serious violations in other countries. If governments do not accept the basic moral premises of international human rights but only pay them lip service, how can international human rights law ever work?

Third, can one hope through international law and institutions to affect the ways governments behave toward their own citizens, or do the roots of repression, discrimination, and other denials of human rights lie in deeper and more complex political, social, and economic problems? And if, as some believe, humanity faces an increasingly uphill struggle against the relentless pressures of increasing population, resource depletion, environmental degradation, and economic scarcity, can one ever hope to reach conditions of economic well-being in which social competition will become less intense and human rights can flourish?

These problems must be taken seriously. It is neither realistic nor useful to pretend that international human rights law can produce an immediate change in the way human beings and their governments have behaved for millennia or to promise any quick and dramatic improvement in the human condition.

But there is some basis for optimism. For example, it is evident that the concept of international human rights has taken firm root and acquired its own dynamic. Even if governments do not often take international human rights seriously, common people in countries throughout the world—in Eastern Europe, Latin America, and elsewhere—are clearly taking it seriously. Even if governments have employed international human rights concepts hypocritically and for selfish political purposes, their actions have served to reinforce human rights principles and establish important and continuing precedents. International human rights institutions have been established which, once in place, have acquired their own momentum, expanding their human rights activities in ways that governments have found difficult to curb. A few significant victories have been won—in Zimbabwe, for example—and many small advances have been made. At the least, international human rights law has probably exerted some check on government actions and kept matters from getting worse.

Certainly, the international human rights movement will encounter reverses as well as advances, and dedication, persistence, and much more work will be needed. The directions such work might take include:

— increasing efforts to embed international human rights norms more firmly within national legal systems and to sensitize lawyers, judges, and other officials to the relevance and usefulness of international human rights law and procedures as tools to advance human rights within national societies;

— strengthening existing international institutions, such as the various human rights commissions and courts, by developing and revising their procedures and utilizing them more fully;

— enhancing the role and influence of NGOs involved in the promotion of human rights and increasing their access to national and international human rights institutions and processes;

— developing new national and international human rights institutions, such as an independent UN High Commissioner for Human Rights or regional human rights arrangements in Africa, the Arab World, and Asia;

— developing better fact-finding mechanisms by which to determine whether nations are violating international human rights obligations;

— expanding the relationships among the various human rights treaties and institutions and revising them where necessary to avoid inconsistencies and duplication of effort;

— developing a broadly acceptable theory of the relationship between human rights and economic development, including practical programs capable of realizing and accommodating both objectives;

— achieving wider dissemination of human rights ideas and documentation among people in every country and insuring access by individuals to national and international institutions to seek redress for violations;

— attempting to depoliticize human rights questions, so as to increase the willingness of governments to address such issues fairly and on their own merits in international forums; and

— persuading government officials that human rights *are* an appropriate and legitimate concern of national foreign policy, not only because support for human freedom and dignity is "decent" and "right," but also because it is in each nation's pragmatic long-term national interest, in order to attain the respect and friendship of other nations and to achieve a world in which people can live securely and in peace.

In many cases, the day-to-day problems involved in work in the field of international human rights law will be undramatic, and broader goals and issues may not be apparent. But practitioners will nonetheless be sharing in an important and exciting enterprise, albeit one whose ultimate success remains elusive.

Notes

1. See generally UNITED NATIONS ACTION IN THE FIELD OF HUMAN RIGHTS, UN Doc. ST/HR/2/Rev. 1, UN sales no. E.79.XIV.6 (1980).

2. For an exposition of some of the major academic viewpoints on the importance of international human rights law, see *Symposium on the Future of Human Rights in the World Legal Order*, 9 HOFSTRA L. REV. (1981), especially Sohn, *The International Law of Human Rights: A Reply to Recent Criticisms, id.* at 347, and Schachter, *The Views of "Charterists" and "Skeptics" on Human Rights in the World Legal Order, id.* at 357.

3. A list of ratifications of the major treaties is contained in appendix E.

4. *E.g.*, prohibition on Export-Import Bank support to private business engaging in business with South Africa, unless the Secretary of State certifies that the South African purchaser is nonsegregationist, Pub. L. No. 95–630, 92 Stat. 3727 (1978); extension of the UN arms embargo to include exports of all goods to South Africa military and police, N.Y. Times, 18 Feb. 1978, at 12, col. 6.

5. *E.g.*, Foreign Assistance Act of 1961, § 502B.

6. *See* chapter 13. 22 U.S.C. 2304 (Supp. 1981).

7. *Cf.* discussion in F. NEWMAN & R. LILLICH, INTERNATIONAL HUMAN RIGHTS: PROBLEMS OF LAW AND POLICY 120, 468–79 (1979).

8. A current listing of human rights treaties in force and the nations parties to them may be found in STATUS OF MULTILATERAL TREATIES ON HUMAN RIGHTS CONCLUDED UNDER THE AUSPICES OF THE UNITED NATIONS, UN Doc. E/CN.4/907/Rev. (revised periodically).

9. For a listing of human rights and other treaties and international agreements to which the United States is party as of 1 January each year, see TREATIES IN FORCE, published each year by the U.S. Department of State.

10. G.A. Res. 488(V), 5 UN GAOR, Supp. (No. 20) at 77, UN Doc. A/1775 (1950).

11. *See* chapter 12.

12. These questions are discussed further in Bilder, *Rethinking International Human Rights: Some Basic Questions*, 1969 WIS. L.R. 171, *reprinted in* 2 HUMAN RIGHTS J. 557 (1969).

2
Strategies for Selecting and Pursuing International Human Rights Matters

DAVID WEISSBRODT

Nongovernmental organizations or lawyers interested in improving the implementation of international human rights are faced with the basic question, Where does one begin? The present chapter will consider possible answers to this question through reference to the experience of domestic and international human rights organizations. The chapter will suggest a modified case-by-case approach, which may be useful to NGOs and individuals faced with assigning priorities or selecting strategies to deal with human rights concerns.

Basic Alternatives

There are at least six not entirely exclusive ways of answering the strategy question of where to begin improving human rights in the world. The *first* approach would focus on improving international human rights law by further elaboration of doctrine and the creation of new procedures. There already exist, however, over fifty international human rights treaties defin-

The author is very grateful for the assistance of Jean Boler in preparing this chapter.

ing human rights, elaborating norms, and, in some instances, creating procedures for implementing those norms. Despite the fact that existing procedures do need strengthening, that a few new treaties would be helpful,[1] that work is needed to assure more domestic implementation of international norms,[2] and that more effort should be devoted to encouraging the universal ratification of present treaties,[3] the basic problem for the human rights movement today is how to use the present norms and procedures to achieve concrete improvement in actual conditions. Fruitful use of existing human rights doctrines and techniques should, in turn, contribute to the credibility and effectiveness of the present human rights structure.

If one rejects human rights law reform work at the international level as a first step that has for the most part already been taken, the human rights activist must then decide upon the next step. There are over 160 countries in the world; all have some human rights problems.

A *second* approach would require the human rights organization or lawyer to undertake an inventory of all the human rights problems in the world and then to derive an overall action strategy that would assign priorities to countries and/or specific rights. Under such an approach one might identify a single right as critical and then set out to abolish violations everywhere in the world. For example, Amnesty International (AI) selected torture in 1972 and the death penalty in 1978 as areas of special concern.[4] Of course, if the human rights problem is widespread, there still remains the question of which violations or violators should be the first targets for action. In addition, one must select rights that will be amenable to international action and around which there is sufficient world consensus.

A *third* approach would attempt to identify the worst violators of human rights in the world and then to focus on those governments.[5] Such rankings of violators have generally been failures, for it is very difficult to compare violations and nearly impossible to achieve consensus as to which rights should be given greater weight in the ranking process. For example, are 700 political executions during a year in Iran[6] worse than the imprisonment of 1,500 political prisoners for several years in Uruguay,[7] or better than the torture of 5,600 people in Argentina[8] or the starvation of 1.5 million people in Kampuchea?[9]

Under a *fourth* approach, one might attempt to assess human rights problems in light of the potential for improvement in each country; then one could attempt to encourage improvements on a country-by-country basis. Since a government must maintain relations with all other nations, this country-by-country technique is to some extent necessary, and the

Carter Administration apparently adopted this approach in its human rights policies. While nongovernmental and individual human rights activists often lack the resources to undertake such a universal inventory of human rights conditions and measures, they can be more selective in targeting areas for action.

A *fifth* approach might permit the human rights organization or activist to take problems on a first-come, first-served basis. Unfortunately, the first case brought to light may not be particularly serious or particularly amenable to improvement. Furthermore, the more established human rights organizations receive information about so many problems each week that it would probably be impossible to determine which case really "came first." This approach would quickly overwhelm the organization with individual cases of relatively slight significance.

A *sixth* strategy combines some aspects of the other approaches but recognizes the limited resources and capabilities of NGOs and other human rights activists. This essentially case-by-case approach requires consideration of a series of factors to determine what actions, if any, should be taken in each case:

a. *Is there sufficient information to document the alleged violations and to justify the measures contemplated?* Different levels of information may imply techniques of differing coerciveness or publicity.

b. *Are violations sufficiently serious to justify particular attention?* Almost all violators will contend that they have been unfairly singled out for attention. Even though this defense is spurious, because all violators should be encouraged to reform, NGOs must allocate their limited resources in such a way as to defuse such allegations of selective persecution. The more egregious situations should be capable of generating the broadest world consensus to ameliorate the situation, and, in addition, would demonstrate the impartial concern for human rights upon which the actor's credibility depends.

c. *Is there reason to believe that the situation may be improved by one or more of the techniques available to the actor?* Indications of the potential usefulness of an action may be garnered from such subsidiary questions as: Have similar techniques for dealing with this type of problem or country been successful in the past? Are the officials of the country receptive to foreign initiatives? What sort of action has the greatest potential for success and the least risk of harm to the victims? Changing conditions in the target country may require tactical shifts or even abandonment of the matter, and there must be regular reevaluation of the considerations that prompted choice of a particular human rights strategy or tactic.

d. *Given the political, financial, and practical constraints on the pro-
    spective actor, is the NGO or individual in a position to take effective
    action in this case?* While most NGOs strive to appear impartial and
    independent in pursuing human rights problems, each has constraints
    arising from the nature of its staff, membership, financial supporters,
    geographical location, and substantive expertise. In each case, the
    need to appear independent and impartial must be balanced with the
    need for self-preservation, and no NGO can pursue cases to which
    major segments of its constituency would object. The broader the NGO's
    political and financial base, the more successful will be its efforts to
    be truly independent, impartial, and effective.

e. *Will the contemplated action be compatible with the political perspec-
    tives of the human rights victims to be aided?* This question does not
    raise an ideological as much as a practical problem; the contemplated
    NGO actions should be useful rather than counterproductive to a reso-
    lution of the problems that gave rise to the alleged rights violations.
    For example, a U.S.-based organization usually cannot concentrate
    on human rights violations in Eastern Europe without appearing to be
    politically biased. Also, U.S. human rights pressure on Eastern Eu-
    rope may be less effective than similar pressure that originates in Eu-
    rope or in the Third World. Similarly, an Israeli organization would
    be ineffective in complaining about human rights violations in Syria,
    and vice versa.

    At the same time, however, support of human rights victims must
    not depend on support of a victim's political goals or methods; for
    example, protests against unfair trials or ill-treatment of Irish Repub-
    lican Army members in Northern Ireland do not imply support of po-
    litical violence.

f. *Having decided that a particular human rights problem deserves at-
    tention, which actions are most appropriate?* The practical measures
    available to most human rights organizations include fact-finding; dip-
    lomatic initiatives; letter-writing campaigns; publicity; on-site mis-
    sions; lobbying sympathetic governments to raise human rights issues
    with violating governments; persuading business, labor, or other pri-
    vate groups to take appropriate measures to support victims of rights
    violations and to condemn violating nations; legal action in the target
    nation or elsewhere; providing aid to victims and their families; and
    invoking international human rights procedures

    No firm rule may be identified as to how available techniques should
    be ordered, although it is generally best to judge the impact of less
    coercive or public measures before resorting to more aggressive tech-

niques. Private and informal actions will often be appropriate if the facts are still uncertain.

NGO Experiences with Specific Human Rights Strategies

Having outlined a number of ways to select those human rights problems to be addressed, it may be instructive to examine how several organizations have actually utilized different techniques in two quite different areas: the public interest law movement in the United States and implementation of the human right to food. While not perfectly analogous, the efforts of U.S. lawyers and activists to end racism and to represent the public interest are more easily analyzed than many international activities, because a single-country context provides a focus not easily found in the world arena. These domestic legal efforts also are relatively well documented. The right to food is a relatively uncharted area and thus offers an excellent opportunity to explore contemporary strategies.

Strategies of the U.S. Public Interest Movement

In this relatively early stage of the development of the international human rights movement, one of the most pressing questions is how to focus the efforts of NGOs and individuals concerned with human rights for the most efficient use of limited resources. This section will examine the experience of public interest law organizations in order to derive useful strategic lessons for the international human rights movement. The "public interest law movement" is broadly defined to include law firms working mainly with environmental and consumer issues, the Legal Services poverty law program, and the National Association for the Advancement of Colored People (NAACP) campaign to end segregation.[10] These diverse organizations possess a common goal of representing groups and values that historically have been slighted by the U.S. political and legal systems. Each organization has made strategic decisions about how best to confront the massive tasks they have chosen.

Analysis of the public interest law movement reveals that, in general, an organization whose goal is to further the public interest has *four* levels of decisions to make about the services it will provide. *First,* it must decide whether to serve every potential client that seeks help. *Second,* if everyone will not be helped, it must devise a policy for determining the general category of cases that will be taken. *Third*, once an overall policy is established, it should formulate criteria to determine which cases and issues further the overall goals of the organization. *Fourth*, the organization must decide whether pursuing specific cases and issues is enough or whether furtherance of the overall policy requires organizational efforts outside the legal system.

The first two levels of decision will be examined in light of the general experience of the Office of Economic Opportunity (OEO) Legal Services Program and public interest law firms. The third level, actual case or issue selection, will be explored by tracing the case selection strategy used by the NAACP in its attack on racial segregation in American institutions. The perceived successes and failures of the public interest law movement as a whole will form the basis for investigating the last decisional level.

The Decision to Select Clients

The first decision a public interest organization must make is whether to assist only some of the clients who seek its help. Although this step seems obvious if an organization is to effectively focus its resources, underlying assumptions about the legal system and the lawyer's role have made this step difficult for some public interest organizations. In fact, early poverty lawyers resisted taking this step to the point of almost permanently emasculating the young OEO-Legal Services program.[11]

There were two reasons for this resistance. First, the Legal Aid program attributed the problems of the poor to their limited access to justice-dispensing institutions and believed that supplying a lawyer to every poor person would cure poverty. The inherent assumption in this approach was that the legal system could rectify all injustice. The second assumption was that a public interest lawyer could effect social change and still retain his or her traditional role as a value-free advocate. Under this view, interjecting a lawyer's own values through client selection was inappropriate, and poverty lawyers should follow the example of their colleagues and let the client choose the issue.[12]

One year after the federal program was funded, the folly of accepting too many clients and trying to reach too many goals became apparent to the Legal Services management. Their offices were being swamped with more clients than they could adequately serve, and the program was drifting toward preoccupation with processing cases while ignoring longer-range pragmatic goals. Accordingly, it was out of necessity and in order to save the program that the Legal Services management devised a selection strategy.

In the area of public interest law, client selection and rejection may raise not only a practical problem but also ethical issues. The service-oriented public interest lawyer feels the tension between the obligation to serve the public (canon 2 of the American Bar Association's Code of Professional Responsibility) and the obligation to provide competent, zealous advocacy even where resources are inadequate (canons 6 and 7). The inevitable corollary to an emphasis on the number of people served with finite resources is that the quality of service received by each person is reduced. Since the Code essentially prohibits falling below a certain level of competence in order to increase the quantity of clients served, client selection seems ethically as well as practically mandated for organizations seeking to further public interest goals.

International human rights workers, many of them lawyers, are also understandably uncomfortable in ignoring some of the pleas for help that reach them. The staffs of human rights organizations are almost invariably overwhelmed by the volume of cases presented and by insufficient guidance as to which cases require attention. The experience of the Legal Services Corporation teaches, however, that the decision to reject some cases in order to pursue others more thoroughly is crucial.

Amnesty International, for example, has struggled with the choice between work for individual prisoners of conscience and efforts on behalf of large groups of prisoners. In some countries such as Indonesia, where there were thousands of often unidentified prisoners, it sometimes seemed pointless to work for the release of a few dozen individuals. In regard to other countries, like Uganda under Idi Amin, it was counterproductive to work for the release of named individuals. Therefore, AI gradually began to exert more effort toward country campaigns and to shift research resources away from individual prisoner adoptions. Individual prisoner adoptions remain, however, the focus of AI work, both because they generate the greatest amount of personal involvement among the membership and because they illustrate in a direct, personal way the human dimension of massive human rights problems.

A General Policy for Case Selection

Once the principle of case or problem selection was accepted by the public interest law movement, an overall selection policy had to be developed. The crucial question at this juncture is whether and to what degree client selection should be a product of the advocate's or organization's judgment. If the lawyer makes this judgment, in order to focus advocacy efforts and consequently improve the quality of service given to the constituency as a whole, accountability to that constituency may become a problem. On one hand is the assumption that the lawyer knows best and that his or her subjective decision based on personal values should control. On the other hand is the view that a community organization representative of the lawyer's constituency should handle the selection process.

Both models have drawbacks. The advocate's own values and perspectives may risk becoming unresponsive to the client group. This danger is particularly real for lawyers who represent diverse interests such as consumer, environmental, civil, political, and economic values rather than an identifiable community. Reliance on an individual perception of the public good, even that of a well-informed individual, may not produce selection decisions that effectively allocate resources.

Conversely, a requirement of rigid accountability deprives unorganized interests of any voice, and the primary impetus for the public interest law movement was the desire to provide representation for powerless, unorganized groups. Even where a defined community exists and an organization could direct the activities of public interest lawyers, such control may not be advisable. Community boards and human rights organizations have been known to ignore the reform potential of certain actions and steer advocates toward cases that have more immediate urgency but no long-term impact.

Many public interest law organizations have resolved the accountability problem by formulating an overall policy which limits the advocates' independent discretion and focuses the energies of the organization on actions that have wide-ranging and long-term effect.[13] Such a policy assures that selected cases will be responsive to the overall needs of the community, yet also conserves resources for the "important cases."

The following factors might be considered by human rights NGOs in formulating an overall policy for issue selection:
1. the organization should have a policy focus, that is, a theory of the underlying causes of the condition(s) it seeks to change;
2. the organization should compare the effectiveness of alternative policies;
3. the feasibility of a proposed policy should be considered in light of current social and political circumstances;
4. the structure and character of the implementing organization should be considered, including the special skills of staff and volunteers; and

5. the degree of independence of an organization vis-à-vis its clientele
   should be taken into account.

Each of these factors will be examined in the context of the public interest
law movement, in order to assist international human rights organizations
in determining what factors are important to their own policy decisions.

The experience of the OEO Legal Services program illustrates the need
for a *policy focus* in formulating an overall strategy for action. When the
Legal Services management decided to deemphasize the service-oriented
approach inherited from the Legal Aid movement, three policy options
were formulated.

One option was based on the "civilian perspective" theory that the government's war on poverty failed because government agencies responsible
for distribution of income and opportunity were uninformed or unresponsive.[14] The poor needed representatives who would force these agencies
to include the "civilian" perspective of the poor in the decision-making
process. Under this theory, neighborhood law offices would have been
required to act as a liaison between the poor community and government
agencies.

The second policy alternative was the "social rescue" theory or New
Haven proposal, which focuses on poor people as the victims of social,
psychological, and educational deficiencies that must be addressed to enable them to compete for a share in the nation's affluence.[15] In this view,
lawyers would form part of a multidisciplinary team that would treat all
the problems of a particular poor family.

Law reform was the third policy option, and the one ultimately chosen
by Legal Services.[16] The foundation of this choice was an underlying belief that the legal system could be transformed from an institution that
discriminated against the poor to one that benefited them.

A different focus is characteristic of public interest law firms concerned
with consumer, environmental, and housing issues. In those firms, a version of the civilian-perspective theory directs the lawyers' work, and the
public interest firm attempts to open the governmental and corporate decision-making process to the public.

It is unclear whether the international human rights movement has even
begun to analyze the underlying causes of the conditions it seeks to change,
much less to begin efforts aimed at altering the basic conditions that cause
human rights violations. Instead, many concerned with human rights seem
to concentrate on describing horrible violations without identifying either
causes or techniques for improving the situation. Other human rights advocates have attempted to cajole the principal violators, the governments,
into accepting human rights norms and then have sought to insure imple-

mentation of these norms. But this strategy may only treat the symptoms represented by the violations without adequate analysis of the causes of human rights problems.

In addition to campaigns to end specific gross violations, for example, some thought might be given to why governments resort to repression. One hypothesis might run as follows: Governments, particularly in developing countries, have accepted an export-led growth model that requires social and political stability. In many countries the army is the only institution sufficiently organized to ensure stability. The army takes control, represses dissent, and violates the human rights of dissenters. But the army cannot deal successfully with the distribution of power and wealth in society. Hence, if development begins to occur, dissatisfaction grows; the army increases its repressiveness in order to maintain control, and strife ensues with very unclear results.

Such an analysis leads to the second factor in developing an overall case of issue selection strategy, the *comparative effectiveness of alternative approaches*. Were an organization to accept the above hypothesis about the cause of human rights violations, antitorture campaigns would be less important than efforts to reevaluate the export-led growth model and to convince the army of the need to distribute the benefits of development more equitably—so as to obviate the need for repressiveness. In contrast, the law reform approach favored by the public interest law movement is unlikely to address fundamental politcal and social issues, but it can produce a large number of beneficiaries at relatively low cost. In any event, attention to the ultimate causes of human rights violations is essential to charting subsequent strategies.

The third factor, *practical feasibility*, eliminates some policy alternatives. For example, a policy option at one time considered by the legal services movement involved a concentrated effort to organize poor people into groups that could exert pressure in the political and private economic spheres. It was, however, predicted (no doubt accurately) that the politicians who controlled the legal services budget would not be enthusiastic about a program that encouraged political unrest and offered a platform for potential political opponents. The source of funding for an organization thus may influence basic policy decisions. Foundation-supported law firms consider themselves freer to take controversial stands and implement politically unpopular programs than their government-financed counterparts. International human rights organizations should be aware of the corresponding practical implications of the policies they choose.

A fourth element to be considered in developing a policy is the *structure of the organization*, including the number of volunteers and people on the staff. The professional structure of the public interest law firm facilitates monitoring government agencies, as permanent staff can keep track of administrative maneuvers and judge potential legal actions. If there are enough staff, each member has an opportunity to develop expertise in complicated areas and keep abreast of developments. Environmental and consumer interests probably could not have been as effectively represented by an organization that relied on a loose volunteer structure. The structure of the international human rights organizations will also effect its overall policy. The volunteer nature and small size of some human rights organizations may preclude close scrutiny of governments, but at the same time may foster greater political commitment and information-gathering through a broad nonprofessional volunteer movement.

The skills of the workers in an organization also influence the policy-making decision. For the public interest law movement, law reform was an attractive strategy because it enabled the lawyers to do what they do best. An international human rights group should assess the skills of its staff and volunteers, and if most are nonlawyers or are unfamiliar with human rights procedures, a test-case strategy may be less appropriate than organizing interest groups and publicizing violations.

Finally, the *degree of control an organization has over its clientele* also shapes policy. Environmental and consumer interest law firms can identify a possible litigation or lobbying opportunity and then either find a client or institute action themselves. Because clients for these firms do not possess a substantial personal stake in the outcome of a case, the firm has a great degree of control. The legal services attorney, by comparison, is much more limited; the welfare of each client must be weighed against the desire to institute test litigation or pursue a legislative remedy.

Many international NGOs pursue human rights violations without much attention to the individual concerns of victims and thus retain a great deal of control. Their obligation to human rights victims, however, like a poverty lawyer's duty to clients, limits their freedom to pursue strategies that may be unacceptable to victims. For example, human rights victims in developing nations may not want their advocates to pursue bilateral governmental measures which take advantage of the economic dependence of developing countries and which may further structures of dependence.

Choosing Specific Cases or Issues

The experience of the public interest law movement suggests a type of test-case strategy as the most cost-effective policy for an organization of limited resources. In choosing cases or issues, the initial and fairly obvious rule that emerges is a preference for cases and problems with the widest possible impact at the least cost. The most attractive suit, administrative action, or legislation for a public interest lawyer is the one that modifies the law in a way which directly benefits a great number of his or her constituency. The poverty law field provides many examples of legal techniques that increased the flow of resources to the poor community by, for example, liberalizing welfare eligibility requirements and increasing the minimum wage for migrant farm workers. Generally, however, an organization cannot meet social reform goals by winning one case or even gaining the passage on one statute; the reform process is incremental and requires strategic decisions at each stage.

One example of this strategy can be found in the NAACP's efforts to end racial segregation in U.S. education.[17] Almost since the establishment of the NAACP in 1910, it was agreed that this national organization should confront national issues concerning blacks, not run a local legal-aid clinic. From 1910 on, lawyers and activists for the NAACP frequently met to discuss which strategies would be most effective in eliminating the racism that then had the sanction of U.S. law.[18]

Initially, the NAACP considered litigation aimed at equalizing separate facilities in the seven most discriminatory states. They later abandoned this approach in favor of one that challenged segregation itself. The futility of a frontal attack on the nineteenth-century Supreme Court decision that upheld "separate-but-equal" racial segregation was recognized.[19] Hence, the NAACP concentrated on the inequality of education for blacks as a way of impugning the states' *application* of *Plessy* v. *Ferguson*. This strategy led to a plan to attack segregation at the graduate- and professional-school levels.

The immediate object of these lawsuits, admission of blacks to the institutions, was overshadowed by the larger goal of establishing that due process and equal protection imposed upon the states the obligation to supply opportunities that were in fact equal. The NAACP anticipated that the enormous expense of maintaining two sets of genuinely equal facilities would compel the abandonment of segregation in higher education. Attention could then be turned to desegregation of undergraduate colleges, secondary schools, and, finally, public elementary schools. There would also be less white resistance to desegregating higher education rather than the more socially sensitive primary schools.

Law schools were the initial target, on the theory that judges, themselves lawyers, should see the inequality and thus illegality of theoretically "separate-but-equal" facilities. In 1936 *Murray* v. *Maryland*[20] became the first victory for blacks, when the Maryland Court of Appeals upheld a lower court order to admit the black plaintiff to the University of Maryland Law School. A few years later the Supreme Court reached a similar decision.[21]

In 1950 the Supreme Court decided two cases that encouraged the NAACP and black litigants, while still holding firm to the separate-but-equal doctrine.[22] Graduate and professional schools were begrudgingly being desegregated, while *Plessy* remained viable law. Within the next few months, courts in Delaware and Missouri required desegregation because educational facilities were actually unequal.[23]

Coincidentally with the NAACP's legal efforts, the mood of the country was changing. Beginning in the 1920s, social scientists launched an extensive attack on racism, and the NAACP made substantial use of sociological and psychological data in its struggle. In the 1940s, the patriotism that condemned facism seemed to prescribe equality for black citizens within the United States; in 1948, President Truman issued executive orders ending discrimination in federal employment and segregation in the armed forces.

Finally, in the landmark 1954 case of *Brown* v. *Board of Education of Topeka*,[24] the Supreme Court directly confronted the constitutionality of the separate-but-equal doctrine in education. In a unanimous decision, it ruled that school segregation was unconstitutional as a violation of the equal protection clause of the Fourteenth Amendment. Recognizing the problems of implementing *Brown* in light of a hostile political climate, however, the Court delayed a decision on implementation until it heard arguments from state and local authorities regarding the proper mode of enforcement. In 1955, the Court decided to let the federal district courts retain jurisdiction and to implement the Court's order with concern for "varied local school problems" and "with all deliberate speed."[25]

The South took full advantage of the vagueness of this mandate and successfully resisted integration in many areas for years. It was not until 1969 that the Court reconsidered the pace of desegregation and stated that "'all deliberate speed' . . . is no longer constitutionally permissible . . . [T]he obligation of every school district is to terminate dual school systems at once."[26]

The *Brown* decision created a mass political movement that did more to end desegregation than did Supreme Court decisions. Its principles were extended by courts into other areas such as public transportation, use of public facilities, and, eventually, the overturning of antimiscegenation laws.[27] The growing political activism also made possible the adoption of legislative measures against discrimination in voting, housing, and employment.

The international human rights movement has a number of lessons to learn from this brief history of the civil rights movement. First, in order to be effective one must identify a specific evil, such as racism. Second, one cannot expect to achieve an easy or quick victory, but must often pursue a gradualist strategy identifying the targets that are most amenable to change, such as graduate schools in the border states. Ideally, initial targets should elicit the least resistance possible from human rights violators and should, at the same time, be capable of generating broad public support and enthusiasm within the organization itself. The selection of initial targets also might be substantially influenced by where complainants and informants can be found.

Third, activists must make use of a broad range of information about the causes of evils and should, in turn, attempt to generate scholarly and public awareness to combat it. Where early victories are achieved, they must be used to create a broad basis of public concern and embarrassment to the violator, nationally and internationally. Indeed, sometimes a case may be pursued primarily to dramatize an underlying problem rather than to gain immediate redress. The possibility of remedy, even if remote, may attract far more public attention and may better contribute to the ultimate resolution of problems than standard ways of seeking publicity, such as press releases and press conferences. In the words of California Supreme Court Justice Frank C. Newman, such techniques constitute "publicity plus."

Fourth, activists can be most effective in using the contradictions between the promises of governments and the reality of repression. Hence, even if an international agreement contains no enforcement mechanism, its ratification by a country should be utilized to highlight the hypocrisy of paying lip service to human rights while instigating or tolerating violations. Similarly, useful embarrassment may be created if nations which proclaim that human rights are a major concern are publicly confronted with evidence of violations in so-called friendly countries and are asked to pressure those allies for reforms.

Finally, human rights activists should not be distracted from their ultimate objectives by momentary procedural victories or by merely identifying violators to dramatize the evil at early stages. At the same time, the advocate should consider what benefits might accrue from the establishment of a precedent that could be used in later cases. For example, the UN Working Group on Chile helped to establish a precedent that later aided the formation of a working group on disappeared persons.[28] Similarly, the UN Trust Fund for Human Rights Victims in Chile was converted into a trust fund for human rights violations throughout the world.[29]

There are, however, some basic criticisms of the test-case option. One criticism is that test cases divert energy that should be devoted to alleviating the real causes of poverty and powerlessness. In this view, legal reform without social reform has little impact, and, while cases may create rights and grievances that innundate the courts, the status quo survives. Adherents of this viewpoint advocate a more direct attack on economic systems through organizing powerless groups into political forces and using test cases to bring people together rather than to reform the law.

Other critics maintain that the test-case strategy makes the powerless community overly dependent on the "foreign aid" of the public interest lawyer.[30] They say that the most cost-effective way to bring about social change is to concentrate on educating people about their rights and developing ways for them to be vindicated without the need of a legal go-between. These critics contend that the main bars to developing legal self-sufficiency for the poor are lawyers' reluctance to relinquish control over the movement and institutional racism which cannot be overcome solely through the legal process.

Both of these criticisms should be considered carefully by the international human rights movement. Each calls for less emphasis on the role of the advocate-worker and an increased emphasis on devising means for traditionally powerless groups to exert direct pressure on the system.

Beyond the Test Case

In many ways the promise of *Brown* is still unfulfilled. Equal access to educational institutions exists as a matter of law, and there are more non-whites in schools, colleges, and graduate programs than there were in 1954. Whites, however, have left the cities for the suburbs, thus resegregating schools and leaving many blacks trapped in financially deprived school systems. The courts have refused to respond to such challenges as white flight. Indeed, governments have encouraged white flight through tax deductions for mortgage interest, poorer services in the city, and other means.

It was necessary for courts and activists to attack the evils of overt and de jure racism in the early stages of the civil rights movement in order to dramatize the plight of blacks and to end segregationist laws. U.S. courts and society, however, have retained this simplistic, violator perspective and have failed to pursue actual equality for all black citizens.[31] It could be argued that, in some ways, the civil rights activities of the NAACP and similar organizations have served to legitimize American social structures by ending overt racism and by promoting an ideology of equality of opportunity without achieving such equality in reality.

People or groups trying to institute change are naturally inclined to act as if their own skills and training define the best route to change. Although the public interest law movement has succeeded in altering legal doctrine, it is debatable whether the movement can alleviate the problems that precipitated its creation. Likewise, the international human rights worker may eventually find that creating means for intervening when human rights violations occur is not enough. At some point, the human rights worker must begin to address the political, economic, and social structures that create oppression.

Strategies for Implementing the Human Right to Food

Food, clothing, housing, and health care are necessities of life. Nonetheless, while the U.S. Constitution establishes rights to speech, assembly, religious freedom, liberty, and other civil rights, the United States has not thus far regarded the basic necessities a matter of fundamental legal entitlement. Accordingly, the right to food and other economic rights present unique strategic challenges that might be usefully, albeit tentatively, examined.

First, it is necessary to explain why food ought to be considered a fundamental human right.[32] Certainly, no one would contend that food is less critical to human existence than, for example, freedom of speech. The right to food, however, may need the same sort of elaboration and development that freedom of speech or due process has required. Therefore, it seems appropriate to suggest ways in which one might develop an understanding and implementation of the right to food or its complementary freedom from hunger.

One may find that the right to food may be better implemented through technical and assistance programs rather than through police officers, courts, and other means for implementing political rights familiar to lawyers. Nevertheless, it may be useful to examine violations of the right to food in order to develop an understanding of implementation procedures. Consequently, one must identify possible violators of the right to food, and this chapter then concludes by suggesting some techniques for dealing with such violators.

The Universal Declaration of Human Rights sets forth not only the more familiar civil and political rights but also the principle that "Everyone has

the right to a standard of living adequate for . . . health and well-being
. . . , including food, clothing, and housing." Furthermore, the International Covenant on Economic, Social and Cultural Rights, which entered
into force in 1976, requires governments to take appropriate steps "with a
view to achieving progressively the full realization" of economic rights
"to the maximum of . . . available resources." Article 11 of this treaty
recognizes "the fundamental right of everyone to be free from hunger"
and requires governments "to improve methods of production, conservation and distribution of food" and "to ensure an equitable distribution of
world food supplies in relation to need."

It is clear that international human rights law goes beyond U.S. law in
explicitly declaring the right to food and the related right to be free from
hunger. Having signed but not yet ratified the Covenant, the United States
is legally bound to avoid any action that would violate the Covenant, but
is not subject to its implementation procedures.

Even granting that the international human right to food is firmly established, there remains considerable question as to the content of the right.
It should be remembered, however, that U.S. courts are still in the process
of defining freedom of speech after two hundred years. Similarly, it may
take some time to achieve understanding and implementation of the right
to food.

In order to further elaborate the right to food, the UN General Assembly
convened a World Food Conference in 1974, which issued the Universal
Declaration on the Eradication of Hunger and Malnutrition. The Declaration provides,

Every man, woman and child has the inalienable right to be free from hunger and
malnutrition. . . . It is a fundamental responsibility of Governments to work together for higher food production and a more equitable and efficient distribution
of food between countries and within countries. Governments should initiate immediately a greater concerted attack on chronic malnutrition and deficiency diseases among the vulnerable and lower income groups.[33]

In a statement relevant to the infant formula issue discussed below, the
Food Conference declared, "The importance of human milk . . . should
be stressed on nutritional grounds."[34]

The World Food Conference and other international efforts have concentrated on implementation techniques that promote the right to food by
such measures as development programs, education, agrarian policies, the
promotion of cooperatives, technical and financial assistance, the provision of fertilizers and high-quality seeds, and arrangements for stabilizing

world food markets to avoid famine. These measures are very different from those involved in the implementation of political rights that have a strong legal component. Instead, the right to food is largely implemented in programs run by agronomists, biologists, managers, doctors, engineers, trade experts, and other technicians.

Implementation of the right to food in the United States is achieved through such programs as the food stamp program,[35] the school breakfast program,[36] and the school lunch program.[37] Although not enshrined in the U.S. Constitution, these programs are now a matter of statutory entitlement. U.S. foreign development aid[38] and Food for Peace[39] programs were also intended to help implement the right to food in developing countries, although their success has been questioned.[40]

The principal international agencies that try to implement the right to food are the Food and Agriculture Organization (FAO), the World Health Organization (WHO), the International Fund for Agriculture and Development, the World Food Council, the World Food Program, the World Bank, UNICEF, and the International Monetary Fund. The FAO is a specialized agency of the UN that provides technical assistance for improving the production, processing, marketing, and distribution of food. The World Food Program, a joint undertaking of the FAO and the UN, collects food commodities, services, and cash from producing countries and distributes food so as to meet emergency food needs, chronic malnutrition, preschool children's needs, and school feeding. UNICEF distributes food and other assistance to children. WHO provides technical assitance for nutrition, sanitation, and maternal and child care; it also develops international standards for food products.

These efforts to implement the right to food are motivated by tremendous world needs. Of the four billion people in the world, at least one billion are undernourished. But grave problems of hunger do not belie the existence of the right to food—just as the persistence of racial discrimination in the United States one hundred years after the adoption of the Fourteenth Amendment does not make the equal-protection clause any less binding. It takes time to achieve implementation, and complete enforcement is never achieved. If it were, society would long ago have seen an end to theft and murder.

The existence of hunger does not always imply violations of the right to food. Hunger may stem from natural disasters, wars, or simply from a lack of adequate resources. Nevertheless, one *can* identify violations of the right to food, for example, in regard to failures to distribute world food supplies equitably, which is a particular concern of the Covenant on Economic, Social and Cultural Rights. Such maldistribution might include the conversion of cereals to cattle fodder despite human needs or the use of food as a political weapon.

The direct transfer of food from surplus to deficit nations is an obvious answer to maldistribution problems and may be critical to deal with emergencies such as famines, but these transfers can create long-term dependence and do not encourage people to strive for greater food production. Instead, most international food programs are intended to encourage local agricultural methods such as terracing, fertilizing, irrigation, crop rotation, use of new seed varieties, pest control, better storage facilities, and improved transport. In addition to the transfer of appropriate agricultural technology, there is a desperate need to redistribute land to those who till the land, whether through individual, collective, or cooperative ownership systems. In order to be achieved fairly, such redistribution depends on meaningful participation by the people in the decision-making processes of a country, that is, the guarantee of civil and political rights in order to ensure the implementation of economic rights.

The promotion of infant formula in Third World countries as equivalent or superior to mother's milk is one area in which the right to food may be "violated" by private parties, that is transnational corporations. It has been estimated that some ten million cases of diarrhea and marasmus, related in part to inadequate bottle feeding, occur annually among infants in developing countries.[41] One study of 35,000 infant deaths in Latin America showed that over half the infants dying of diarrheal disease and malnutrition were not breast fed.[42] In an Indian study, formula-fed infants were hospitalized ten times more often than breast-fed infants.[43] A study in Papua New Guinea indicated that 89 percent of the bottle-fed babies suffered from malnutrition, whereas only 26 percent of the breast-fed infants were malnourished.[44]

Mothers in Third World countries may be persuaded to use infant formula because it is the modern thing to do, but they often lack clean water to mix with the formula and the means to sterilize bottles. They may not be able to read the instructions or to afford sufficient formula to feed their babies adequately, leading to dilution of the formula with impure water in unsterile bottles. The result is malnourishment and diarrhea, frequently resulting in permanent, nutritionally caused defects and death.[45]

A number of partially successful strategies have been adopted to combat this promotional activity, which results in denial of the right to food. At the international level, since 1970, the UN Protein Advisory Group, UNICEF, the International Pediatric Association, the Pan American Health Organization, and WHO have called upon the food industry to change infant formula marketing methods. In response, the companies established a self-regulating council that promulgated a voluntary code, but the code did not cover most of the critical marketing abuses.[46]

In 1979, a joint FAO/WHO Codex Alimentarius Commission proposed a Code of Ethics for the International Trade in Food, which Third World nations could adopt and which forbids "claims in any form . . . that would directly or indirectly encourage a mother not to breast feed her child, or imply that breast milk substitutes are superior to breast milk."[47]

NGOs such as War on Want and the Infant Formula Action Coalition (INFACT) publicized the problem. The Swiss-based Nestlé Corporation, the largest producer of infant formula, sued an activist Swiss organization for libel because of an article entitled "Nestlé Kills Babies." While a Swiss court held that it could not be proven that the infant formula itself killed infants, the court admonished Nestlé to change its marketing practices.[48]

The international conferences, voluntary code, national publicity campaigns, and Swiss court judgment failed to change substantially the marketing practices of the multinational infant formula companies.[49] A more effective technique utilized to influence U.S.-based companies was the submission of proposals by shareholders to educate management about the problem. Two large companies, Borden and Abbott Laboratories, responded by altering their advertising practices. The largest U.S. formula producer, Bristol-Myers, which initially resisted the shareholder proposal, was challenged in court for making misleading statements about the use of infant formula and finally settled out of court by promising to change its promotional practices.[50]

The U.S. Congress has held hearings on the infant formula marketing problem but has not adopted legislation to prohibit misleading promotional activities by U.S.-based multinational infant formula companies. Despite U.S. congressional concern, the Reagan Administration directed the U.S. delegation to cast the only vote against the adoption of a WHO voluntary code that would ban promotion of infant formulas. Other possible U.S. domestic actions might be Federal Trade Commission action against companies that engage in misleading advertising or private suits by parents misled by infant formula advertising.[51] Such U.S. solutions are, at best, problematic, and they do not affect non-U.S. formula producers. Third World efforts to control the distribution of infant formula have generally failed, owing to a lack of resources to develop and enforce appropriate standards.

INFACT and other NGOs have attempted to monitor compliance with the WHO Code of Ethics and with other norms against the promotion of infant formula, particularly in Third World nations. On each occasion, when WHO or another intergovernmental organization discusses this problem, NGO representatives present evidence of promotional activities by the companies. While this evidence is helpful, WHO or the Alimentarius Commission might establish a more formal monitoring system in order to collect relevant information about promotional practices and adjudicate alleged violations.

Strategies for implementing the right to food are not yet well developed. Very few human rights organizations and activists have devoted much attention to the right to food or to devising a sensible approach to its implementation. The infant formula problem affords a useful opportunity to identify violators, dramatize the violations, establish techniques that might be helpful to many infants, and explore application of these techniques to similar problems in the areas of economic and social rights.

Conclusion

Most human rights organizations and advocates are so overwhelmed by the terrible pressures of their work that they often lack the time or resources to evaluate or plan their efforts dispassionately. Nevertheless, they are forced each day to make strategic choices which often end up defining broad policies for the organization. The present chapter has suggested a number of policy questions that should be addressed before strategies are selected, in order to advance both short-term and long-range human rights goals. While the present effort can be considered only a tentative beginning, one can hope that others will continue to refine the approach suggested here in the light of greater experience.

Notes

1. *E.g.*, in the areas of protection against torture and the rights of the child.

2. *Compare* Filartiga v. Pena-Irala, 630 F.2d 876 (2d Cir. 1980) *with* Fujii v. State, 38 Cal. 2d 718, 242 P.2d 617 (1952). See chapter 13.

3. *See* Sub-Commission on Prevention of Discrimination and Protection of Minorities Res. 1B, UN Doc. E/CN.4/Sub.2/452 and Add. 1 and 2 (1979); Weissbrodt, *United States Ratification of the Human Rights Covenants*, 63 MINN. L. REV. 35 (1978).

4. The organization convened an international conference in Paris in 1973 to gather information on torture and to publicize the problem. *See* AMNESTY INTERNATIONAL, CONFERENCE FOR THE ABOLITION OF TORTURE, PARIS 10–11 DECEMBER 1973, FINAL REPORT (1973). Subsequently, Amnesty International also published a book discussing the international norms against torture and describing the use of torture in each country where it occurred. AMNESTY INTERNATIONAL, REPORT ON TORTURE (1975). In addition to publicity, the organization developed new international techniques for attempting to stop torture, including an "Urgent Action Network," created to respond immediately to threats of torture anywhere in the world. Whenever the AI Secretariat learns of an arrest or disappearance where torture is likely, it sends thousands of Urgent Action appeals to members throughout the world. The members then send letters and telegrams to identified government officials. This approach has achieved considerable success in abating the practice of torture.

With respect to the death penalty, AI held a series of regional conferences and then a December 1978 world conference in Stockholm. *See* AMNESTY INTERNATIONAL, REPORT OF THE CONFERENCE ON THE ABOLITION OF THE DEATH PENALTY, STOCKHOLM 10–11 DECEMBER 1977 (1978). Again, the organization published a very substantial book on the subject. AMNESTY INTERNATIONAL, THE DEATH PENALTY (1979). Since capital punishment is such a widespread problem, the organization selected several nations chosen for geographical, political, and ethnic diversity, where the death penalty was a grave problem. Having targeted representative states, AI has experimented with new techniques for changing attitudes on the death penalty, including use of the Urgent Action Network; raising the issue in UN forums, such as the Congress on Crime Prevention and Control; and asking local AI groups to study the death penalty situation in the target countries, to write letters to officials, and to publicize the death penalty.

5. *See, e.g.*, the annual reports published by Freedom House, which rank countries on a scale of one through seven from most free to least free.

6. U.S. DEPT. OF STATE, COUNTRY REPORTS ON HUMAN RIGHTS PRACTICES FOR 1979, at 744 (1980).

7. AMNESTY INTERNATIONAL, ANNUAL REPORT 1979–1980, at 167 (1980).

8. U.S. DEPT. OF STATE, COUNTRY REPORTS ON HUMAN RIGHTS PRACTICES FOR 1980, at 329 (1981).

9. U.S. DEPT. OF STATE, COUNTRY REPORTS ON HUMAN RIGHTS PRACTICES FOR 1979, at 463 (1980).

10. A definition of public interest law reasonably begins with an idea of what constitutes "the public interest." Some commentators characterize the public interest as a single interest presumably shared by all citizens. *See, e.g.*, M. MEYERSON & E. BANFIELD, POLITICS, PLANNING AND THE PUBLIC INTEREST 322 (1955). Other commentators doubt that any one interest could be shared by an

entire society, but submit that the public interest is based on consensus among the "preponderance" of people. *See, e.g.*, Downs, *The Public Interest: Its Meaning in a Democracy*, 29 Soc. RESEARCH 5 (1962). Still others describe the public interest as a balancing of private interests for the common good. *See, e.g.*, F.R. MARKS, K. LEWSING & B. FORTINSKY, THE LAWYER, THE PUBLIC AND PROFESSIONAL RESPONSIBILITY 51 (1972). John Rawls provides a recent and important ethical delineation of the public interest in his concept of "justice as fairness." J. RAWLS, A THEORY OF JUSTICE 7 (1971). Finally, Burton Weisbrod offers an economics-oriented definition that emphasizes efficiency in the allocation of resources and equity in the division of society's income, output, and opportunities as relevant dimensions of the public interest. B. WEISBROD, J. HANDLER, & N. KOMESAR, PUBLIC INTEREST LAW: AN ECONOMIC AND INSTITUTIONAL ANALYSIS 8 (1978). For a comprehensive review of the literature on the public interest see NOMOS V: THE PUBLIC INTEREST (C. Fredrich ed. 1962); V. HELD, THE PUBLIC INTEREST AND INDIVIDUAL INTERESTS (1970).

In general, public interest law is defined as the representation of the underrepresented. S. JAFFE, PUBLIC INTEREST LAW: FIVE YEARS LATER 11 (1976). "Issues to which [public interest law] directs itself may run the gamut from the protection of wildlife to provision of adequate housing for urban poor." Woods & Derrick, *Symposium: The Practice of Law in the Public Interest—Introduction*, 13 ARIZ. L. REV. 797, 798 (1971). Although the antecedents of the modern public interest law movement can be traced back to the early 1900s, the movement mushroomed in the late 1960s as part of the nationwide protest against individual and public powerlessness in the face of big business and bureaucratic government. *See* Berlin, Roisman, & Kessler, *Public Interest Law*, 38 GEO. WASH. L. REV. 675, 678 (1970); Riley, *The Challenge of the New Lawyers: Public Interest and Private Clients*, 38 GEO. WASH. L. REV. 547, 582–87 (1970).

For descriptions of some modern public interest law firms, including structure, objectives, and estimates of effectiveness, see B. WEISBROD, J. HANDLER, & N. KOMESAR, PUBLIC INTEREST LAW: AN ECONOMIC AND INSTITUTIONAL ANALYSIS 149–470 (1978); G. HARRISON & S. JAFFE, THE PUBLIC INTEREST LAW FIRM (1973); Adams, *Responsible Militancy—The Anatomy of a Public Interest Law Firm*, 29 REC. A.B. CITY N.Y. 631 (1974); Halpern & Cunningham, *Reflections on the New Public Interest Law: Theory and Practice at the Center for Law and Social Policy*, 59 GEO. WASH. L. REV. 1095 (1971); Comment, *The New Public Interest Lawyers*, 79 YALE L.J. 1069 (1970).

For description and analysis of public interest law outside the United States, see Sward & Weisbrod, *Public Interest Law: Collective Action in an International Perspective*, 3 URB. L. & POL'Y 59 (1980); Cappelletti, *Government and Private Advocates for the Public Interest in Civil Litigation: A Comparative Study*, 73 MICH. L. REV. 793 (1975).

11. Earl Johnson, Jr., director of the Legal Services program through its early years, has said that the decision to switch from a service orientation to the more focused law reform strategy was the most significant of his career. He predicted that if it had not been made, the program could not have made an impact on poverty. E. JOHNSON, JUSTICE AND REFORM: THE FORMATIVE YEARS OF THE OEO LEGAL SERVICES PROGRAM 132–33 (1974) [hereinafter cited as JUSTICE AND REFORM].

12. For a discussion of the ethics of rejecting clients under the Code of Professional Responsibility, see Bellows & Kettleson, *From Ethics to Politics: Confronting Scarcity and Fairness in Public Interest Practice*, 58 B.U.L. REV. 337, 343–53 (1978).

13. For example, the following guidelines are used in the selection of cases for the Center for Law and Social Policy, Washington, D.C.:

1. an important public interest is involved;
2. the individuals and groups involved do not have the financial resources to retain and compensate competent counsel for the matter involved;
3. no other legal institution is likely to provide effective representation;
4. the area of the law has not been adequately explored;
5. opportunities for innovation are present;
6. the subject matter is one in which the staff of the Center has competence;
7. the activity is one in which there is substantial room for participation by students at the Center; and
8. the resources of the Center required are commensurate with the gains likely to be achieved.

14. *See* Cahn & Cahn, *The War on Poverty: A Civilian Perspective*, 73 YALE L.J. 1317 (1964).

15. *See* JUSTICE AND REFORM, *supra* note 11, at 26.

16. *Id.*

17. *See generally* R. KLUGER, SIMPLE JUSTICE (1975) for a detailed account of the history of Brown v. Board of Education, 347 U.S. 483 (1954).

18. It has been suggested that there is a parallel between the status of the Universal Declaration of Human Rights now and the status of the Fourteenth Amendment before 1954 (when the latter was on the books, but not actually enforced). Blacks turned to the courts to achieve enforcement of the Amendment. Ultimately, the constituency for human rights must also make itself felt in the courts.

19. Plessy v. Ferguson, 163 U.S. 537 (1896).

20. 169 Md. 478, 182 A. 590 (1936).

21. Missouri *ex rel.* Gaines v. Canada, 305 U.S. 337 (1938).

22. Sweatt v. Painter, 339 U.S. 629 (1950); McLaurin v. Oklahoma State Regents for Higher Education, 339 U.S. 637 (1950).

23. *See* R. KLUGER, SIMPLE JUSTICE 289–90 (1975) (the Delaware case was not officially reported); State *ex rel.* Brewton v. Board of Education of the City of St. Louis, 361 Mo. 86, 233 S.W. 2d 697 (1950).

24. 347 U.S. 483 (1954).

25. Brown v. Board of Education of Topeka, 349 U.S. 294, 300–01 (1955) (*Brown* II).

26. Alexander v. Holmes County Board of Education, 296 U.S. 1920 (1969).

27. *See, e.g.*, Gayle v. Browder, 352 U.S. 903 (1956), *aff' g per curiam* 142 F. Supp. 707 (M.D. Ala., 1956) (buses); Holmes v. City of Atlanta, 350 U.S. 879 (1955), *vacating per curiam* 223 F.2d 93 (5th Cir. 1955) (municipal golf courses); Mayor of Baltimore v. Dawson, 350 U.S. 877 (1955), *aff' g per curiam* 220 F.2d 386 (4th Cir. 1955) (public beaches and bathhouses); Loving v. Virginia, 388 U.S. 1 (1967) (antimiscegenation).

28. Comm. on Human Rights Res. 20(XXXVI), 36 UN ESCOR, Supp. (No. 3) 180–81, UN Doc. E/CN.4/1408 (1980); *see* Kramer & Weissbrodt, *The 1980 U.N. Commission on Human Rights and the Disappeared*, 1 HUM. RTS., Q 18, 19 (1981).

29. Comm. on Human Rights Res. 35(XXXVI) 37 UN ESCOR, Supp. (No. 5) 236; UN Doc. E/CN.4/1475 (1981); G.A. Res. 33/174, 33 UN GAOR, Supp. (No. 45) 158, UN Doc. A/33/45 (1979).

30. Cahn & Cahn, *Power to the People or the Profession?*, 79 YALE L.J. 1005 (1970).

31. Freeman, *Legitimizing Racial Discrimination Through Antidiscrimination Law; A Critical Review of Supreme Court Doctrine*, 62 MINN. L. REV. 1049, 1052–57 (1978).

32. *See generally* S. GEORGE, HOW THE OTHER HALF DIES (1979); Barnet, *Human Rights Implications of Corporate Food Policies*, in THE POLITICS OF HUMAN RIGHTS 143 (1980); M. Ganji, THE REALIZATION OF ECONOMIC, SOCIAL AND CULTURAL RIGHTS: PROBLEMS, POLICIES, PROGRESS, UN Doc. E/CN.4/1108/ Rev. 1, E/CN.4/1131/Rev.1, sales no. E.75.XIV.2 (1975).

33. *Report of the World Food Conference*, UN Doc. E/CONF. 65/20, at 2 (1974).

34. *Id.*

35. 7 U.S.C. § 2011 (1975).

36. 42 U.S.C. § 1773 (1976).

37. 42 U.S.C. § 1751 (1976).

38. 22 U.S.C. § 2151 (1976).

39. 7 U.S.C. § 1427, *et seq.* (1973); *see also* Food for Peace Act of 1966, Pub. L. No. 89–808, 80 Stat. 1526 (1967).

40. For an exploration of Food for Peace program abuses and a proposal for a

massive overhaul of U.S. food policy see, *U.S. Food Aid: Beneficence or Blackmail?* 1 MULTINATIONAL MONITOR (January 1981).

41. *Marketing and Promotion of Infant Formula in the Developing Nations: Hearing before the Sen. Subcomm. on Health and Scientific Research*, 95th Cong., 2nd Sess. 72 (1978) (statement of Derrick and E. F. Patrice Jellife).

42. Puffer & Serrano, *Patterns of Mortality in Childhood*, 262 PAN AM. HEALTH ORGANIZATION SCI. PUBLICATIONS 267–68 (1973). [hereinafter cited as Puffer].

43. Ellestat-Sayed, et al., *Breast-feeding Protects Against Infection in Indian Infants*, 120 CAN. MED A.J. 295, 295–98 (1974).

44. *Senate Subcomm. Hearings, supra* note 41, at 810 (statement of Julian Lambert).

45. Puffer, *supra* note 42.

46. *Code of Ethics and Professional Standards for Advertising, Product Information and Advisory Services for Breast-Milk Substitutes* (20 Nov. 1975, amended 14 Sept. 1976) in INTERNATIONAL COUNCIL OF INFANT FOOD INDUSTRIES, A REVIEW OF ITS OBJECTIVES AND ACTIVITIES (1977).

47. FAO/WHO Codex Alimentarius Commission, *Draft Code of Ethics for the International Trade in Food*, ALINORM 79/35, app. IV (1979).

48. A. CHETLEY, THE BABY KILLER SCANDAL: A WAR ON WANT—INVESTIGATION INTO THE PROMOTION AND SALE OF POWDERED BABY MILKS IN THE THIRD WORLD 108–11 (1979).

49. Post & Baer, *The International Code of Marketing for Breastmilk Substitutes: Consensus, Compromise and Conflict in the Infant Formula Controversy*, 25 INT'L COMM. JUR. REV. 52 (1980).

50. *See, e.g.*, Hewson, *Influencing Multinational Corporations: The Infant Formula Marketing Controversy*, 10 N.Y.J. OF INT'L L. 125, 126–52 (1977).

51. Scott, *Innocents Abroad: Infant Food Technology at the Law's Frontier*, 20 VA. J. INT'L L. 617, 646–54 (1980).

3

Protection of Human Rights through the United Nations System

THEO C. VAN BOVEN

The role of regional organizations such as the European and Inter-American Commissions on Human Rights and the potential of the Human Rights Committee established under the International Covenant on Civil and Political Rights should not be underestimated, yet many highly important procedures for the protection of human rights that are accessible to individuals and nongovernmental organizations (NGOs) exist within the UN system. This overview of UN procedures is designed to acquaint the reader with the range of options available within the UN context; more detailed explanations and suggestions for action are contained in subsequent chapters.

What Are the Primary Human Rights Forums in the UN?

The primary UN forums may be classified on the basis of their *composition*, their *competence*, and their *purposes*. As each is important in se-

This chapter is a revised and updated version of Van Boven, *Human Rights Fora at the United Nations. How to Select and to Approach the Most Appropriate Forum. What Procedural Rules Govern?*, in INTERNATIONAL HUMAN RIGHTS LAW AND PRACTICE (J. Tuttle ed. 1978).

lecting the proper forum in which to raise a particular human rights issue, certain preliminary determinations should be made:

1. Is the forum an *intergovernmental* body, composed of representatives of governments, or is it an *expert* body, composed of persons serving in their individual capacity?
2. Does the forum derive its powers directly or indirectly from the *UN Charter* or from a *special convention*?
3. Is the purpose of the forum *to make policy and decisions* or *to investigate and/or report*?

Many UN bodies deal partly or incidentally with human rights issues, including the General Assembly, the Security Council, the Economic and Social Council, the Trusteeship Council, the International Court of Justice, and the International Law Commission. Some of these forums will be discussed briefly at the end of this chapter; the focus, however, will be on those bodies whose activities and procedures fall squarely within the domain of human rights. These include:

a. *The Commission on Human Rights*—an intergovernmental body, based on article 68 of the UN Charter and which serves as the central policy organ in the field of human rights. Much of the Commission's activity is initiated by working groups or other arrangements, which should not be overlooked. The Commission annually establishes a working group to consider situations of alleged gross violations of human rights referred to it by its Sub-Commission under the Resolution 1503 procedure discussed in detail in chapter 4. The Commission also has a working group that examines the situation of human rights in South Africa and Namibia. Formally, this is only an ad hoc body, but it has become, in fact, permanent. There is currently a Working Group on Enforced and Involuntary Disappearances, which was established in 1980 for an initial period of one year, and whose mandate has been extended annually since that time.

Ad hoc arrangements to deal with human rights situations in particular countries are also important. For example, the Commission has appointed special rapporteurs, representatives, or envoys to examine the human rights situations in Chile, El Salvador, Guatemala, and Bolivia. In the course of preparing their reports, these rapporteurs may examine reliable information submitted to them in good faith, interview interested persons, or make on-site visits, with the cooperation of the government concerned.

b. *The Sub-Commission on Prevention of Discrimination and Protection of Minorities*—composed of people serving in their individual capacity, established by the Commission on Human Rights pursuant to Resolution 9 (II) of the Economic and Social Council with powers inherently deriving from the UN charter. Its powers are subordinate to the Commission. The Sub-Commission has established relevant working groups on communications, slavery, and indigenous populations with powers in the nature of investigation and recommendation.

c. *Investigatory groups*—on (1) *southern Africa* (to which reference was made above) established by the Commission on Human Rights and composed of individual experts; (2) *Israeli-occupied territories*, established by the General Assembly and composed of representatives of member states; and (3) *apartheid*, established by the General Assembly and composed of governmental representatives. The powers of these investigatory bodies can be considered as inherently deriving from the UN Charter.

d. *The Committee on the Elimination of Racial Discrimination*—established on the basis of the International Convention on the Elimination of All Forms of Racial Discrimination and composed of experts serving in their personal capacity. The Committee has supervisory and examining powers pursuant to the Convention.

e. *The Human Rights Committee*—established under the International Covenant on Civil and Political Rights and composed of experts serving in their personal capacity. The Committee has supervisory and examining powers pursuant to the Covenant and the Optional Protocol thereto (relating to communications or complaints).

Selecting the Most Appropriate Forum[1]

Chapter 2 discusses some of the considerations that should guide the selection by a NGO of those human rights issues or cases to which it should devote its resources. Once an issue has been selected, the next problem is selection of the most appropriate forum. In the UN context, three questions might be asked as guidelines:

a. *What are the objectives of bringing a case or issue to the United Nations?* If the objective is to seek *publicity or exposure* of a certain human rights situation, one could address oneself, if applicable, to the various investigatory groups or rapporteurs. Their public reports, submitted to the General Assembly and/or the Commission on Human Rights, are partly based on oral testimony and written statements received from individuals, NGOs, and institutions. These reports can be considered as a means of exercising public pressure upon the authorities of the countries and territories concerned. The reports and their conclusions also serve as a basis for decision making by UN policy organs such as the General

Assembly and the Commission on Human Rights. Presently, southern Africa (South Africa and Namibia), the occupied Arab territories in the Middle East, Chile, El Salvador, Guatemala, and Bolivia are included in this category.

If the situation does not fall within the competence of one of these geographically specific investigative groups or rapporteurs, and the situation complained of is serious and widespread, the best avenue for publicity might be an oral intervention before the Commission or Sub-Commission under the agenda item concerning gross violations of human rights.[2] This may also result in *further action by appropriate UN bodies* and could lay the foundation for direct, informal contact with the government in question by the UN, NGOs, or other governments.

If the objective is *to call the attention of the government in question to the alleged violations*, the best strategy may be to use the confidential "1503 procedure," which begins with the filing of a communication with the UN Human Rights Centre, destined for the Sub-Commission.[3] This procedure may be particularly appropriate if it is believed that the accused government may be embarrassed by, and therefore responsive to, such an international complaint.

If the objective is to seek *individual redress*, the only procedure that is operative and intended to deal with the human rights concerns of individuals is found in the Optional Protocol to the International Covenant on Civil and Political Rights.[4] This procedure can be invoked only if any of the rights set forth in the International Covenant are violated by a state party to the Protocol.

b. *Who is the actor or complainant in the case?* If a complaint is filed by a person who is personally the *victim* of a human rights violation, the Optional Protocol to the Covenant on Civil and Political Rights may offer the appropriate procedure—if the country that is the alleged violator has ratified the Optional Protocol and the violation occured subsequent to that ratification. The victim may be represented by a lawyer, a family member, or perhaps a NGO. If the victim is unable to act on his or her own behalf or to assign someone to do so, third persons may be permitted to represent him, although the Committee has declined to consider communications where the authors have failed to establish any link between themselves and the alleged victims.

If the actor or complainant is *not a victim* of a violation of human rights, any of the forums discussed here may be potentially appropriate. The choice of forum will depend on such subfactors as the particular rights violated (prohibition of slavery and slaverylike practices; prohibition of torture or cruel, inhuman or degrading treatment or punishment); the consistency and massive character of the violations (consistent pattern of gross and reliably attested violations of human rights); and whether the violation occured in areas officially declared by policy organs to be of serious international human rights concern (southern Africa, occupied territories of the Middle East, Bolivia, Chile, Guatemala, El Salvador).

Except for the procedure concerning the human rights of persons subjected to any form of detention of imprisonment, which provides no possibility of access by individuals or groups of persons, all other nontreaty procedures mentioned may be utilized by individuals, groups of individuals, and NGOs in consultative status alike. In all these cases, the actors may be considered as making their submissions on behalf of the common interest (*actio popularis*), although these types of procedures are in the nature of identification and investigation and not of (quasi-) adjudication.

Participation in the activities of the Sub-Commission's Working Groups on Slavery and Indigenous Populations and in inquiries relating to southern Africa, occupied Middle Eastern territories, Bolivia, Chile, Guatemala, and El Salvador may be more direct in that the various working groups or rapporteurs concerned may allow written and *oral* submissions and, if those testifying agree, the divulgence of their names in the reports. The written submissions of NGOs under the procedure relating to detention or imprisonment, on the other hand, are compiled in a synopsis without explicit mention of countries concerned.

Under the 1503 procedure, the authors of communications have no capacity for any direct involvement or participation, once the original communication has been filed. They are not even entitled to receive any information on the handling of the matter, although the practice in the Commission is to announce publicly the names of those countries considered (but not the actions taken, if any).

c. *What action should be taken if more than one procedure is available?* A case of alleged violation of the rights of a detainee in Bolivia, Chile, Guatemala, or El Salvador may be submitted to the respective rapporteur of the Commission, may be communicated for eventual handling under the 1503 procedure, may be reported by a NGO to the Sub-Commission in relation to the agenda item on detention or imprisonment, or may be referred to in an oral presentation by a NGO in the Commission on Human Rights itself at a time when the human rights situation in the country in question is under discussion. A case of alleged ill-treatment of a prisoner in a country that is party to the Optional Protocol may be the subject of a communication to the Human Rights Committee under the Protocol, may be communicated to the UN for eventual handling under the 1503 procedure, or may be reported to the Sub-Commission in relation to the procedure on detention or imprisonment. A case of alleged economic exploitation of a miner in South Africa may be communicated to the *Ad Hoc* Working Group of Experts on southern Africa, to the Special Committee against Apartheid, to the Sub-Commission Working Group on Slavery, or to the Commission on Human Rights when the human rights situation in southern Africa is under examination.

While in the above examples several concurrent procedures are available, this is not the general rule. The most common duplication of procedures occurs in the three special cases of southern Africa, the Israeli-occupied territories, and Chile; many assume the support or cooperation of a NGO that has consultative status with the UN, allowing the NGO to make direct submissions to UN bodies under certain circumstances.

Generally speaking, there do not seem to be any persuasive *legal* arguments against invoking these various procedures either simultaneously or successively. Article 5(2)(a) of the Optional Protocol does prohibit consideration of a communication if "the same matter" is being examined under another international investigation or settlement. In practice, the Human Rights Committee has recognized that cases considered by the Inter-American Commission on Human Rights under the instruments governing its functions *are* under examination in accordance with another procedure of international investigation or settlement within the meaning of article 5(2)(a). On the other hand, the Committee has determined that the procedure set up under Resolution 1503 does *not* constitute a procedure of international investigation or settlement within the meaning of article 5(2)(a), since it is concerned with the examination of situations that appear to reveal a consistent pattern of gross violations of human rights, and a situation is not "the same matter" as an individual complaint. The Committee has also determined that article 5 of the Protocol can only relate to procedures implemented by interstate or intergovernmental organizations on the basis of interstate or intergovernmental agreements or arrangements. Procedures established by nongovernmental organizations, as, for example, the procedure of the Inter-Parliamentary Council of the Inter-Parliamentary Union, cannot, therefore, bar the Committee from considering communications submitted to it under the Optional Protocol.

With regard to the application of article 5(2)(a), the Committee has further determined that it is not precluded from considering a communication, although the same matter has been submitted under another procedure of international investigation or settlement, if it has been withdrawn from or is no longer being examined under the latter procedure at the time that the Committee reaches a decision on the admissibility of the communication submitted to it.

Even if there may be no legal impediment to the simultaneous filing of communications or raising of issues, some discretion may nevertheless be needed in choosing a forum. One may decide, for example, that it would be better not to overwhelm a single body such as the Sub-Commission by raising the same issue in every possible context; progress in the Commission, on the other hand, may not be possible without the cooperation of a friendly governmental delegation.

If one approaches the question of the choice of a UN forum from the perspective of the *kind of human rights violation* each considers, the following list identifies in summary form the appropriate UN body and the necessary standing or qualification an individual, group of persons, or NGO must meet in order to present information to that body. The order is somewhat arbitrary but roughly proceeds from the most general to the more specific categories of violations.

a. *Situations that appear to reveal a consistent pattern of gross violations of human rights.* The Sub-Commission and the Commission (and their respective working groups) are the competent forums.

If a NGO has consultative status with ECOSOC, it may present oral and/or written information directly to the Sub-Commission or Commission under the provisions of ECOSOC Resolution 1235 (XLII) and the relevant resolutions governing the activities of NGOs. This may provide the opportunity for (although it will not require) public debate on the allegations made. It should be borne in mind, however, that there are quantitative as well as qualitative criteria to be observed as regards written statements by NGOs.

The confidential proceedings under ECOSOC Resolution 1503 (XLVIII) can be initiated by an actual victim or victims of the alleged violations; by anyone with direct and reliable knowledge of the violations; by a NGO acting in good faith; and by individuals who, even though they may have only secondhand knowledge, present clear evidence of the substance of their communication.

b. *Human rights of persons subjected to any form of detention or imprisonment, in particular practices of torture and other forms of cruel, inhuman, or degrading treatment or punishment.* NGOs in consultative status are entitled to submit any reliably attested information on the subject, provided that such NGOs act in good faith and that their information is not politically motivated and contrary to the principles of the UN Charter. Under current practice, the materials received from NGOs are presented to the Sub-Commission in the form of a synopsis prepared by the Secretary-General.

c. *Enforced or involuntary disappearances.* The Commission's Working Group on Enforced or Involuntary Disappearances is the competent forum.

The working group consists of five persons serving in their personal capacity. It may receive written information from governments, intergovernmental organizations, NGOs (whether or not they have consultative status), and individuals. The working group has authorized its Chairman to transmit urgent reports of enforced or involuntary disappearances received between sessions of the group and which require immediate action to the government of the country concerned, together with a request that the government transmit to the group such information as it might wish.

d. *Slavery and slaverylike practices,* including the slave trade in all its practices and manifestations, traffic in persons, the exploitation of the prostitution of others, and such related issues as the sale of children or exploitation of child labor. The Sub-Commission and its Working Group on Slavery are competent forums.

NGOs in consultative status may submit reliable information on the subject in writing and may also attend the annual meetings of the working group to assist it in its work through oral and written interventions.

e. *Discrimination against indigenous populations.* The Sub-Commission's Working Group in Indigenous Populations is the competent forum.

This working group was established only in 1981 and held its first meeting in August 1982. Its primary task is the identification and development of standards concerning the rights of indigenous populations, including the definition of indigenous populations from an international viewpoint and paying urgent attention to cases of physical destruction of indigenous communities (genocide) and destruction of indigenous cultures (ethnocide). Both NGOs in consultative status and representatives of indigenous groups, even if they do not have consultative status, may attend the working group's annual sessions and present information through oral and written interventions. While the working group does not technically deal with specific complaints, it has indicated its intention to consider the application of existing standards "giving special attention to gross and consistent violations of human rights."

f. *Civil and political rights* set forth in the International Covenant on Civil and Political Rights. The Human Rights Committee is the competent forum.

Individuals who are victims of alleged violations of protected rights in a country that is a party to the Optional Protocol may submit complaints to the Committee. As discussed in chapter 10, NGOs may informally direct information to individual members of the Committee which may be relevant to the Committee's consideration of the human rights reports required of each state party to the Covenant.

g. *Economic, social, and cultural rights* set forth in the International Covenant on Economic, Social and Cultural Rights. The Economic and Social Council and its sessional working group on reports under the Covenant are the competent forums.

Only the specialized agencies of the UN are formally entitled to bring information to the attention of ECOSOC in its consideration of reports under the Covenant, although NGOs in consultative status could present information discreetly and informally to members of the working group or of ECOSOC (see chapter 10).

h. *Racial discrimination* in violation of the International Convention on the Elimination of All Forms of Racial Discrimination. The Committee on the Elimination of Racial Discrimination is the competent forum to receive complaints from individual or group victims, although it became operative only in March 1983; its procedures are set forth in article 14 of the Convention.

i. *Apartheid and the human rights situation in South Africa and Namibia*. The General Assembly's Special Committee against Apartheid, the United Nations Council for Namibia, and the Commission are the competent forums.

No special rules govern the submission of information or petitions to these three bodies, and oral and written material may be received from individuals, NGOs, or other bodies.

As regards the human rights situation in South Africa and Namibia, particularly with reference to such practices as torture, ill-treatment and death of political prisoners, conditions of Africans in "Transit Camps" and in "Native Reserves," grave manifestations of colonialism and racial discrimination, and infringements of trade union rights, the Commission on Human Rights and its *Ad Hoc* Working Group of Experts on southern Africa are the competent forums.

Persons or organizations possessing relevant information concerning the situation may be invited to appear as witnesses before the working group or to submit written communications.

j. *The human rights situation in the territories occupied as a result of the hostilities in the Middle East in 1967*. The Special Committee to Investigate Israeli Practices Affecting the Human Rights of the Population of the Occupied Territories is the competent forum.

Persons or organizations possessing relevant information concerning the situation under investigation may be invited to testify before the Special Committee or to submit written communications.

k. *The human rights situation in Chile*. The Rapporteur on Chile and the Commission on Human Rights are the competent forums.

Information may be received from "all relevant sources," including individuals and organizations, either in writing or through invited oral testimony.

Differences between Domestic and UN Human Rights Forums

It should be kept in mind that very significant differences exist between various domestic human rights forums and UN human rights forums. Although the UN has developed a comprehensive set of international norms for the promotion and protection of human rights, its system of actual implementation and supervision is still rudimentary. At national levels well-developed, independent judicial systems and rules may exist. Another difference stems from the fact that at national levels the legal factor may prevail, whereas in the UN, particularly in forums with an intergovernmental membership, the political factor is dominant.

Finally, although the UN might be able to provide a remedy in certain cases and situations, this can only be considered a supplemental or complementary avenue of redress. The primary and most direct remedy should ideally be available at the national level, and recourse should be sought at the international level only where domestic remedies are inadequate and ineffective.

As a result of the differences mentioned above, certain methods and techniques that may be relevant to the domestic judicial or administrative process are not as appropriate or relevant within the UN system. One example is the role of precedent, which is very important in the Anglo-American and many other domestic judicial systems. Within the UN, however, it should not be automatically assumed that the procedures adopted to investigate the human rights situation in Chile, for example, will necessarily serve as a model or precedent for other countries where a military coup occurs and results in gross violation of human rights. Rather, much will depend on political considerations in any organization whose structure is predominantly intergovernmental, such as the UN.

This ultimate political factor in an intergovernmental setting may render less meaningful other elements common to the domestic legal process, such as the force of logical argument or the conclusive character of evidence determined by a fact-finding body. But even if sound legal argument or well-proved facts may yield to political considerations, the value of well-prepared, nonideological submissions by NGOs should not be underestimated. Individual members who serve in their personal capacity on such bodies as the Sub-Commission on Prevention of Discrimination and Protection of Minorities or the Human Rights Committee are often receptive to approaches by informed NGOs, and clear legal and factual presentations can be of great value.

Finally, one should be aware of the fact that most of the UN procedures mentioned above are the result of developments in the last few years. These procedures are admittedly still rudimentary and their functioning leaves much to be desired. Nevertheless, these means of implementing human rights norms reflect widespread concerns and strong policy commitments on the part of the international community. Many people both inside and outside the UN have invested a great deal of time, energy, and talent in their development, and that commitment is, in itself, powerful evidence of the vitality and value of these procedures.

Notes

1. *Also see* the Checklist in Appendix B.
2. *See* chapter 11.
3. *See* chapter 4.
4. *Id.*

PART II

International Procedures for Making
Human Rights Complaints

4
Individual Complaint Machinery under the United Nations 1503 Procedure and the Optional Protocol to the International Covenant on Civil and Political Rights

DINAH L. SHELTON

Through the activities of its internal organs and through the elaboration of separate human rights treaties, the United Nations has developed two specific avenues for individual communications concerning human rights violations, which may be utilized by victims of such violations and/or their representatives. The procedures discussed here vary enormously both in aim and practice: the internal UN procedures were developed by existing bodies to consider situations of widespread, massive violations; that provided under the Optional Protocol to the International Covenant on Civil and Political Rights is designed to offer redress to individuals whose rights have been violated.

Although the procedures may seem limited from the perspective of due process for the complainant and the limited relief which may be sought, it should be borne in mind that the older of the two procedures was instituted in 1970, and the newer went into effect only in 1978. Each remains in an evolutionary stage and will depend upon well-prepared cases to set helpful precedents for the implementing bodies.

The Resolution 1503 Procedure

The procedure established by UN Economic and Social Council Resolution 1503 (XLVIII) (1970) is designed for consideration of systematic, massive violations of human rights, and it involves the entire hierarchy of the UN's human rights organs: the General Assembly, ECOSOC, the Commission on Human Rights, and the Sub-Commission on Prevention of Discrimination and Protection of Minorities. It is intended to identify and correct, if possible, "situations which appear to reveal a consistent pattern of gross violations of human rights." Communications which allege individual violations may be taken as evidence of such patterns or practices if they are received in sufficient quantity, but they will not be treated as cases for remedial action in and of themselves.

Substantive Requirements for the Communication

a. *Who may file.* Any individual or group may submit communications; it is not necessary for the author to have been a victim or even to have firsthand knowledge of violations. "Direct and reliable" knowledge is sufficient, provided it is accompanied by clear evidence. A communication will not be considered if it appears to be based exclusively on newspaper or other mass media reports, although such reports may contribute to the proof offered.

There is no requirement that the complainant be a national of the state complained against, but the communication must be attributed to someone: anonymous communications cannot be accepted. The author may request that his or her identity be concealed from the government and others during the proceedings. In practice, the Secretariat of the UN Human Rights Centre will delete identifying information in preparing its summary for the Sub-Commission, Commission, and government if the petitioner is an individual not related to the victim. The identity of petitioners who are relatives of victims or NGOs is ordinarily released unless they request deletion of their identities.

b. *States complained against.* Any country, even if it is not a member of the United Nations, may be the subject of a complaint/communication under the 1503 procedure. The Commission has, in practice, considered communications involving nonmembers of the United Nations such as the Republic of (South) Korea.

c. *Subject matter.* The scope of 1503 subject matter is not precisely defined in the resolution, which refers to "gross and reliably attested violations of human rights and fundamental freedoms, including policies of racial discrimination and segregation and of apartheid." The phrase "gross violations" may have a qualitative as well as a quantitative aspect, particularly insofar as the resolution distinguishes "gross" *and* systematic violations. Thus, the Commission or Sub-Commission may refuse to consider a situation which is either not sufficiently serious in terms of the rights allegedly violated or which is not "systematic" becaue it relates to only a few individuals or was restricted by a very short period of time.

The content of the rights covered by the 1503 procedure is broad and undoubtedly includes those contained in the UN's International Bill of Human Rights (the Universal Declaration of Human Rights and the two UN-sponsored International Covenants). In submitting a complaint, one should relate the violations alleged to specific articles of the Declaration and/or Covenants, as this will facilitate consideration of the communication by the Sub-Commission's working group (who divide preliminary work among themselves between sessions). The early cases considered under the 1503 procedure generally dealt with violations of civil and political rights (e.g., arbitrary detention, torture, discrimination on political grounds), but economic, social, and cultural rights are also within the procedure's purview.

Most of the situations forwarded by the Sub-Commission for consideration by the Commission have concerned countries in which human rights violations have been widespread, such as Argentina, Equatorial Guinea, Ethiopia, Indonesia, Uganda, and Uruguay. There have also been more specific complaints, such as persecution of Jehovah's Witnesses in Malawi or discrimination against the Korean minority in Japan.

Formal Requirements

Communications may be addressed to any organ or body of the United Nations, though it is recommended that they be addressed to the Secretary-General of the United Nations, in care of the Human Rights Centre (formerly the Division of Human Rights), Geneva, Switzerland. It is the Centre, that part of the UN Secretariat specifically concerned with human rights, which initially processes the complaints. The Centre summarizes the communications in a confidential list, which is circulated to members of the Human Rights Commission, the Sub-Commission, and the state against which the communication is directed. The communications themselves are placed in a confidential file. Although it is not a formal requirement, the Secretariat requests that *twelve* copies of each communication be submitted. If the length of the communication or the limited resources of the author make this impossible, copies will be made by the Secretariat.

A description of the rules to be followed in considering 1503 communications is set forth in Sub-Commission Resolution 1 (XXIV)(1971). Complaints may be submitted in any language and must contain "a description of the facts and must indicate the purpose of the petition and the rights that have been violated." As is true for other procedures, abusive or insulting language should be avoided and may lead to a communication's rejection. Communications will also be inadmissible if they constitute an abuse of the right of petition, are manifestly political in violation of the UN Charter, or seek to impinge upon the rights and freedoms of others.

The Sub-Commission initiates consideration of all communications when it meets for four weeks each year in August and September. The timing of a communication is therefore important, as a communication received in September or October will not be considered until the following August. In order to assure consideration, communications should be received *at least* two months prior to the opening of sessions in mid-August, and preferably earlier.

Communications must be submitted within a "reasonable time after exhaustion of domestic remedies," provided such remedies are effective and not unreasonably prolonged. The exhaustion requirement is a common procedural barrier, based on the presumption that there are effective domestic remedies available to the individual claimant and the belief that a state should be given the opportunity to remedy violations before such questions are dealt with internationally. Where all available remedies have been attempted without obtaining satisfaction, this fact should be clearly stated and supported with evidence of the author's personal experience with the domestic system of judicial and administrative remedies.

However, if such evidence is not available, the author should excuse failure to attempt remedies by providing evidence of attempts made by individuals similarly situated or by showing that attempts at remedies would be obviously futile because of a deliberate state policy to the contrary. Where a challenged government policy is expressed in legislation, domestic remedies will normally be inadequate unless the state's judiciary has the power to invalidate a law on constitutional grounds (as is the case in the United States). If the alleged practice is so widespread that government officials must be aware of it, its continued existence may imply that the authorities cannot or will not remedy the situation. Evidence of exhaustion of domestic remedies or the ineffectiveness of such remedies must be included in a communication, although the burden of proof to establish failure to exhaust domestic remedies is on the country concerned.

Means of Consideration

Resolution 1503 cases are considered by previously established organs of the United Nations. Preliminary review of each communication is by a five-member working group of the Sub-Commission, which meets immediately prior to each August session and which receives summaries of communications, arranged by rights, throughout the year.

As thousands of communications are received each year, preliminary screening must be done by the Secretariat. It is unlikely that the Sub-Commission's working group would recommend that more than ten to twenty situations be referred to the Commission in any given year. The Sub-Commission may not actually transmit more than a dozen of those situations to the Commission.

The cases that are initially deemed acceptable are then reviewed by the full Sub-Commission, a body of independent experts who serve in their individual capacities. The Sub-Commission decides whether to refer each situation to the Human Rights Commission, a forty-three-member organ composed of governmental representatives.

The Sub-Commission's working group makes a determination, based upon the content of the communication and the reply (if any) of the state complained against, whether there are "reasonable grounds to believe that the communication reveals a consistent pattern of gross and reliably attested violations of human rights and fundamental freedoms." This decision is reached by majority vote of the working group, which meets in closed sessions.

While no rule prohibits the working group from requesting additional information from either the government involved or from the author of the communication, there is no right to a hearing or even to information as to the course of the proceedings. This near-total confidentiality is one of the most distinctive (and often criticized) characteristics of the 1503 procedure, and once the author of a communication receives an acknowledgment that the communication has been received, all correspondence concerning the procedure ceases.

If the working group recommends further consideration, the communication and state's reply is forwarded to the Sub-Commission in confidential reports. The Sub-Commission decides, based on the communications and other "relevant information" transmitted by the working group, which *situations* "appear to reveal a consistent pattern of gross and reliably attested violations of human rights requiring consideration by the Commission." Thus, several communications regarding the same country may be considered together as constituting a single "situation."

There is no definition of what constitutes "relevant information," nor is there any right for the author of a communication or a NGO to present such information. As noted in chapter 11, however, informal contacts with Sub-Commission members are permitted, although it is unlikely that any discussion of the confidential proceedings themselves will be possible.

The Sub-Commission is not obligated to forward situations to the Commission; it may hold over a case for consideration at the following session, or it may request that the working group reexamine a communication. If the Sub-Commission does decide to foward a situation to the Commmission, the state involved—but *not* the author of the communication—is notified and invited to present written comments to the Commission. Neither the Sub-Commission's findings nor its recommendations are published.

The Human Rights Commission meets during February and March each year in Geneva. Consideration of the recommendations of the Sub-Commission occurs in private session, following initial review by a five-member working group of the Commission. Each of the five members represents a different geographical region, and, similar to the Sub-Commission's working group, it meets in private session.

If the Commission decides to consider a situation under the 1503 procedure, the state concerned is invited to participate in the debate and to answer Commission questions. Once again, the author of the communication is neither invited to participate nor informed of the status of the communication.

Kind of Decision Reached

Prior to consideration by the full Commission, a communication essentially passes through several different decisions on admissibility, although there must be at least a prima facie showing of the merits of the complaint. Although there are no fidings on the merits prior to action by the Commission, it is nevertheless true that referral of a situation to the Commission by the Sub-Commission is often interpreted as at least demonstrating that the allegations in a communication have some merit.

At the Commission level, Resolution 1503 offers several alternative courses of action. First, the Commission may terminate consideration, either through finding that no gross violation has occurred or that other circumstances require discontinuance of the procedure. Second, the Commission may continue consideration of a case until a later session.

Third, it may decide to initiate a "thorough study" of the situation, with *or without* the consent of the government involved. The procedures involved in undertaking "thorough studies" are within the discretion of the Commission, which has recently decided to make public one such study in the case of Equatorial Guinea, despite the confidentiality requirements of Resolution 1503.[1]

Finally, *with the consent* of the government concerned, the Commission may make an investigation through an ad hoc committee. Such a committee would have power to receive communications and hear witnesses, although its procedures would be confidential and its meetings private.

It should perhaps be noted here that the 1503 procedure is not the only avenue of investigation open to the Commission in the face of gross violations of human rights, as outlined in chapter 3. To avoid confusion with the rapporteur or ad hoc committee option under Resolution 1503, the Commission in 1981 appointed a "Special Representative" and a "Special Envoy" to investigate alleged violations of human rights in El Salvador and Bolivia, respectively.

As result of an informal agreement in 1978, the Commission has begun announcing the names of countries that have been the subject of 1503 decisions. In the period 1978–82, these have included Afghanistan, Argentina, Bolivia, Burma, the Central African Republic, Chile, El Salvador, Equatorial Guinea, Ethiopia, German Democratic Republic, Guatemala, Haiti, Indonesia, Japan, the Republic of Korea, Malawi, Mozambique, Paraguay, Uganda, Uruguay, and Venezuela. The content of the decisions is not revealed, however, although the names are published in the Commission's annual report to ECOSOC.

Reference to ECOSOC and the General Assembly

In its annual report to the Economic and Social Council, the Commission may recommend action regarding 1503 cases. At this point all confidentiality regarding the proposals is removed. ECOSOC may accept the recommendations of the Commission, adopt its own proposals, or draft recommendations for adoption by the General Assembly.

Tactics and Strategies

Given the almost total secrecy of the 1503 procedure, the opportunity to respond to government allegations or to supplement the initial communication is limited. It is therefore essential that complete information be included in the initial communication. Both qualitative and quantitative details of violations should be presented: data on mass arrests, disappearances, or other widespread violations; individual examples; government responses, if any; NGO and press reports. In particular, specific evidence of violations of those rights from which no derogations are permitted even in times of national emergency (see, e.g., article 4 of the International Covenant on Civil and Political Rights) will underscore qualitative characterization of "gross" violations.

While many communications might involve a whole range of serious violations of human rights, consideration should be given to limiting the scope of a communication so that it does not appear to be an attack on the entire political or economic system of a country. A 1981 communication on Iran, for example, might focus on religious persecution instead of general political repression; a complaint against Paraguay might emphasize the violation of basic rights of specific indigenous peoples.

The author of a communication can and should assist the procedure by preparing a one- or two-paragraph summary of its contents, which may be on an index card attached to the communication itself. Although there is no guarantee that the summary will be circulated to members of the Commission and Sub-Commission, in most cases the Secretariat will welcome being relieved of the burden of preparation and will make use of the author's summary. This permits emphasis on the salient facts of the communication and ensures that the summary is prepared in time for consideration by the working group of the Sub-Commission.

Supplementary information may be offered at any time, including directly to the Commission if a situation has been referred by the Sub-Commission, but there is no requirement that such information be considered.[2] Informal personal representation at all stages of the procedure could further assist in ensuring that full consideration is given to the issues raised.

Relationship to Other Procedures

The 1503 procedure may be utilized without jeopardizing the availability of any remedy for *individual* violations of human rights. Certain types of cases, however, may be considered more appropriate for submission to specialized procedures; for example, petitions concerning trade union rights and forced labor may be forwarded by the UN Secretariat to the International Labor Organization (ILO) for consideration.[3] Some complaints must be excluded by the Sub-Commission "if their admission would prejudice the functions of the specialized agencies of the UN system."

Public discussion of "gross and reliably attested violations of human rights" under the provision of ECOSOC Resolution 1235 (XLII) (1967) is a procedure of similar substantive scope to that of the 1503 procedure, and its relationship to the 1503 procedure has provoked much debate.[4] It is not, however, a complaint procedure directly accessible to individuals. A discussion of NGO participation in the public discussions under Resolution 1235 is contained in chapter 11.

The Optional Protocol to the International Covenant on Civil and Political Rights

The Optional Protocol creates a right to individual petition and establishes procedures for implementing the International Covenant on Civil and Political Rights. As the name indicates, it is subject to separate ratification by parties to the Covenant, and only 28 of the 71 parties (as of 31 December 1982) have agreed to the provisions of the Optional Protocol.[5]

The Covenant establishes an eighteen-member Human Rights Committee, one of whose functions in implementing the Covenant is to receive and consider individual communications.[6] The Committee consists of nationals of states parties to the Covenant (not necessarily the Protocol), elected by the parties; Committee members serve in their individual capacities and not as government representatives. The Committee draws upon several sources of law in its work: the Protocol itself, the Covenant, the Rules of Procedure of the Committee,[7] and precedent established in consideration of prior communications.

Substantive Requirements for Complaints

a. *Who may file*. Article 1 of the Protocol states that any individual claiming to be a victim of a violation by a state party may submit a communication. Thus, unlike the 1503 procedure, NGOs or other interested parties are prohibited from filing communications under the Protocol, unless they themselves are victims of rights violations. Nonetheless, the Committee has taken the view that the term "victim" does not mean that in every case the individual affected must personally sign the communication. He or she may act through an appointed representative. Further, the Committee may accept a communication submitted on behalf of an alleged victim when it appears that the victim is unable to submit the communication personally, provided there is a sufficient link between the author and the victim. A close family connection has been considered sufficient, such as a petition submitted on behalf of the author's husband, stepfather, and mother. The burden of proving a sufficient link rests with the author, and failure to establish such a link will render the communication inadmissible.

b. *States complained against*. The state complained against must be one of those that have specifically ratified the Protocol, in addition to the Covenant itself. Complaints concerning a state that has not adhered to the Protocol are in practice not transmitted to the Committee by the Secretariat, and the author is informed of the unavailability of the procedure.

c. *Subject matter*. The primary criterion for a complaint under the Protocol is that it must allege violation of a right guaranteed by the Covenant. These rights cover a wide range, including, inter alia, the right not to be tortured or arbitrarily detained; to a fair trial; to freedom of expression, thought, and religion; and to participate in political life. They do not include some rights that are contained in the Universal Declaration of Human Rights, such as the right to property or the right to work. The substantive rights protected are contained in Parts II and III of the Covenant; interpretation of the scope of these rights is the task of the Committee.

The alleged violation must have occurred within the territory and subject to the jurisdiction of the alleged violating state. In addition, several communications have been considered incompatible with the Covenant because the events complained of took place prior to the entry into force of the Covenant and the Protocol for the state concerned. On the other hand, reference to such events may be taken into consideration if the violations have continued or have had effects after ratification and entry into force.

Even if a communication concerns a right protected under the Covenant, it may be inadmissible if the state concerned has made a reservation which rejects or limits that particular provision. Under article 4 of the Covenant, a state also may derogate from its obligation "in time of public emergency which threatens the life of the nation and the existence of which is officially proclaimed . . . to the extent strictly required by the exigencies of the situation." Such derogations are common where a country faces a real or imagined threat, and communications in such situations should be careful to meet the argument likely to be raised by a government that certain rights violations are necessitated by an emergency. This can be done either by submitting evidence that the acts complained of do not fall within the limits outlined above (e.g., there is no threat to "the life of the nation," or the restrictions are beyond those "strictly required") or that the acts violate rights from which *no* derogation is permitted under the Covenant, that is, freedom from torture or slavery; the right to life; prohibition against imprisonment for contractual debt; nonretroactivity of criminal laws; the right to recognition as a person before the law; and freedom of thought, conscience, and religion. Even if a derogation may be generally proper, article 4 prohibits any discrimination "solely on the ground of race, colour, sex, language, religion or social origin."

The Protocol provides that the Committee shall not consider any communication from an individual unless it has ascertained that all available domestic remedies have been exhausted. The author must submit information showing that exhaustion of domestic remedies has occured or that there exist no effective remedies. If the state concerned disputes the contention that all available remedies have been exhausted, the state is required to give details of the effective remedies available to the alleged victim in the case. A general description of the rights available to accused persons under the law and general description of the domestic remedies designed to protect and safeguard those rights have been deemed insufficient. Further, the Protocol expressly provides that the domestic remedies clause does not prevent a case from being considered if the application of remedies is unreasonably prolonged.

The Committee is also prohibited from considering a communication if "the same matter is . . . being examined" under another procedure of international investigation or settlement, in order to prevent simultaneous or duplicative procedures. When the competing procedure is completed, however, the Committee may proceed. It should be noted that several countries have filed reservations to bar consideration of any communications that are being *or have been* considered in another forum, thus preventing an "appeal" to the Committee. Finally, the Committee has determined that the 1503 procedure is *not* "the same matter" as an individual complaint under the Protocol, since the former procedure is concerned with situations rather than with individual communications.

Formal Requirements

Communications should be addressed to the Human Rights Committee in care of the Human Rights Centre of the United Nations, in Geneva. To assist petitioners, the Committee has outlined a model communication, which may be used in filing. This model includes information as to the author and the victim (name, nationality, address, justification for acting as representative if not a direct victim); identification of the state concerned; the articles of the Covenant allegedly violated; steps taken to exhaust domestic remedies; whether any other international procedure has been invoked; and a detailed description of the facts, including relevant dates. The communication must be signed and dated.

Means of Investigation

Once a communication is transmitted by the Human Rights Centre to the Committee, it is considered first by a working group established by the Committee. If the communication passes the first admissibility hurdles of not being anonymous, or an abuse of the right of submission, or incompatible with the Covenant, it is then brought to the attention of the state concerned. The state is allowed six months to submit to the Committee "written explanations or statements clarifying the matter and the remedy, if any, that may have been taken by that State."

While there is no direct prohibition on the consideration of other material, the Committee is directed under article 5 of the Protocol to consider all communications "in the light of all written information made available to it by the individual and by the State Party concerned." In practice, the author of a communication may be given the opportunity to respond to observations by the country concerned.

All Committee and working-group discussions of communications take place in closed meetings. At each semiannual session, the Committee has before it a list of communications, summaries of their contents, fact sheets for each case based on the submissions of the author, any additional information submitted by the individual or state concerned, and recommendations from the working group.

There is currently no provision for oral hearings, although some members of the Committee have indicated that oral proceedings might be considered in the future. The Protocol also does not give the Committee competence to conduct on-site investigations of complaints.

Decisions and Implementation

The Covenant provides that all decisions shall be reached by a majority vote of the members present, but efforts have thus far been made to arrive at all decisions by concensus. It is not clear if the actual results of a vote (were one to be taken) would necessarily be included in the formulation of the Committee's views on a communication.

If a communication is found to be inadmissible prior to its transmittal to the country concerned, that decision is communicated to the author, and that is the end of the procedure. A finding of inadmissibility after transmission also terminates the procedure, after notification to both the individual and country concerned.

Even where a communication is considered admissible and a decision is reached on the merits of the allegations, the Committee's only formal obligation is to "forward its views" to the individual and government concerned. It does not issue judgments, but the first precedents set indicate that the differences between "views" and judgments may be more semantic than real.

Over 70 communications had been considered by the Committee by the end of 1980; they alleged violations of the Covenant in Canada (17), Columbia (4), Denmark (4), Finland (3), Iceland (1), Italy (1), Madagascar (1), Mauritius (1), Norway (2), Sweden (1), Uruguay (36), and Zaire (1).

The first seven petitions considered on the merits concerned Uruguay, which ratified the Protocol prior to the 1973 coup.[8] Violations were found to have occured in six of the seven cases, and the Committee published its "views" on all seven. In these decisions, the Committee made it clear that general denials by the government were insufficient to overcome the evidence offered by the complainants; a majority of the members simply concluded that they could not find that a violation had not occurred, while six members joined in a separate opinion stating that violations had been established. In the seventh case, which alleged denial of a passport in violation of the Covenant, the government of Uruguay issued a valid passport to the individual concerned after the Committee declared that the communication was admissible and transmitted it to the government. The Committee "noted with satisfaction" the action taken by Uruguay and closed the matter without deciding whether or not there had been a violation.

Among subsequent decisions, perhaps the most important is the "Lovelace Case" (communication no. R.6/24), in which it was alleged that loss of Indian status and the right to live on a reservation through marriage violated various provisions of the Covenant. The Committee agreed that the facts disclosed a breach of article 27 of the Covenant, which guarantees the right of ethnic minorities to enjoy their own culture "in community with the other members of their group."[9] The Committee also has published its views on communications concerning Finland, Mauritius, and Sweden.[10]

The Committee is not a UN organ, and there are no formal provisions for oversight or implementation of the Committee's decisions by other bodies. However, the Committee's Annual Reports provide a detailed description of the Committee's work and developing jurisprudence. They are submitted to the UN General Assembly and made available for sale at UN and other bookstores. At present, the "views" of the Committee are issued in press releases for general distribution, although the Committee is considering also publishing these in a separate sales document.

Notes

1. For a fuller discussion, *see* Fegley, *The U.N. Human Rights Commission: The Equatorial Guinea Case*, 3 HUM. RTS. Q. 34 (No. 1, 1981).

2. The total confidentiality of the 1503 procedure means that the Secretariat will not even inform the author if a communication is still under consideration, so that supplementary information should be sufficiently self-explanatory to be understandable without reference to the original communication.

3. *See* chapter 5.

4. The UN Secretariat has prepared a report on the relationship between Resolutions 1235 and 1503, UN Doc. E/CN.4/1237/Add.1 (1978).

5. A list of the parties to the Optional Protocol is set forth in appendix E.

6. The same Committee also considers state reports filed under article 40 of the Covenant, which is discussed in chapter 10.

7. The Committee's Rules of Procedure are available in UN Doc. CCPR/C/3/Rev.1 (1979).

8. Human Rights Committee Annual Report, 35 UN GAOR, Supp. (No. 40), UN Doc. A/35/40 (1980) at 111–37.

9. Human Rights Committee Annual Report, 36 UN GAOR, Supp. (No. 40)

111, UN Doc. A/36/40 (1981). An instructive selection of documents in the Lovelace Case may be obtained from the New Brunswick Human Rights Commission.

10. *Id.*, at 111–89.

5

Human Rights Complaint Procedures of the International Labor Organization

LEE SWEPSTON

The procedures developed by the International Labor Organization (ILO) form part of what may be the most effective and thorough international mechanism for the protection of human rights. However, the first thing to be aware of about these procedures is that they probably cannot be used directly by individual complainants—only by a government, a trade union or employers' association, or a delegate to the International Labor Conference.

In order to understand and learn how to use the ILO procedures, it is necessary first to understand something about the ILO and how it works.

Basic ILO Structure

The ILO was established in 1919 by the Treaty of Versailles. It was the only element of the League of Nations to survive the Second World War

The views expressed herein are solely those of the author and do not necessarily represent those of the ILO.

and became a specialized agency of the United Nations system in 1945. In 1969, the ILO was awarded the Nobel Peace Prize.

The tripartite structure of the ILO (governments, employers, and workers) is unique among intergovernmental organizations. It is composed of three organs: (1) the General Conference of representatives of member States (the "International Labor Conference"); (2) the Governing Body; and (3) the International Labor Office. The International Labor Conference and the Governing Body are composed half of government representatives and half of representatives of employers and workers of member states. The presence and voting power of these nongovernmental elements give the ILO a unique perspective on the problems before it and offer possibilities of dealing with practical problems facing ILO members.

The ILO and Human Rights

The general perception of the ILO is that it deals purely with social matters; in fact, it has a more practical, day-to-day involvement in human rights than do organizations whose concern is crisis-oriented.

If one takes a modern definition of human rights, which would include the subjects covered by the International Covenants on Civil and Political Rights, and on Economic, Social and Cultural Rights, the ILO's competence is seen to include a wide range of rights in addition to those that might be considered purely "labor" issues. "Human rights" are not simply the rights to be free from discrimination, to practice one's religion, to speak one's opinion—though all these are covered by the ILO's work, to greater or lesser degree. The ILO's work focuses on the human rights that are perhaps more immediately important to more people: to form trade unions, to protection from child labor and compulsory labor, to safe and healthful working conditions, and to social security. The ILO has adopted conventions which deal with, among other subjects, freedom of association the right to organize, collective bargaining, the abolition of forced labor, discrimination in employment, indigenous peoples, minimum ages for child labor, vocational guidance and training, protection of wages, occupational safety and health, social security, employment of women, migrant workers, and labor administration.

These rights are implemented through the adoption and implementation of *international labor standards*. The ILO adopts conventions and recommendations at the annual International Labor Conference, requires governments to examine whether conventions should be ratified, and closely supervises and criticizes how countries apply the conventions they do choose to ratify. *Recommendations* are intended as guidelines for legislation and practices countries may wish to adopt on certain subjects. They cannot be ratified, and a state can thus undertake no legal obligation to implement them. They often supplement *conventions*, which are normally less detailed but which lay down minimum standards of performance. Member states of the ILO may (but are not obliged to) ratify them, in which case they become legally obligated to comply with the terms of the conventions and to report regularly to the ILO on how they are complying. By mid-1981, there had been nearly 5,000 ratifications of the 156 ILO conventions.

Supervision of Ratified Conventions

It is not the existence per se of conventions and recommendations that makes the ILO effective, but rather the fact that their implementation is regularly and systematically monitored. This supervision is carried out mainly by two bodies, the Committee of Experts and the Conference Committee on the Application of Conventions and Recommendations.

The Committee of Experts on the Application of Conventions and Recommendations is composed of nineteen independent experts on labor law and social problems, from all the major social and economic systems and all parts of the world. It meets annually to examine reports received from governments, which are obligated to report every two or four years (and more frequently on request) on how they are applying the conventions they have ratified. Workers' and employers' organizations in countries that have ratified conventions may also submit comments on how conventions are being applied in practice, thus offering a valuable supplement to governments' reports.

If the Committee of Experts notes problems in the application of ratified conventions, it may respond in two ways. In most cases it makes "Direct Requests," which are sent directly to governments and to workers' and employers' organizations in the countries concerned. These are *not* published, and if governments furnish the information or take the measures requested, the matter goes no further. For more serious or persistent problems, the Committee of Experts makes "Observations," which, in addition to being sent to governments, are published as part of the Committee's annual report to the International Labor Conference.

The comments the Committee makes are as rigorous as the information it possesses allows. As an example, its Observations, which are much less frequent and often shorter than Direct Requests, filled more than two hundred pages in 1980. The thoroughness of the Committee's analysis and its reputation for independence and objectivity mean that many problems are resolved at the Direct Request stage. Between 1964 and 1980, the Committee noted more than thirteen hundred cases in which governments took the measures requested of them.

The Conference Committee on the Application of Conventions and Recommendations is the next level of supervision. Established each year by the International Labor Conference, it reflects the ILO's tripartite structure of governments and of workers' and employers' representatives. On the basis of the report of the Committee of Experts, the Conference Committee selects a number of especially important or persistent cases and requests the governments concerned to appear before it and explain the reasons for the situations commented on by the Committee of Experts. At the end of each session, it reports to the full Conference on the problems governments are encountering in fulfilling their obligations under the ILO Constitution in regard to labor standards or in complying with conventions they have ratified. The Conference Committee's report is published in the Proceedings of the International Labor Conference each year, along with the Conference's discussion of the Committee's report.

The ILO also employs "direct contacts" as an important method of supervising the application of ratified conventions. This means simply that when a government encounters difficult problems in applying ratified Conventions, the International Labor Office, at the request of the government or with its consent, sends an official, or, in some cases, an individual expert, to discuss the problems with the government and to help it arrive at a solution. Since its institution in 1969, this system has been highly successful and is often used by governments to resolve problems in order to avoid public criticism.

Complaint Procedures

The supervisory mechanism described above is generally an effective way of ensuring that ratified conventions are implemented. However, it has also been considered necessary to provide procedures to consider complaints that ILO conventions or basic principles are not being adequately applied. There are four basic procedures, each of which is discussed in detail below. "Representations," under articles 24, 25, and 26(4) of the ILO Constitution and "complaints," under articles 26 to 29 and 31 to 34 of the Constitution, must concern ratified ILO conventions. The third procedure, which deals with freedom of association, is one of the most widely used international complaint procedures for the protection of human rights. Such complaints, alleging violation of the ILO's basic principles on freedom of association, may be filed whether or not the state concerned has ratified any ILO conventions on this subject.

The final type of complaint procedure provides for special surveys on discrimination in employment, but it has not yet been used since its creation in 1974.

Table 5.1 indicates the basic requirements of each of the kinds of complaint procedures.

Under each of the four complaint procedures discussed below the material will be arranged as follows:

a. Substantive requirements:
    What may the complaint concern?
    Against what states may it be submitted?
    Who may submit a complaint?
b. Formal requirements:
    To whom must it be submitted?
    Are there special form and language requirements?
c. Means of investigation
d. Kind of decision reached
e. Implementation of the decision

Representations under Article 24 of the ILO Constitution[1]

Substantive Requirements

Under article 24 of the ILO Constitution, a representation may be filed if a country "has failed to secure in any respect the effective observance within its jurisdiction of any Convention to which it is a party."

A representation thus may be filed only against a state that has ratified the convention concerned. The state must be a member of the ILO or, if it

Table 5.1 *Quick Guide to ILO Complaints Procedures*

Kind of Complaint	Subject	Ratification Necessary?	Who Begins the Procedure?	Who Investigates?
Article 24 "representa-tion"	Any ILO convention	Yes	Any workers' or employers' organization	ILO Governing Body
Article 26 "complaint"	Any ILO convention	Yes	1. State that has ratified same convention 2. Delegate to the International Labor Conference 3. ILO Governing Body	Commission of Inquiry
Special procedures for freedom of association	Freedom of association	No	1. Workers' or employers' organization concerned 2. ILO bodies, state concerned, ECOSOC	1. Committee on Freedom of Association 2. Fact-Finding and Conciliation Commission
Special surveys on discrimination	Discrimination in employment	No	1. State concerned 2. Another state concerned 3. Workers' or employers' organization concerned	Special panel of experts *or* International Labor Office

has withdrawn, still be bound by a convention it had ratified. There are approximately 5,000 ratifications of ILO conventions, increasing by over 100 each year, so it is impossible to reproduce here all ratifications; a complete list may be obtained directly from the ILO (1211 Geneva 22, Switzerland).

A representation may be submitted by "an industrial association of employers or of workers" (article 24, ILO Constitution), that is, a trade union or an employers' organization. There is no restriction on which "industrial associations" may file representations, and the determination of what constitutes an industrial association is made by the ILO. They may be local or national organizations, or regional or international confederations, and they need have no direct or indirect connection with the subject of the complaint. However, when the ILO Governing Body is deciding how the representation should be handled, a representation may be given more credence if it is received from an organization that has international standing or some connection with the subject of the complaint.

Formal Requirements

The representation should be submitted to the Director-General of the International Labor Office in Geneva. The only restrictions as to form are that the representation must be in writing and must refer specifically to article 24 of the ILO Constitution.

There are no restrictions as to language. As a matter of information, the "official" languages of the ILO are English, French, and Spanish, and the "working" languages are these three plus German and Russian.

A representation is receivable if it fulfills the conditions outlined above: it must come from "an industrial association of employers or workers"; it must concern a member state of the ILO; it must refer to a convention ratified by the state against which it is made; and it must allege that that state "has failed to secure in some respect the effective observance within its jurisdiction of the said Convention." A representation can be filed without anything more, but two of the above items may require further substantiation before a representation is receivable. First, the filing organization should include some proof of its status, unless it is well known. The Governing Body has stated in the past that it alone will determine whether an organization qualifies, whether or not it is an officially registered trade union or employers' association in its own country.

A representation also should contain the best-documented and most complete information available to substantiate the alleged violation. A bare allegation alone will engage the procedure, but it will be slowed down unless the Governing Body has enough facts to make an initial assessment of the situation.

Means of Investigation

After a representation has been declared receivable with regard to form, a special committee of the Governing Body examines the substance of the representation itself. In effect, the committee decides whether a prima facie case has been made out, that the facts as stated by the complaining organization would, if not contradicted, constitute a violation of the convention. This is the reason that as much documentation of the allegations as possible should be included with the representation.

If it decides to continue the examination of the representation, the committee may then communicate with the filing organization asking for any additional information it may wish to submit, and with the government concerned. The government is asked to comment on the allegations and to "make such statement on the subject as it may think fit." When all the information from both parties has been received, or if no reply is received within the time limits set, the committee makes its recommendations to the Governing Body.

The Governing Body decides whether or not it accepts the government's explanations, if any, of the allegations. If the Governing Body decides in favor of the government, the procedure is closed, and the allegations and replies may be published. If the Governing Body decides that the government's explanations are not satisfactory, it may decide to publish the representation and the government's reply, along with its own discussion of the case. This was the case, for example, with respect to a representation by the International Confederation of Free Trade Unions that alleged the nonobservance by Czechoslovakia of the Discrimination (Employment and Occupation) Convention, 1958 (No. 111).[2]

Kind of Decision Reached

The decision of the Governing Body that it is or is not satisfied with the government's explanations amounts to a finding of violation of or compliance with the Convention. Publication of a finding of violation constitutes the final decision, although it is also possible for the Governing Body to decide that a case should subsequently be handled under the "complaints" procedure provided for under article 26 of the ILO Constitution (see next section).

Implementation of the Decision

Whether or not the Governing Body decides that it is satisfied with the government's explanations, the questions raised in the representation are normally followed up by the ILO's regular supervisory machinery, the Committee of Experts and the Conference Committee on the Application of Conventions and Recommendations. Even if the Governing Body is satisfied, these committees may raise questions that they feel require further examination.

Complaints under Article 26 of the ILO Constitution

Substantive Requirements

As with representations, a complaint must be based on the obligations of an ILO convention that the country concerned has ratified. A complaint may be filed against any state which has ratified the relevant convention and which is a member of the ILO. In addition, if a state has withdrawn from the ILO but still has obligations under a convention it ratified while a member, a complaint may be filed.

Under article 26, the complaint procedure may be instituted by:

Governments. Any member state of the ILO that has ratified a convention may make a complaint alleging that the convention is being violated by another state party to the convention. The motive of the state that makes a complaint is irrelevant, and there is no requirement that the state filing the complaint, or any of its nationals, should have suffered any direct prejudice. There have been five cases in which governments have complained under this procedure.

Delegates to the International Labor Conference. Any delegate to the Conference may, during the Conference session, file a complaint against a state which has ratified a convention. In one case a single delegate did so, although it is more common for a group of delegates to institute complaints.

The Governing Body on its own motion. The ILO Governing Body has the power to begin the complaints procedure at any time, and the Standing Orders concerning representations (see previous section) provide that the Governing Body may decide to make a representation into a complaint at any time. In the one case in which it has followed this procedure, the Governing Body instituted complaint proceedings and established a Commission of Inquiry following the adoption by the Conference of a resolution concerning Chile in 1974. Thus, although the Governing Body does not actually *submit* a complaint, it may institute the procedure at any time.

Formal Requirements

A complaint must be submitted to the Director-General of the International Labor Office. There are no formal requirements as to form and language, except for the substantive requirements set forth in the relevant articles of the Constitution: the complaint must originate from a government, Conference delegate, or the Governing Body; it must refer to a present or former member of the ILO; and it must refer to a convention ratified by the state against which it is made.

To be receivable, a complaint must allege that a country is not "securing the effective observance" of a convention it has ratified. As noted for representations, a complaint should also contain as much substantiation as possible.

Means of Investigation

When the Governing Body begins to consider a complaint, it forwards the complaint to the government for its comments. It then normally establishes a Commission of Inquiry, although this is technically a matter of discretion. A Commission of Inquiry has almost invariably been formed to investigate a receivable complaint.

Commissions of Inquiry are free to set their own rules and procedures, but certain practices have gradually become established. First, written submissions have been requested from both parties (often at several stages in the procedure), and submissions from each party are usually communicated to the other for information and comments. A Commission may also request information from other governments (under article 27 of the Constitution) or from nongovernmental organizations. Commissions of Inquiry have decided to hear representatives of the parties and witnesses presented by them and have summoned witnesses themselves. They have also conducted on-site visits to the countries concerned.

Kind of Decision Reached

Commissions of Inquiry are considered to be "quasi-judicial" in nature. Once the accumulation of evidence is complete, a Commission arrives at conclusions and may make recommendations to the parties (article 28 of the Constitution). The report of the case is communicated to the ILO Governing Body and published in the *Official Bulletin* of the ILO.

A decision states whether or not the situation in a given country is in conformity with the relevant convention. A recommendation may, for example, suggest changes in national legislation or practical measures to give effect to a convention's provisions. A recommendation may even address broader questions, such as the necessity of ending a state of emergency in order to promote civil liberties.

Implementation of the Decision

The normal steps that follow the adoption of a report of a Commission of Inquiry include communicating the report to the Governing Body and to each of the governments concerned, and publishing it in the ILO's *Official Bulletin*. In most cases, the Committee of Experts and the Conference Committee on the Application of Conventions and Recommendations will continue to examine the application of the conventions concerned, with reference to the findings of the Commission of Inquiry, as is done in connection with representations.

In addition, under article 29(2) of the ILO Constitution, any government concerned in a complaint may refer the complaint to the International Court of Justice if it does not accept the Commission's recommendations. Although this has never occurred, it remains a legal possibility. The decision of the International Court in such cases is final, and the Court may affirm, vary, or reverse the findings or recommendations of the Commission of Inquiry. (See articles 31 and 32 of the ILO Constitution.)

Article 33 of the ILO Constitution provides that if a government does not implement the recommendations of a Commission of Inquiry (or of the International Court of Justice) within the time specified, "the Governing Body may recommend to the Conference such action as it may deem wise and expedient to secure compliance therewith." No such action has yet been taken, but there are no restrictions in the Constitution on the measures that might be adopted under this provision.

Finally, under article 34 of the ILO Constitution, a government that has been found to be in violation of a convention by a Commission of Inquiry may request the Governing Body to constitute another Commission of Inquiry to verify that the government has complied with the recommendations made to it. Again, no action under this provision has yet been instituted.

Special Procedures for Complaints concerning Freedom of Association

The most widely used ILO petition procedure is the special procedure that has been established for complaints concerning violations of freedom of association. By 1980, the Committee on Freedom of Association had considered over 1,000 cases, and between 1976 and 1980 noted the release of over 400 detained trade unionists following its interventions. These procedures are not specifically provided for by the ILO Constitution, but were established in the early 1950s by agreement between the ILO and the UN Economic and Social Council.

There are two bodies that may consider complaints in this area. The Governing Body's Committee on Freedom of Association (CFA) receives complaints directly from workers' and employers' organizations. The Fact-Finding and Conciliation Commission on Freedom of Association (FFCC) may deal with complaints that are referred to it by the Governing Body on the recommendation of the CFA or by the state concerned. The FFCC may also examine complaints against nonmember states of the ILO which are referred to it by ECOSOC.

The Committee on Freedom of Association

Substantive Requirements

The special complaint procedures were created for the protection of trade union rights, which have been codified by the International Labor

Conference in conventions dealing with freedom of association. These include the Freedom of Association and Protection of the Rights to Organize Convention, 1948 (No. 87) and the Right to Organize and Collective Bargaining Convention, 1949 (No. 98). However, there is *no* requirement that a state must have ratified either of these conventions for a complaint to be filed, since it is considered that the basic authority for the examination of complaints lies in the ILO Constitution itself, which consecrates the principle of freedom of association. A complaint may therefore be made against any member of the ILO.

Thus, the CFA is guided by this constitutional principle as well as by the provisions of ILO conventions in this area. It has gradually developed a set of principles supplementing the conventions and the ILO Constitution, which have been summarized in a publication entitled *Freedom of Association: Digest of Decisions of the Freedom of Association Committee of the Governing Body of the ILO*, last published by the International Labor Office in 1976.

The principle of freedom of association includes:
— the right of all workers and employers to establish organizations;
— free functioning of such organizations;
— the right to join federations and confederations and to affiliate with international groupings of occupational organizations;
— the right of organizations not to be suspended or dissolved by administrative authorities;
— protection against antiunion discrimination;
— the right to collective bargaining;
— the right to strike; and
— the right to basic civil liberties, which are a necessary precondition to the free exercise of trade union rights.

Complaints may be submitted either by governments or by organizations of employers or workers.

A government may submit complaints to the CFA alleging violations by another government, but no government has ever done so. The complainant government does not itself have to have ratified any of the Conventions on freedom of association.

Three categories of employers' and workers' organizations may file complaints:
— national organizations directly concerned with the matter;
— international organizations which have consultative status with the ILO; and
— other international organizations without consultative status, if the al-

legations relate to matters directly affecting their affiliated organizations.

The CFA reserves the right to determine whether an organization filing a complaint is, in fact, an "organization of employers or workers." It has, for instance, decided that a complaint may be receivable even if a government has dissolved the complainant organization. The situation would probably be similar if the organization making the complaint had not been registered or recognized by the government concerned. However, a complaint will not be accepted from bodies with which it is impossible to correspond, either because they have only a temporary address or because the complaint does not contain an address. The Committee may request the complainant organization to furnish additional information about itself, such as its size, statutes, or affiliations.

Formal Requirements

All complaints must be submitted to the Director-General of the International Labor Office. They must be submitted in writing, duly signed by a representative of a body entitled to present them, and must contain the address of the complainant organization. They should be as fully supported as possible by evidence of infringement of trade union rights.

A complaint will be receivable if it is from a proper organization of employers or workers, concerns an ILO member, and alleges a violation of the right of freedom of association. Substantiation of an organization's status should be included, as well as all available proof of the violations alleged.

Means of Investigation

Once a complaint is received, the Director-General may allow the complainant time to furnish additional substantiation. The complaint is then communicated to the government concerned, which is asked to comment on the substance of the allegations.

It is normally on the basis of the documentation received from both parties that the CFA makes its decisions. However, in recent years the CFA has decided to make more frequent use of oral representations by governments and complainants, contacts with governments during the annual Conference, and on-site visits to gather evidence by representatives of the Director-General of the ILO.

What Kind of Decision Reached

If the CFA finds that no violation has been committed or that the alleged violation has ceased, it will simply decide to halt further examination. On the other hand, if it finds that violations have occurred, it will make recommendations to the parties to correct the situation. It may, for instance, recommend to governments that they institute or refrain from certain actions or that they amend existing legislation. It may also make recommendations to the organization which filed the complaint if it finds that its activities have contributed to the situation.

Implementation of the Decision

If the CFA finds that there are problems in guaranteeing the principles of freedom of association, it may ask the government concerned to continue reporting to it, or it may refer the case to the Committee of Experts on the Application of Conventions and Recommendations (if the relevant conventions have been ratified). In exceptional cases, the CFA may recommend referral of the case to the FFCC.

Procedures before the Fact-Finding and Conciliation Commission

The FFCC is an ad hoc body of independent experts appointed by the Governing Body to examine allegations of infringement of freedom of association. It was originally intended to form the only procedure for the examination of such complaints, but, when the CFA was created in 1951, the FFCC became a forum for the examination of the more serious cases. Although it has been convened only five times (noted below), it has been utilized in cases of particular political delicacy.

Substantive Requirements

As in the case of complaints before the CFA, cases before the FFCC deal with freedom of association. A complaint may be submitted against any state, whether or not it has ratified the freedom of association conventions or is a member of the ILO. If a state is not a member of the ILO but is a member of the United Nations, a complaint concerning it may be referred to the Commission by ECOSOC. In all cases, however, the state concerned must consent to the referral of the case to the FFCC. The only exception to this rule is when a complaint under article 26 of the ILO

Constitution concerns ratified freedom-of-association conventions (and is referred to the special procedures on this subject.)

Cases may be referred to the FFCC in four ways, each of which requires the participation of a government or international body:

By the Governing Body on the recommendation of the CFA. When the CFA has dealt with a case, it may recommend to the Governing Body that it should be referred to the FFCC. This has happened in cases concerning Japan and Chile.

By the Governing Body on the recommendation of the International Labor Conference. This procedure has not yet been used.

At the request of the government concerned. A government may request that a situation concerning freedom of association be examined by the FFCC. This occurred with respect to Greece, when the government requested that a complaint against it be transferred from the CFA to the FFCC.

By the UN Economic and Social Council. With the consent of the government concerned, ECOSOC can refer allegations against states that are members of the United Nations but not of the ILO. This has been done in cases concerning Lesotho and the United States, both of which had been ILO members but which had withdrawn at the time of the complaint. (Both have since rejoined the ILO.)

Formal Requirements

As this procedure is not directly accessible to individuals or NGOs, the formal requirements need not be noted here. Cases referred to the Commission by the CFA are discussed above.

Means of Investigation

FFCCs are free to work out their own procedures, but all have based themselves on documentary evidence furnished by the parties, have heard witnesses, and have visited the countries concerned (except in one case in which the complaint was withdrawn before the visit could take place). Representatives of the complainant organizations and the governments against which complaints are made are allowed to be represented in the proceedings before the FFCC.

Kind of Decision Reached

The mandate of a Commission is to ascertain the facts and to discuss the situation with the governments concerned with a view to securing the adjustment of the difficulties by agreement or friendly settlement. In its dual role of investigator and conciliator, therefore, it makes a thorough examination of the facts and formulates recommendations designed to provide a common ground for the resolution of a dispute. Once a decision is reached, it is published in a special report on the case.

Recommendations of the FFCC have concerned the direction in which the trade union movement in a country should be allowed or encouraged to develop, legislative proposals, calls for the ratification of ILO conventions, and even recommendations for the restoration of civil liberties that are essential to the exercise of trade union rights. It may also make recommendations to other parties, such as the trade unions concerned, as it did in the case of Japan.

Implementation of the Decision

A commission's recommendations have no legal force, and it has no specific enforcement measures available to ensure that its recommendations are implemented. Since a Commission is convened to examine a particular case, it is not even able systematically to monitor the effect, if any, of its recommendations.

However, compliance with the FFCC's recommendations may be monitored by other ILO bodies, such as the CFA. If the country concerned has ratified one of the ILO conventions on freedom of association, the regular supervisory bodies continue to examine the effect given to FFCC recommendations and may refer to the FFCC's conclusions in subsequent comments on the application of the convention in question. The situation may also be followed by the Conference Committee on the Application of Conventions and Recommendations, by the International Labor Conference in plenary session, and by the Governing Body.

Special Surveys on Discrimination in Employment

In 1974, the ILO Governing Body adopted arrangements under which requests for special surveys of the situation in individual countries with regard to discrimination could be considered. While not a complaint procedure per se, it does share some of the features of the complaint procedures examined above. No such special survey has yet been instituted, although the procedure remains in place.

Substantive Requirements

In determining the procedures, the Governing Body stated that surveys might be based on criteria "such as those laid down in the Discrimination (Employment and Occupation) Convention, 1958 (No. 111)." Convention No. 111 defines discrimination, in part, as "any distinction, exclusion or preference made on the basis of race, color, sex, religion, political opinion, national extraction or social origin, which has the effect of nullifying or impairing equality of opportunity or treatment in employment or occupation." Requested surveys should not, however, concern "individual cases unrelated to broader issues of policy."

A survey may be carried out in relation to any member state of the ILO, whether or not it has ratified a convention concerning discrimination. However, the state concerned must consent to the survey.[3]

A request may be submitted by the government of the state concerned; another state, if there are specific issues of concern to that state; employers' or workers' organizations directly concerned with the issues raised or which have consultative status with the ILO; or other international or regional employers' or workers' organizations, if the question raised directly concern organizations affiliated with them.

Formal Requirements

A request is submitted to the Director-General of the International Labor Office and need meet no particular conditions as to form.

Form of Investigation, Decision Making, and Implementation

No procedures have yet been set forth for carrying out surveys, so it may only be supposed that some or all of the methods ILO bodies have used in examining other kinds of complaints would be used—submissions of documentation from interested parties, hearing of witnesses, and visits to the country concerned. Equally, no standards have been set for the form of decisions or recommendations to be reached, or for any oversight that might be exercised thereafter.

Conclusions

The procedures outlined above form part of the most comprehensive international system for examining the implementation of international human rights standards. With the major exception of the procedures for examining complaints by the Governing Body's CFA, they have not been widely used, although the frequency of complaints has accelerated in recent years. Does this mean that they are not effective? The author's experience with the ILO leads him to conclude that this is not the case.

If these procedures are used infrequently, it is because they are but one part of a comprehensive and active system of regular supervision. Thus, a situation which violates internationally recognized labor standards rarely reaches the stage that would provoke a complaint, without its being dealt with by the Committee of Experts or the conference.

When complaints are filed, however, they signal to the government concerned that the ILO intends to undertake a thorough, objective, and prompt examination of the situation, and to reach firm and public conclusions on the rights and wrongs of the case. It is rare indeed that governments do not cooperate fully in the ILO's investigations in such cases. Even if a government does not implement the ILO's conclusions immediately, the longer term often results in the adoption of legislation and practices that closely follow the recommendations made.

The case should not be overstated. Complaints do not invariably result in improvements, and there are sometimes gaps in the information made available to the ILO. Such cases may arise when the government feels that it faces such serious internal difficulties that it must postpone taking measures to fulfill its international human rights obligations. Even in such cases, however, the ILO continues to work with the government to attempt to implement the recommendations which have followed the examination of a complaint.

Above all, it should be noted that the complaint procedures would not be nearly as effective if they did not form part of the ILO's overall machinery for supervising the implementation of ILO principles and instruments. It is not simple for human rights NGOs to have access to the ILO machinery, except with the cooperation of trade unions. However, NGOs should be aware of the ILO's work in the field of human rights as a valuable source of information, and as a defender and promoter of human rights on a daily, working level.

Notes

1. While fewer than two dozen cases have thus far been filed, use of the article 24 procedure seems to be increasing, and it represents a potentially important means of raising complaints. [ed. note]

2. ILO, LXI OFFICIAL BULLETIN, Series A, No. 3 (1978).

3. One might ask whether this requirement of prior consent is responsible for the nonutilization of the procedure. [ed. note]

6

The Complaint Procedure
of the United Nations Educational,
Scientific and Cultural Organization
(UNESCO)

STEPHEN MARKS

In addition to being the main organization within the UN system for the promotion of teaching and research on human rights, UNESCO is also concerned with alleged violations of human rights under several different procedures. Implementation of the twenty-six recommendations, twenty-six conventions, and five declarations that have been adopted by UNESCO, most of which concern human rights, is primarily carried out through a reporting system which does not include individual petitions or complaints. There are special procedures for the implementation of certain instruments, but these also exclude individual petitions.

The most important complaint procedure available to individuals and NGOs is that described in this chapter. It was initiated by the UNESCO Executive Board in 1976 and its procedures finalized in 1978 in Decision 104 EX/3.3 of the Board [hereinafter "the Decision"].[1] Before examining in detail how this procedure works, a brief summary of its history and development may be helpful.

The author is responsible for the choice and presentation of the facts contained in this chapter and for the opinions expressed therein, which are not necessarily those of UNESCO and do not commit the organization.

Like all UN organizations well known to the public, UNESCO has always been a body to which people who feel they have been victims of injustice or mistreatment write and request help. Their letters range from complaints of remote psychic manipulation by obscure evil forces, sent by persons of dubious mental health, to well-substantiated allegations of clear violations of human rights falling within one of the four fields over which UNESCO has competence: education, science, culture, and communication.

In 1952, the Executive Board noted in one of its decisions that the Director-General and the Chairman of the Executive Board "receive communications from private persons or associations alleging violations by States . . . of certain human rights."[2]

At its following session, the Board decided that its Chairman could examine such communications and submit to the Board those which seemed to him to call for some action by the organization.[3] Although this decision had the potential to become a procedure for considering complaints, it was never actually utilized.

It was not until fifteen years later that the Board adopted a rudimentary procedure for considering complaints. In 1967, the Board adopted a procedure modeled on (and expressly referring to) ECOSOC Resolution 728 F.[4] In accordance with this new procedure and the practice under it, a communication received by the Secretariat would be transmitted to the Committee on Conventions and Recommendations in Education (which is composed of governmental representatives and was formerly called the Special Committee on Discrimination in Education) if it was found (a) to be addressed to UNESCO by an identifiable author, and was not a copy of a communication addressed elsewhere; (b) to concern a specific case, that is, refer to an identifiable victim or victims; (c) to involve human rights; and (d) to relate to UNESCO'S fields of competence.[5]

If these conditions were not fulfilled, the author was simply notified that note had been taken of the communication. If the conditions were met, the author was informed of Decision 77 EX/8.3 and asked if there were no objection to divulging his or her name (or organization) and transmitting the communication to the government concerned. If an affirmative reply was received, which was not always the case, the communication was sent to the government, which was invited to reply. The communication and reply, if any, were transmitted to the Committee, which met in private sessions and which permitted oral submissions by the government concerned. Finally, the Committee reported on its activities to the full Executive Board, but it did not normally provide any details about the cases examined.

The only exception to the confidential nature of this procedure was the case of Chile. The Board publicly endorsed the conclusions of the Committee's report in 1976 and expressed its "profound disquiet at the continuing infringements, according to the information received, of human rights in the fields of education, science, culture and information."[6] The Board renewed its appeal to the Chilean authorities to take all necessary measures to restore and safeguard human rights and decided that the Committee should continue its examination of appropriate communications. This public decision was highly unusual and reflects the political stance of the Board (Pablo Neruda had been a member of the Board during the Allende government) rather than an advance in the implementation of Decision 77 EX/8.3.

As part of the same 1976 decision, the Board asked the Committee to review and improve its procedures. Before this review had been completed, the General Conference of UNESCO invited the Director-General and the Executive Board "to study the procedures which should be followed in the examination of cases and questions which might be submitted to UNESCO concerning the exercise of human rights in the spheres to which its competence extends, in order to make its action more effective".[7] This study resulted in adoption by the Board of Decision 104 EX/3.3 in 1978.

Substantive Requirements under the 1978 Procedure

The ten conditions for admissibility of a communication are set out in paragraph 14(a) of Decision 104 EX/3.3, all of which must be met. Clearly, the most important criteria concern the subject matter, as defined in conditions (iii), (iv), and (v) of paragraph 14(a). Most communications which are declared inadmissible by the Committee which examines them fail on one or more of these counts.

A communication must concern "human rights falling within UNESCO's competence in the fields of education, science, culture and information." There can be no doubt that this formulation includes each of the four rights directly derived from the enumerated fields of competence:
— the right to education;
— the right to share in scientific advancement;
— the right to participate freely in cultural life;

— the right to information, including freedom of conscience and expression.

Four other rights are so closely related to the former that they may also
be included:

— the right to freedom of thought, conscience, and religion;
— the right to the protection of the moral and material interests resulting
from any scientific, literary, or artistic production;
— the right to freedom of assembly and association for the purposes of
activities connected with education, science, culture, and information;
— the right of children to special protection.

Finally, two collective rights may be relevant, since they both have a
cultural dimension:

— the right of minorities to enjoy their own culture, to profess and practice their own religion, and to use their own language;
— the right of peoples to self-determination, including the right to pursue
cultural development.

Of these ten rights, only the first seven have been specifically noted in
official UNESCO documents.[8] However, all but the right to self-
determination have been mentioned in representations by UNESCO before
the UN Human Rights Committee.[9]

In practice, these rights are defined as they appear in the International
Bill of Human Rights (the Universal Declaration and the two International
Covenants). It also would appear to be within the spirit of the decision
and the work of the Committee to define the rights covered by condition
(iii) in light of their development in UNESCO's own normative instru-
ments dealing with human rights, although these are not frequently cited.
They would include, inter alia, the Universal Copyright Convention; the
Convention against Discrimination in Education; the recommendations
concerning the status of teachers and artists; the Declaration of Guiding
Principles on the Use of Satellite Broadcasting for the Free Flow of Information, the Spread of Education and Greater Cultural Exchange; and the
Declaration on Race and Racial Prejudice.

Condition (iii) also excludes communications that are motivated *exclusively* by non-human rights considerations. Taken literally, this condition
would only exclude communications that had nothing but political (or other
non-human rights) motivations. However, the fact that the author is from
a country or an organization hostile in some way to the state concerned is
usually enough for the representative of that state to claim that the only
motivation is political.

Condition (iv) is closely related to condition (iii). Compatibility with
the principles of UNESCO, the UN Charter, and other basic human rights

instruments does not appear to be a difficult condition to meet if condition (iii) is fulfilled.

Condition (v) requires that the communication "must appear to contain relevant evidence" and "must not be manifestly ill-founded." Taken literally, the first condition does not require that any evidence be produced (at least at the preliminary stage of admissibility), only that the matter be presented in such a way that the Committee can expect to examine some evidence at the merits phase of the case.

In practice, many states tend to assert that a communication is manifestly ill-founded. That assertion usually implies that the state challenges the allegations on the merits but wants the case dismissed immediately. In theory, this condition should serve as a barrier only to communications that are obviously outside the scope of the procedure, owing either to misunderstanding of the rights protected or clearly unsupportable allegations.

A communication may originate "from a person or group of persons who, it can be reasonably presumed, are victims of alleged violations" or "from any person, group of persons or non-governmental organization having reliable knowledge of these violations."

There is no definitive interpretation of what constitutes "reliable" knowledge, although it is later provided that a communication "must not be based exclusively on information disseminated through the mass media." This would not seem to exclude press reports as important sources of information (although the reliability or credibility of the author may be challenged by a state if these sources are relied on too heavily).

Under the UNESCO procedure, it is not necessary to demonstrate a connection between the person or organization filing the communication and the alleged victim. However, a communication cannot be anonymous, a requirement that must be considered by any potential complainant who may fear reprisals.

A complex issue falling between the questions of *what* may be complained about and *who* may submit a complaint concerns the status of the alleged victim. It has not yet been decided whether a communication concerning rights which are *not* among those considered to fall within UNESCO's competence but which concerns a victim whose professional activity *does* fall within UNESCO's competence is admissible. For example, a teacher, scientist, writer, musician, or journalist who has been arbitrarily detained, would, by virtue of the alleged violation of human rights, be prevented from exercising his or her rights relating to education, science, culture, or information.

To the extent that humanitarian considerations prevail over political factors, the Committee may be expected to accept such an interpretation and has done so in cases of disappearances. However, the political implications of an allegation that a government's policy toward members of a group or minority is preventing the exercise of "UNESCO rights" are serious. In such a case, stretching the UNESCO procedures by linking a non-UNESCO-related violation and a UNESCO-related victim may meet with resistance and, conceivably, jeopardize the limited implementation of the system. Nevertheless, such a link *has* been presumed, at least at the admissibility stage.

A communication may be filed against any country. However, the necessary dialogue with the authorities would be virtually impossible if a country is not a member of UNESCO.

Formal Requirements

There are no rules governing the form of communications; they are normally in the form of letters addressed to the Director-General of UNESCO. As long as the author is identifiable and the communication refers to human rights violations, it will usually be handled in accordance with the procedure outlined in this chapter. There are, however, several formal hurdles that must be overcome if a communication is to be declared admissible and considered on its merits.

Conditions (vi) through (x) of paragraph 14 of the Decision refer essentially to formal requirements. Offensive and abusive wording is not allowed, although the offensive or abusive parts may simply be eliminated. It is in the author's interest to avoid any wording that may be so interpreted, since it is likely that the author or the Secretariat would be instructed to eliminate such passages, thus delaying examination of admissibility until the next session, that is, for six months. The requirement that a communication must be submitted within a "reasonable time limit following the facts" is interpreted according to the circumstances. In practice, this time limit is not considered to run while a victim or organization is endeavoring to obtain redress through domestic and international channels.

Condition (ix) refers to exhaustion of local remedies, but the requirement is not one of *prior* exhaustion of those remedies; it is rather that the author must "indicate whether an attempt has been made to exhaust" them. One could argue that the author could merely state that no attempt has been made and thereby meet the requirement. However, for this condition to be meaningful, the Committee should be expected to hesitate to admit a communication if it appears to be the first or only forum to which the author is appealing. Any international body may be reluctant to seek an international solution to a problem for which effective remedies may be available within the country concerned. However, the wording of this condition gives the Committee considerable flexibility and avoids a detailed examination of local procedures. Where local judicial or administrative remedies have been explored without success, this fact would be relevant to the consideration of the communication.

The final formal condition is one that is similar to a rule of lis pendens. Condition (x) allows the Committee to declare inadmissible communications that have been settled, whether under municipal law or international human rights procedures, as long as the Committee is satisfied that the principles of human rights have been respected in the settlement. Although the Secretariat has been instructed by the Committee to request information from other international organizations on the status of a communication being handled simultaneously by both institutions, the fact that the case is before another body is not a cause for inadmissibility.[10]

The initial letter to the Director-General is not considered to be the "communication" formally examined by UNESCO. Rather, each letter or communication received is acknowledged by the Secretariat (the Office of International Standards and Legal Affairs), which also sends to the author a UNESCO-prepared form on which information relevant to the complaint must be entered. The form requests information as to the author's name, nationality, and address; relationship of the author to the alleged victim; factual information, including the connection between the violation and education, science, culture, or information; and any attempts to exhaust domestic remedies. This form must be signed and returned, with the agreement that it will be transmitted to the government concerned and the name of the author divulged. It is only after the return of this form to UNESCO that a "communication" is formally deemed to exist.

Means of Investigation

The primary investigatory body is the Executive Board's Committee on Conventions and Recommendations (formerly the Committee on Conventions and Recommendations in Education), which meets every six months, generally in April and September. The committee first decides whether a communication is "admissible," that is, whether it appears to meet the formal and substantive requirements set forth in paragraph 14(a) of Decision 104 EX/3.3. If a communication is admissible, the Committee then proceeds to an examination of the "merits" of the claim, in order to determine whether it warrants further action.[11]

As is the case in most international investigative procedures, much of the actual work in analyzing and summarizing the information contained in a communication, especially in the earlier stages of the procedures, is done by the UNESCO Secretariat. After receipt of the returned UNESCO form from the author, the Secretariat sends a copy of the form to the government concerned. All correspondence is addressed to the Permanent Delegation of the government to UNESCO; in practice, it is delivered by hand to the delegation. The letter of transmittal explains that the communication will be brought to the notice of the Committee at its next session, together with any reply the government may wish to make.

A summary of each communication is prepared, giving the identity of the author, the procedural status, the essential elements of the claim, the recourse attempted, and the purpose of the communication.[12] The important correspondence, including any reply from the government concerned and the UNESCO form, is included.

The communications are grouped according to whether they are to be examined as to their admissibility or as to the merits. In accordance with paragraph 14(f) of the Decision, which allows the Committee to "avail itself of the relevant information at the disposal of the Director-General," the Committee's documentation may contain other pertinent information, which can be provided orally or in writing.[13] Once the Committee has begun its session, the Secretariat's role is to service the Committee and to notify the authors and governments concerned of the decision concerning admissibility or subsequent dismissal of an admissible communication.

In addition to the "Secretariat" (the officials acting under the authority of the Director-General), the procedure also provides a direct role for the Director-General. This role, set forth in paragraphs 8 and 9 of Decision 104 EX/3.3, is often referred to as "humanitarian intercession," and it includes "initiating consultations, in conditions of mutual respect, confidence and confidentiality, to help reach solutions to particular problems concerning human rights."

Thus, even before a communication is transmitted to the government concerned, the matter may be considered by the Director-General to justify intercession. While intervening in any way in the internal affairs of Member States is expressly prohibited by the UNESCO Constitution, the

Director-General can use his or her authority to draw the attention of a country to a specific human rights problem and seek, confidentially, to obtain a satisfactory solution. Solutions reached in this way, which are not unusual, are of course preferable to awaiting the outcome of the procedure before the Committee.

Once the Committee is satisfied that the conditions of paragraph 14(a) have been met, a communication is normally declared admissible and the merits considered at the next session. Unlike the 1503 procedures discussed in chapter 4, the Committee notifies both the author and the government of its decision on admissibility. The Committee's deliberations on admissibility are in private session, although the government concerned is permitted to attend the Committee's meetings "in order to provide additional information or to answer questions from members of the Committee."[14]

The Committee's Decision on the Merits

Upon examining the merits of a communication, the Committee may decide that no further action is warranted. In this case, the communication is dismissed, and both the author and the government concerned are notified. If further action is warranted, the Committee's task is to help "bring about a friendly solution designed to advance the promotion of the human rights falling within UNESCO's fields of competence."[15]

A preambular paragraph of Decision 104 Ex/3.3 states that "UNESCO should not play the role of an international judicial body," and the most characteristic feature of the merits phase of the procedure is the search for a dialogue with the government. As long as the government is cooperative, the Committee is willing to be patient.

The Committee submits confidential reports to the Executive Board at each session. These reports are to contain "appropriate information arising from its examination of the communications which the Committee considers useful to bring to the notice of the Executive Board . . . [as well as] recommendations which the Committee may wish to make either generally or regarding the disposition of a communication under consideration."[16]

The Committee's practice is to report on each communication examined at the session (approximately fifty at the present time), whether it has been declared admissible or not. The report on each communication usually includes a brief summary of the facts and the state of the procedure, the point of view expressed by the members of the Committee and by the representative of the government concerned, and the decision reached by the Committee. The decision on a communication which has been examined as to its admissibility is that it is either admissible, inadmissible, suspended (for further information), or postponed (due to practical or technical considerations). As regards admissible communications, the Committee reports that it has decided either to apply the special procedure concerning disappeared persons, described below; to request further information from the government concerned, the author of the communication, or both; or to recommend some other action. It can, for example, request the Executive Board to invite the Director-General to address, on its behalf, an appeal to the government concerned for clemency or for the rapid release of a detained person.

The Board examines the report of the Committee in closed meetings. Members of the Board express whatever views they may have on the content of the report, and then the Board "takes note" of the report. When the report contains recommendations for action, the record shows that the Board has endorsed the wishes of the Committee.[17]

To offer a quantitative idea of the Committee's decisions, the following statistics are from the Committee's April 1980 session: forty-five communications were examined as to admissibility, of which five were declared admissible, thirteen inadmissible, twenty suspended, and seven deleted from the agenda. Ten communications were examined on the merits, of which six were considered under the special procedure on disappearance; "considerable progress" toward settlement was noted with respect to one case; one communication was the subject of a recommendation to appeal for clemency; one was postponed; and one was deemed settled.[18]

Special Procedure on Disappearances

A special procedure has been adopted by the Committee to deal with cases of disappeared persons. Referring to General Assembly Resolution 33/173, the Committee decided in 1979 that "communications, declared admissible, concerning enforced or involuntary disappearances of persons as a result of actions imputed to law enforcement authorities or similar organizations" would be placed on a special list "if the Committee has not obtained sufficient information about the fate of the missing persons from the government concerned."[19] Such disappearances are examined again by the Committee whenever new information is provided by either the governments concerned, the author of the communication, the family and friends of the missing persons, or an humanitarian NGO. Even in the absence of such information, the communications on the list must be reexamined at least once a year by the Committee.

The governments concerned are requested "to devote appropriate resources to searching for such persons and to keep UNESCO informed of any new development concerning each case of disappearance that is brought to the attention of the Organization."[20] Of the eight admissible communications considered at the September 1979 session, five were handled under this special procedure; it was applied to six of the ten admissible communications considered at the April 1980 session.[21]

After the creation of the Working Group of the UN Commission on Human Rights in 1980 under Commission Resolution 20 (XXXVI), the April 1980 session of the Committee decided to transmit communications to which the special procedure was applied and similar future communications to the working group and to defer examination of them for one year, with the exception of communications concerning disappearances that have occured within the past two years. The deferred communications are to be reexamined in the light of the deliberations of the working group.

Examination of "Cases" versus "Questions"

Paragraph 10 of Decision 104 EX/3.3 distinguishes between UNESCO's competence in individual, specific "cases" and "questions of massive, systematic, or flagrant violations of human rights committed *de jure* or *de facto* by a State or from an accumulation of individual cases forming a consistent pattern." Paragraph 18 further defines such "questions" as including (but not limited to) aggression, interference in internal affairs, foreign occupation, colonialism, genocide, apartheid, racism, and "national and social oppression."

This dual mandate resulted from negotiations that occurred during the adoption of the Decision, as certain Executive Board members felt that only large-scale violations of human rights should be considered, while others felt that UNESCO should be authorized to deal with individual cases. There are as yet no precedents for the examination of "questions," and it is not clear at what stage of the procedure a communication is to be designated as a "case" or a "question."

The essential difference between a "case" and a "question" is that the latter is considered *in public* by both the Executive Board and, ultimately, the General Conference of UNESCO.[22] All aspects of the procedure for the examination of a "question" are currently under study as part of the Committee's confidential work.[23]

Conclusions

The confidential nature of the UNESCO procedure described in this chapter, the emphasis on friendly settlement, and the lack of strong implementation or oversight mechanisms suggest that the procedure is rather weaker than some of those established by the ILO or regional organizations. At the same time, however, the confidentiality is less complete than that imposed by ECOSOC's Resolution 1503 procedure and provision is made for the consideration of individual cases as well as large-scale violations. Both the author of a UNESCO communication and the government concerned are informed of the disposition of a communication, and the Committee's role in friendly settlement also implies at least an indirect role for the complainant.

Given the fact that these procedures were not established pursuant to a specific convention but are based rather on the inherent constitutional authority of UNESCO, they should be viewed as an important step forward in the protection of human rights. All international procedures designed to protect human rights ultimately depend on the good faith and cooperation of the governments concerned, and the informal, mediating character of the UNESCO procedure can be equally, if not more, effective than many more public actions. The potential for the as yet untried public consideration of "questions" of mass violations may also provide a meaningful forum in those instances where publicity and public pressure are needed to combat such major violations.

Notes

1. UNESCO Doc. 104 EX/Decision 3.3 (1978).
2. UNESCO Doc. 29 EX/Decision 11.3 (1952).

3. UNESCO Doc. 30 EX/Decision 11 (1952).

4. E.S.C. Res. 728F(XXVIII), 28 UN ESCOR, Supp. (No. 1) 19, UN Doc. E/3290 (1959).

5. UNESCO Doc. 77 EX/Decision 8.3 (1967).

6. UNESCO Doc. 99 EX/Decision 9.5 (1976).

7. UNESCO Doc. 19 C/Resolutions 6.113 and 12.1 (1976).

8. Executive Board, Part C, Annex II, at 53 (1981).

9. UN Doc. CCPR/C/SR.78 (1978); see chapter 10.

10. UNESCO Doc. 112 EX/CR/HR/5, para. 56 (1981).

11. The substance of the Committee's discussions of a communication often blurs the formal distinction between admissibility and the merits, even though separate decisions may be rendered. It has been suggested that every complaint is, in effect, examined on its merits by the Committee and that a responding government thus is made aware of other governments' concerns even if a communication is formally declared inadmissible. [ed. note]

12. While there is no guarantee that it will be utilized, it is recommended that the author of a communication prepare a short (two-paragraph) summary of the complaint and, if the facts are particularly complex or supporting documentation lengthy, a somewhat longer précis (perhaps two to three pages) of the substance of the communication, which should be submitted with the communication. If essential documents have been included as annexes to the communication, it is probably advisable to incorporate some direct reference to them in these summaries. Complete copies of communications are *not* prepared for each delegation, although they are available for consultation. [ed. note]

13. There is no formal procedure for submission of such other material. At least in theory, the Committee could draw upon any material available to UNESCO, and NGOs and others should not hesitate to send relevant information on human rights to the Division of Human Rights and Peace of UNESCO, even outside the context of a communication under Decision 104 EX/3.3. *See* Alston, *UNESCO's Procedure for Dealing with Human Rights Violations*, 20 SANTA CLARA L. REV. 665, 680 (1980). [ed. note]

14. *Supra* note 1 at para. 14(e).

15. *Id.*, para. 14(k).

16. *Id.*, para. 15.

17. The public record is very vague in reporting the Committee's recommendations, and specific countries are not mentioned. For example, the announcement of decisions taken at the 110th session stated merely that "the Board examined the report of the Committee on Conventions and Recommendations concerning this item [the Committee's report under Decision 104 EX/3.3], *took note* thereof and *endorsed* the Committee's wishes expressed therein." UNESCO Doc. 110 EX/Decisions at 34 (1980).

18. 21st UNESCO General Conference, UNESCO Doc. 21 C/13, para. 65 (1980).

19. Decision of the Committee, 10 Sept. 1979, UNESCO Doc. 108 EX/CR/ HR/PROC/2 Rev. (1979) (confidential).

20. *Id*.

21. 21st UNESCO General Conference, note 18 *supra*.

22. *Supra* note 1 at paras. 17 and 18.

23. It is possible that the Committee has decided, in effect, not to act on any "questions" presented to it; indeed, authors of some communications have been requested to rephrase their complaints in such a way that they could be dealt with as a series of individual "cases" rather than as "questions." [ed. note]

7

The Individual Petition Procedure of the Inter-American System for the Protection of Human Rights

ROBERT E. NORRIS

As a result of the entry into force of the American Convention on Human Rights in 1978, the Inter-American Commission on Human Rights (IACHR) was reorganized in 1979 under a new Statute, which establishes separate petition procedures for complaints against member states of the Organization of American States (OAS) that are parties to the Convention as well as those that have not ratified. Parties to the Convention are subject to the petition procedure set forth in article 19(a) of the Statute, pursuant to articles 44–51 of the Convention, while other member states continue to be subject to the former procedure of the IACHR, preserved in its basic form in article 20 of the Statute.

The essential aspects of the two procedures have been harmonized by the Commission's new Regulations. The prerequisites for admissibility of the petition, the stages of processing, and methods of fact-finding and reporting or publication of findings are essentially the same under both procedures. In either case, an admissible petition initiates an inquiry that may result in a decision on the merits of the complaint and in specific recommendations to the government of the state concerned. Although the Commission's recommendations are not binding, its inquiry and final report may have a salutary effect by focusing attention upon the alleged violation or situation of the victim. The Commission is explicity authorized to work toward a friendly settlement under the procedure provided for state parties to the Convention, and it is not precluded from seeking this type of remedy in the case of states that are not parties. The principal difference between the remedies available under either procedure is that petitions brought against state parties may eventually be referred to the Inter-American Court of Human Rights for a binding decision, if the state concerned has accepted the Court's jurisdiction.

The following pages present the substantive and technical requirements for filing a petition with the Commission, a description of how the petition is processed, and the kinds of decisions that may be reached by the Commission. The final section summarizes the procedure before the Inter-American Court.

Substantive Requirements

Rights Protected

The Commission is empowered to act upon petitions that allege the violation of the human rights of any person by the government of a member state of the OAS. The relevant human rights are those defined by the American Convention on Human Rights in the case of parties to the Convention and those found in the 1948 American Declaration of the Rights and Duties of Man in the case of nonparty states. The violation may have occurred within or outside the national boundaries of the state accused.

The civil and political rights set forth in the Declaration and the Convention are similar, although these rights are better defined in the latter. The principal distinction between the two systems is the broad range of economic, social, and cultural rights included in the Declaration, such as the rights to property, the benefits of culture, work and a fair remuneration, the preservation of health and well-being, education, leisure time, and social security. In contrast, the Convention protects only the right to property and rights of the family and children.[1]

Although the Regulations do not require that the petitioner identify the right or rights allegedly violated, it is in the petitioner's interest to do so. In many cases, the rights in question may be apparent; in others, the facts may fail to direct the Commission's attention to violations of related rights or to particular aspects of those rights that the petitioner deems important. And, as a general rule applicable to any international procedure, a petitioner should not rely entirely on the assumption that the petition will be processed with a high degree of competence or care. Any relevant omission may result in a delay of several months or more.

In more complicated cases, particularly those involving rights in the American Declaration, which are not well defined, the petitioner may have to interpret a specific right and demonstrate how the circumstances of the case constitute a violation. Relevant sources for such an interpretation would include the constitution and internal laws of the state concerned; the Charter of the OAS;[2] and other multilateral conventions related to human rights, such as those of the International Labor Organization (ILO) or treaties on refugees, asylum, or extradition. Even treaties which have not been ratified by the state concerned, but which have been accepted by a significant number of the member states of the OAS, may assist in defining a right in the American Declaration or the American Convention. The Convention itself may be used to interpret the Declaration,[3] as may pertinent resolutions of various organs of the inter-American system such as the earlier Inter-American Conferences, Meetings of Consultation, and the OAS General Assembly. Finally, some guidance may be found in the resolutions, reports, and studies adopted by the Inter-American Commission itself.

The scope of the rights protected is limited in various manners. Article 32(2) of the Convention contains a general restrictive clause, which acknowledges that "the rights of each person are limited by the rights of others, by the security of all and by the just demands of the general welfare, in a democratic society." Some of the other rights are limited by specific "clawback" clauses, which permit restrictions "in the interest of national security, public safety or public order, or to protect public health or morals or the rights or freedoms of others."[4] In certain situations of an exceptional nature, article 27 permits a state party to take measures derogating from the Convention "to the extent and for the period of time strictly required," so long as those measures do not conflict with that state's other international obligations and do not involve discrimination. Even in emergency situations, however, certain rights, such as the right to life and the right to humane treatment, are considered nonderogable.[5]

The rights of the American Declaration are also limited by a general restrictive clause, almost identical to that of the Convention, and, by implication, by the duties set forth in Chapter Two of the Declaration.

The scope of restrictions on rights is limited in turn by Commission practice. In a 1968 resolution, the Commission declared that certain fundamental rights contained in the Declaration were not subject to suspension and that a state of siege must be officially decreed under a constitutionally established procedure and limited to the requirements of the situation.[6] This same resolution served as the basis for the derogation clause of the American Convention. In 1974, however, the Commission referred to the standards of article 27 of the Convention to determine the compatibility of the state of siege in Chile with that country's obligations to respect the rights proclaimed in the Declaration, even though Chile had not ratified the Convention.[7] Accordingly, a petitioner may look to the 1968 resolution as well as to the American Convention for guidelines in questioning the legality of an alleged violation that occurred under the aegis of a suspension of guarantees.

Since mere assertion of a derogation under article 27 is not sufficient to remove jurisdiction from the Commission, a petitioner may be able to challenge the validity of a purported derogation on several grounds, for example:

1. Are the rights allegedly violated within those not subject to suspension under article 27(2), i.e., right to juridical personality, right to life, right to humane treatment, freedom from slavery, freedom from ex post facto laws, freedom of conscience and religion, rights of the family, right to a name, rights of the child, right to nationality, right to participate in government, and the judicial guarantees essential to protect those rights?
2. Was the Secretary-General of the OAS properly informed of the suspension, and does the text of the government's derogation sufficiently describe the rights affected?
3. Even if the notice is technically correct, do the circumstances cited by the government fit within the definition of "war, public danger, or other emergency that threatens the independence or security" of the nation?
4. Are the measures taken limited in scope and in time to those "strictly required by the exigencies of the situation"?
5. Are the measures taken inconsistent with any of the state's other obligations under international law?
6. Are the measures illegal because they discriminate on the basis of "race, color, sex, language, religion, or social origin"?

Similar arguments may be made with respect to a state that has not ratified the Convention, utilizing the principles set forth in the Commission's 1968 Resolution on "The Protection of Human Rights in Connection with the Suspension of Constitutional Guarantees or 'State of Siege.'"[8]

Who May File a Petition

There are almost no restrictions with regard to standing. Any person or group of persons, without regard to nationality, citizenship, or age, may bring a complaint before the Commission. The complainant may be a direct victim or a third party acting with or without authorization of the victim. Third parties may include NGOs "legally recognized in one or more member states of the Organization,"[9] and even this requirement may be avoided by designating one or more of the organization's members to bring the complaint on an individual basis.

General and Collective Petitions

There are circumstances in which a complainant may wish to consider filing a petition of a *general* or *collective* character. This terminology distinguishes two types of petitions which, while not formally recognized in the Regulations, have developed in the Commission's practice.[10] A general petition is not one phrased in general terms, but rather a petition that alleges the existence of a widespread or general disrespect for human rights not limited in its effects to a particular group or to a single fact situation. Specific cases of violations should be cited as evidence, and examples should support, both numerically and in scope, the allegation of a "widespread" or "general" disrespect for human rights founded upon a government's actions or failure to act. In presenting a general petition, the petitioner might subdivide the text of the petition in such a manner as to focus upon each type of violation separately.

A collective petition also refers to multiple victims and violations and should be supported by specific cases, but the examples cited should have certain common elements that would enable them to be treated more effectively as a collective case than as a series of individual cases. These common elements may include, inter alia, situations where

1. the victims constitute an identifiable group, based upon circumstantial or other relationships (e.g., members of a family, an indigenous tribe, or the same race or members of a particular political, religious, or professional group);
2. the alleged violations arise out of a particular incident or common fact situation (e.g., a massacre, a group kidnapping, or events related to a strike); or

3. the violations involve the same right or related rights (e.g., freedom of religion or of the press, or the right to due process).[11]

The advantages of a general or collective petition may be practical as well as procedural. Though the petition may, and should, identify individual victims, needless repetition of the basic fact situation or legal arguments may be avoided. The result is less paperwork and economy of time for all parties.

The primary advantage, however, is procedural, as allegations of general or widespread violations may obviate the need to demonstrate the exhaustion of specific domestic remedies. Under generally recognized principles of international law, ineffective or inadequate remedies need not be attempted, and the existence of a large number of well-substantiated violations may support an argument that domestic legislation or practice of the state concerned does not afford due process or adequate remedies for the protection of the rights concerned.[12]

Exhaustion of Domestic Remedies

The Commission may not admit petitions unless all remedies available under domestic law have been invoked and exhausted in accordance with generally recognized principles of international law.[13] Administrative or judicial decisions must be appealed, wherever possible, unless it can be shown that such appeal would be futile.[14]

Some exceptions to the requirement of exhaustion of domestic remedies are recognized in the Regulations. Proof of exhaustion need not be presented if the complainant can show that the domestic legislation of the state concerned does not afford due process of law for the protection of that right; the victim has been denied access to the remedies under domestic law or otherwise prevented from exhausting them; or there has been unwarranted delay in rendering a final judgment under those remedies. Other circumstances that may relieve the petitioner of the exhaustion requirement are the existence of a consistent pattern of governmental interference with due process of law, the absence of an independent judiciary,[15] or a consistent pattern of gross violations of human rights in the context of a "general" or "collective" case (discussed above).

If a petitioner is unable to prove exhaustion of remedies because of inadequate documentation, unavailability of counsel, or other factors, he should state the reasons. In such instances, the burden of proof in demonstrating that remedies have not been exhausted may shift to the government.[16]

Technical Requirements

Although procedures for bringing petitions against OAS members that are parties to the American Convention differ from procedures for those that are not, the only difference affecting the preparation of the petition is that the rights in reference will be those of the American Convention in the first instance and those of the American Declaration in the second.[17]

A sample form for petitions is reproduced in the Commission's *Handbook of Existing Rules Pertaining to Human Rights*, but a complaint need not follow it precisely. However, each petition should include the signature and sufficient identification of the complainant, a statement of facts, of timeliness, of exhaustion of domestic remedies, and a declaration that the petition is not pending before a similar intergovernmental proceeding.

Identification of the Petitioner

Article 29(a) of the IACHR Regulations requires that a petitioner's name, nationality, profession or occupation, and postal address or domicile be included. If the petitioner appoints an attorney or other person to represent him or her before the Commission, the representative should be identified in the same fashion. Any person who initiates a complaint as a victim's legal representative should present, if possible, a notarized power of attorney. Proof of authorization to act in the name of the victim or complainant may be required in cases in which a friendly settlement is contemplated or in cases that might be presented to the Inter-American Court.

The petitioner's name is not divulged to the government concerned, unless the petitioner so requests.

Statement of Facts

The statement of facts should be a detailed, third-person account of the acts or situation giving rise to the complaint, including the place and date of the alleged violation. If the complaint is brought on behalf of a third party, special care should be taken to identify the victim in the same manner as the complainant is identified. If possible, more specific identification, such as the victim's passport number, social security number, or national identification card number, should be presented.

It is also important to establish the nexus between the act complained of and the government accused of the violation, particularly in cases of so-called "disappearances" or other instances where government involvement is not evident. The Commission is not empowered to examine human rights violations attributable to private persons or groups unless those persons are acting under color of authority or are allowed to act with impunity.[18] If the complaint does not clearly implicate the government either because of its acts or failure to act, the complainant should state why the government is believed to be responsible. If any government official has been notified of the alleged violation, the official's identity and the date, time, and place (as well as a copy, if possible) of that notification should be included. The complainant should include the name, rank, or other description of the official responsible for the alleged violation or of any person believed to be acting upon official orders.

The statements of any eyewitness or other person with special knowledge of the case should be attached to the petition, and the petitioner should take care to state whether such testimony must be held confidential.

Timeliness

In cases in which domestic remedies have been pursued and exhausted, the petition must be filed with the Commission within six months of the date on which "the party whose rights have allegedly been violated has been notified of the final ruling."[19] There may be room for exceptions if, for example, a prisoner is able to show that late filing was due to serious infirmity while imprisoned, interference with freedom of communication, or the fact that his or her life would have been endangered. In the case of a party acting on behalf of a victim, this requirement may not be applicable if the victim was unable to submit a petition, and the third party acted within a reasonable time after having been informed of the alleged violation or the final decision.

The six-month period is inapplicable in the same circumstances in which the exhaustion requirement is waived, that is, where there is no real opportunity to avail oneself of domestic remedies or where they are unduly delayed. In such cases, the petition must be presented within a reasonable period of time.[20]

If the date of filing is not clearly within the six-month period, the petitioner should include a statement indicating why the petition should be considered under one of the exceptions.

Cases Pending before Other International Bodies

The Commission will not examine a petition that "essentially duplicates" a petition pending before or already examined and settled by another intergovernmental organization, but there are several exceptions to this rule. A petition is admissible if the other organization to which it had been submitted "is one limited to an examination of the general situation on human rights in the state in question and there has been no decision on specific facts that are the subject of the petition submitted to the Commission, or is one that will not lead to an effective settlement of the violation denounced."[21] This exception avoids duplication of efforts and conflicting decisions with similar individual complaint procedures, such as that of the Optional Protocol to the International Covenant on Civil and Political Rights,[22] yet allows simultaneous access to general procedures, such as that provided by ECOSOC Resolution 1503,[23] which do not lead to specific findings of facts or settlement of individual cases.

However, even at the risk of conflicting jurisdiction, the Commission will not renounce competency when the petitioner before the Commission is the victim or a family member, and the petitioner in the other proceeding is a third party who does not have specific authorization from the victim.[24]

Means of Investigation of a Petition

Preliminary Decision on Admissibility

The Secretariat of the Commission has a legal staff to process petitions, prepare country reports, and provide expertise and counsel to the Commission and the OAS within the area of human rights. Each attorney is responsible for the processing of petitions related to one or more member states. When a petition is received in the Secretariat, it is forwarded to the designated attorney, who determines whether it meets, prima facie, the requirements for admissibility. If any important elements are missing, the attorney may request the petitioner to submit additional information, and the processing is suspended until the missing elements are supplied.

The staff attorney makes only a preliminary decision on admissibility for the purpose of initiating the procedure. As more information is obtained from the petitioner or the government concerned, it may become apparent that the petition was not filed within the required time limit, that domestic remedies were not properly exhausted, or that the petition is manifestly unfounded. If so, the petitioner is informed that the complaint is inadmissible. In a difficult case, the Secretariat may consult the Commission at its next session. Under recent practice, the Commission has not made formal decisions on admissibility and has simply proceeded with consideration of the merits of a case, if no questions are raised by the Secretariat or the government concerned. This process is much less formal than that utilized by the European Commission of Human Rights, which rejects the vast majority of complaints as inadmissible.[25]

Transmittal of the Petition to the Government

If a petition is admissible on its face, it is assigned a number and officially registered as a case. A confidential case file is prepared, which contains all correspondence, decisions, and other information related to the case.

Once the case is opened, the "pertinent parts" of the petition are prepared for transmittal to the government concerned. Since the petition procedure is open to individuals, and legal counsel is not required, some complaints are less well drafted than others, and many reflect the sense of urgency and emotional state of the petitioner. The staff attorney transcribes the parts of the complaint that are considered pertinent, taking special care to delete any insulting language and any information that would tend to identify the author of the petition. Accordingly, the narrative may be changed to third person, and personal relationships may be suppressed. Though there are often details in the narrative that suggest the authorship, the petitioner cannot be identified with certainty, because such accounts almost inevitably become known to friends and relatives of the victim, some of whom may live outside the country, or by professional, labor, or human rights organizations who may assert the victim's rights without his or her knowledge.

The pertinent parts of the petition are forwarded to the government concerned through its Minister of Foreign Affairs and, at the same time, the Secretariat acknowledges receipt of the petition and informs the petitioner of the action taken and the date of transmittal to the government. The letter of transmittal requests that the government supply any relevant information with respect to the facts alleged and the exhaustion of internal legal remedies and procedures. The government is expected to reply "as quickly as possible" and no later than within 120 days of the date on which the request was sent. Justifiable extensions of up to 60 days may be granted by the Commission, and a petitioner should request to be informed of the basis upon which an extension was granted.

Should the government fail to respond within the allowable time, the Commission may presume the truth of the pertinent parts of the petition, so long as other evidence "does not lead to a different conclusion."[26] If the government does not respond to any one of the principal allegations and fails to make a general denial, its silence may provide the basis for a presumption of the truth of the allegation.[27] The petitioner should be prepared to bring any nonresponsive pleading to the Commission's attention and to request the Commission to presume the truth of the allegations.

When the government's reply is received by the Commission, the pertinent parts of the reply and any accompanying documents are forwarded to the petitioner (or the petitioner's representative), who is requested to comment and to supply within thirty days any additional evidence to support the complainant's allegations or to rebut the government's reply. The Regulations do not mention a possible extension of the time limit, but it is unlikely that the Commission would deny the petitioner the same extension as that allowed the government, so long as the petitioner shows justifiable cause. The petitioner should take care to respond to the legal arguments or factual statements contained in the government's reply. If appropriate, the petitioner may request that the Commission submit an interrogatory based on the reply or ask the government to supply specific documents or elements of proof.

This process of reply and rejoinder may continue so long as the staff attorney or Commission feels that it would be useful in establishing the facts of the case.

Special Fact-Finding Procedures

The usual method of establishing the facts in cases before the Commission is through the system of reply and rejoinder described above, but the petition system has provided for two other fact-finding procedures, which may be invoked in special circumstances: the hearing and the on-site investigation.

The Commission may decide to conduct a hearing at any time during the investigation. There are no formal requirements, and a hearing may or may not be adversarial in nature.[28] The Commission may request the representative of the state to supply any pertinent information, and either party may present oral or written statements.

On-site investigations may be held for the purpose of investigating an individual case or cases or for the purpose of studying the general situation of human rights in a member state. Parties to the Convention are obligated to furnish the necessary facilities for such an investigation, but other member states have no specific treaty obligations to accede to the Commission's request.[29]

Serious or Urgent Cases

When there is an imminent threat to a person's life or physical integrity, the petitioner should inform the Commission by the most expedient means. A telephone call to the Executive Secretary or the appropriate staff member may be helpful as advance notice, but the Secretariat, even in urgent circumstances, may require a communication in writing. A cablegram would suffice if it contains sufficient details of the situation and the return address or phone number of the sender.

In such a case, the Secretariat may by cablegram request a prompt reply from the government concerned.[30] If the government's response is not satisfactory, consideration of the petition will continue under the normal procedure, but the mere fact of an urgent inquiry by the Commission may alleviate the immediate threat by informing the government that the case is being considered by the Commission.

Kind of Decision Reached

Friendly Settlement

At any stage of the proceedings, but generally after the Secretariat has made a prima facie determination of admissibility and has concluded a preliminary consideration of the evidence, the Commission or either of the parties may invoke the friendly settlement procedure.[31] While the possibility of friendly settlement is specifically provided for only in the case of states parties to the Convention, the Regulations do not preclude such an initiative in the case of other OAS members.

The Commission has not yet developed a formal procedure for assisting in friendly settlements, but one may presume that the Secretariat will play a major role in the actual negotiations and then submit the proposed settlement to the Commission for its approval. Any settlement must be reached "on the basis of respect for the human rights recognized" in the Convention,[32] and the Commission must be satisfied that the terms of the settlement protect the general interest as well as that of the individual claimant or victim. If a friendly settlement is achieved, the Commission prepares a brief statement of the facts and the settlement, which is transmitted to the parties and made public through the OAS Secretary-General.[33]

Cases Involving States Parties to the Convention[34]

If a friendly settlement is not reached, the Commission prepares a report containing the facts and its conclusions, as well as any proposals or recommendations and a time limit for their implementation. The report is transmitted to the parties, who are not authorized to make it public.

Within three months from transmittal of the report to the parties, either the Commission or the state concerned—but not the individual petitioner —may present the matter to the Inter-American Court. If the state has not accepted the Court's jurisdiction, the Commission may propose, in appropriate cases, that it do so for the specific case under consideration.

If the case is not presented to the Court or the government fails to implement any Commission recommendation, the Commission may decide to publish its findings as part of its *Annual Report* to the OAS General Assembly or in any other manner it considers suitable. Publication is not required, however, and lies within the discretion of the Commission.

Cases Involving States not Parties to the Convention[35]

The procedure for examining petitions lodged against member states not parties to the Convention is very similar, though there is no specific provision for friendly settlement or for reference to the Court. The Commission's report is transmitted to both parties, but the state may request the Commission to reconsider its decision, on the basis of new arguments or facts. After hearing the petitioner's response to such a request, the Commission may ratify or amend the original decision. If the state fails to implement any of the Commission's recommendations within the time alloted, the Commission may publish the report in the same manner as in cases involving states parties to the convention.

Withdrawal or Joinder of a Petition

The petitioner may request that a petition be withdrawn from consideration at any point in the proceeding. The Commission will generally accede to such a request, but it is not obligated to do so. If it is ascertained that the withdrawal was prompted by a threat, or if the question presented in the petition is one which transcends the interest of the individual petitioner or victim, the Commission may decide to continue examining the case.

In some cases, the Commission has joined petitions which present the same question or which have been brought on behalf of the same victim. In such a case, it would likely recognize a request to withdraw as a party to the petition; however, it would have to consider whether the effect of such withdrawal would adversely affect the general interest. If the petitioner who wishes to withdraw is a close relative of the victim, and the other petitioners have no direct relationship to the victim, the Commission might consult with the other petitioners on appropriateness of withdrawal.

Tactics and Strategy

The essential elements of a petition, as set forth in the Commission's Regulations, are outlined in the previous section. There are additional elements which, though not required, may contribute to the effective prosecution of a petition.

Naming a Representative

The petitioner, whether the victim or a third party, may appoint an attorney or other person to represent him or her in proceedings before the

Commission. Although it is not necessary to presentation of a case, legal representation may assist that presentation in several ways. First, the petitioner may be in prison or subject to harrassment and may therefore wish to avoid direct communication with the Commission by working through a representative whose name or address is less likely to attract attention. Naming a representative also will provide a permanent address and a reliable means of communication, which lessens the likelihood of failure to enter a timely plea or rebuttal. In a complicated case or one that might eventually be referred to the Court, the counsel of an attorney with specialized human rights expertise may prove crucial. It is preferable for the petitioner to name a representative by means of a duly executed power of attorney, if possible. In order to proceed expeditiously and with confidence in arranging a friendly settlement, for example, the Commission should be assured that it is dealing with the "legal" representative of the petitioner.

Request for Provisional Measures

Article 26(2) of the Regulations states that the Commission may request that a state take precautionary or provisional measures "[i]n urgent cases when it becomes necessary to avoid irreparable damage to persons," either at its own initiative or at a party's request. The petitioner should indicate why the matter is urgent, in what way the foreseeable damage may be irreparable, and what measures should be taken to avoid such damage. Specific measures should be suggested, such as providing prompt and adequate medical attention for a prisoner; permitting immediate access to a prisoner being held incommunicado and whose life is believed to be in danger; or requesting a stay of deportation, extradition, exile, or execution.[36]

Prayer for Relief

The prayer for relief represents the ultimate objective of the petitioner, and a specific prayer or request for relief may assist the Commission in arranging a friendly settlement or in preparing recommendations to the government concerned. While a demand for compensation in a specific amount might be inappropriate at an early stage of the proceedings, a request for a full and impartial investigation of the facts, for due process guarantees, or for the right to exercise an option to leave a country to avoid imprisonment would be in order in the original petition. The Commission may recommend that compensation be awarded to a victim.

Documentation of a Claim

It is important to attach to the original petition copies (certified, if possible) of any documentation available to support the facts alleged, the assertion of timeliness, or the exhaustion of domestic remedies. A published account of the alleged violation or incidents, legislation, decisions, or official statements related to the violation may be useful. Most important, the petitioner should attach statements of any witnesses, signed and notarized if possible. If testimony is presented on tape, the petitioner should supply a transcription in order to avoid delays in processing or errors in transcription due to poor fidelity or unfamiliarity with the material or idiomatic expressions.

If the matter has been the subject of an administrative or judicial decision, a copy of the decision should be submitted. If a copy is not readily available, the petitioner should give sufficient detail regarding the parties involved, the date of the decision, and the body taking that decision to enable the Commission to request a copy or other confirmation of the decision from the government concerned. Additional information relevant to the case should be sent directly to the Commission as it becomes available, so that it may be referred to the government concerned for comment.

Informal Contact with the Commission

As noted earlier, much of the actual work involved in investigating the facts alleged in a petition and assessing the applicable law is performed by staff attorneys of the Commission's Secretariat, which is based in Washington, D.C. Informal contact, either orally or in writing, with the staff person handling a case is permissible, and it may be helpful to a petitioner or to a Washington-based representative to enter into direct contact with the Secretariat if possible. In that way, informal requests for information may be responded to more quickly, and additional information may be sent directly to the person most concerned.

It should be noted that the government concerned, under current Commission practice, may also have "informal" contacts with the Secretariat.

These contacts are generally initiated by the appropriate member of the government's mission to the OAS and, most often, through the Executive Secretary of the Commission. Unfortunately, the Commission's Regulations do not require that details concerning informal contacts with the parties be made a part of the record of the case.

In practice, questions of admissibility and fact are often considered at the same time, and there may be no formal decision on admissibility taken—unlike the procedure followed by the European Commission of Human Rights. Thus, persuasive evidence of the truth of any allegations made is likely to be considered by the Commission even if the situation with respect to exhaustion of domestic remedies is somewhat unclear. Oral evidence may be offered to the appropriate Commission staff attorney, but a written statement should also be prepared to assist the attorney in evaluating and questioning the evidence presented.

While formal adversarial hearings under article 40 of the Regulations are rare, less formal oral presentations of information by a petitioner to the Commission may be possible. The petitioner or representative should direct a request to present oral evidence to the President of the Commission.

Requests for formal adversarial hearings or for an on-site investigation by the Commission are likely to be granted only in exceptional circumstances, owing to the financial and staff limitations of the Commission and the political sensitivity of such actions. If the petition is one of many that raise similar issues in a particular country, and the Commission decides to conduct an on-site investigation, a petitioner can work informally with the Secretariat and suggest possible witnesses (including government witnesses) or other sources of evidence.

The petitioner also may take the initiative in proposing a friendly settlement. The most appropriate time would be when the petition's allegations are well substantiated, and there have been no serious preliminary objections to the admissibility of the case. At this point, the petitioner should inform the Secretariat on what basis a friendly settlement would be acceptable and indicate his or her willingness to enter into discussions with the government concerned.

Finally, a petitioner may wish to respond to the Commission's report, if one is adopted, particularly if the findings or recommendations to the government appear to be insufficient. If the government fails to carry out any recommendations within the time period specified, the petitioner should report that failure to the Commission and, in appropriate cases, request that the case be presented to the Court. If the case is not referred to the Court, the petitioner may encourage the Commission to publish the case as a separate document and to include it in its *Annual Report* to the General Assembly.

Procedure before the Inter-American Court of Human Rights[37]

An individual does *not* have direct access to the Inter-American Court, and a case may be brought before the Court only under the following circumstances:

1. if the state concerned is a party to the American Convention and has accepted the jurisdiction of the Court, either unconditionally, for a specified period, or for the specific case;
2. proceedings before the Commission under articles 48–50 of the Convention have been exhausted; and
3. either the state party or the Commission submits the case to the Court within a period three months from the date of the transmittal of the Commission's report to the parties concerned.

The Commission is not required to refer a case to the Court merely because the proceedings before the Commission have been exhausted. It is conceivable that the evidence developed in the case may provide sufficient basis for the Commission's opinion and recommendations, yet may not be sufficient evidence in a court of law. As a quasi-judicial body, the Commission is not bound by strict rules of evidence, and may take cognizance of any information it feels is relevant to the case. The Commission may simply feel that the legal issues involved are not important enough to be submitted to the Court.

If the Commission decides to present the case to the Court, the Executive Secretary will notify the Court, the petitioner, and the state in question.[38] If the state takes the initiative, the petitioner will be so informed by the Commission. After notification, the petitioner has the opportunity to make observations on the request submitted to the Court.[39] This opportunity should be utilized to request any measures that may be necessary to avoid irreparable damage in the interim,[40] to notify the Commission if the petitioner wishes to authorize an attorney to assist the delegates of the Commission in the presentation of the case,[41] or to recommend a particular person as an expert witness in the case.[42] The assistance of the petitioner's attorney may be particularly valuable to the Commission if the attorney is an expert in the law of the state concerned and/or international human rights. There is no provision for legal aid within the Inter-American system, however, and the expenses of witnesses must be borne by the interested party.

In a case which fulfills the jurisdictional requirements but which has not yet been submitted to the Court, the petitioner may ask the Commission to request the Court to adopt any interim measure necessary to avoid irreparable damage. Neither the Regulations of the Commission nor the Rules of the Court state exactly at what point interim measures might be appropriate, but presumably they may be requested as soon as the Commission transmits its preliminary report to the parties. So long as the case is before the Commission, the Commission itself may request the state to take precautionary measures to avoid irreparable damage.

The case is presented to the Court by one or more of the Commission's members chosen as delegates, who may be assisted by staff attorneys or any other person. The complainant may be represented by his own agent. The proceedings before the Court are initiated by presentation of a Memorial and Counter-Memorial, followed by any additional written submissions authorized by the Court. The Court's hearings are normally public, unless the Court decides otherwise, but the Court's deliberations are secret.

The Court may strike the case from the list if the parties agree to discontinue or reach a friendly settlement, or the matter is otherwise resolved. However, the Court may verify the equitable nature of any agreement between the parties and may proceed with its consideration of the case if it decides that its responsibilities can only be discharged by a final decision.

If the Court finds a violation of a right or freedom protected by the Convention, it may rule that the situation constituting a breach be remedied and may also require that compensation be paid to the injured party.[43] Costs may also be awarded. The state party is obliged to comply with the judgment, and compensatory damages awarded in the judgment may be enforced in the appropriate domestic courts. The Court's judgment is public, and certified copies are sent to the parties, the Commission, the Chairman of the Permanent Council of the OAS, the Secretary-General, the states parties to the Convention, and any other person directly concerned.

Concluding Observations

Because several American countries are also parties to the Optional Protocol of the International Covenant on Civil and Political Rights, it may be useful in closing to identify the advantages of an individual petition under the American system rather than under the Optional Protocol. The former protects a broader range of substantive rights; derogations from those rights by a state are more limited; and admissibility requirements for an individual petition are less stringent. The Inter-American Commission also has broader powers of inquiry, including the options of on-site investigation and adversarial hearings, and it may be more willing to take precautionary measures to avoid potentially irreparable harm in appropriate situations.

There exists a friendly settlement procedure applicable to the American Convention, and decisions of the Inter-American Court are legally binding on those governments that have recognized the Court's jurisdiction. Petitions brought under the American system are likely to receive greater publicity (at least within the region) than complaints to the Human Rights Committee, and governments appear to be somewhat more disposed to cooperate with a regional organization in resolving human rights problems. Finally, an individual petition or petitions may encourage the Inter-American Commission to undertake a major study of the overall human rights situation in a country, a possibility not open to the more limited competence of the Human Rights Committee.

Notes

1. Many of these economic, social, and cultural rights were added to the OAS Charter itself in 1968 by the Protocol of Buenos Aires. *See* chapter 13 for a discussion of attempts to assert the right to education in U.S. courts. [ed. note]

2. The Commission's Report on El Salvador stated that the members of the OAS have assumed international obligations by ratifying the specific standards concerning human rights found in the Charter of the Organization. *See* IACHR, REPORT ON THE SITUATION OF HUMAN RIGHTS IN EL SALVADOR, OAS Doc. OEA/Ser.L/V/II.46, doc. 23, rev. 1, at 48 (17 Nov. 1978).

3. *See, e.g.*, discussion of art. 27 in IACHR, REPORT ON THE STATUS OF HUMAN RIGHTS IN CHILE, OAS Doc. OEA/Ser.L/V/II/34, doc. 21, corr. 1, at 2–3 (25 Oct. 1974) (Findings of "on-the-spot" observations in the Republic of Chile, 22 July–2 August 1974).

4. Convention, art. 15, concerning the right of assembly, *reprinted in* OAS, HANDBOOK OF EXISTING RULES PERTAINING TO HUMAN RIGHTS (1980), OAS

Doc. OEA/Ser. L/V/II.50, doc. 6 [hereinafter cited as HANDBOOK]. *See also* arts. 6(3)(c), 7(2), 12(3), 13(2), 16(2), and 22(3).

5. Convention, art. 22(2), *id.* See Norris & Desio, *The Suspension of Guarantees: A Comparative Analysis of the American Convention and the Constitutions of the States Parties*, 30 AM. U.L. REV. 188 (1980).

6. IACHR, Resolution on the Protection of Human Rights in Connection with the Suspension of Constitutional Guarantees or 'State of Siege,' OAS Doc. OEA/Ser.L/V/II.19, doc. 32 (16 May 1968) (English).

7. First Chile Report, *supra* note 3, at 2–3.

8. Note 6 *supra*.

9. IACHR, Regulations, art. 23(1), HANDBOOK, *supra* note 4.

10. The term "general case" was first applied in the Commission's study of case 1684, which alleged violations of the right to life, liberty, and personal security; the right to protection from arbitrary arrest; and the right to due process of law in Brazil. The rapporteur described the case as "one of the most involved cases ever presented to the Commission" and classified no. 1684 as a "general case," which he proceeded to define as one "in which the object of the communication is the denunciation that in a given State, or a given region, by action of the authorities, or of some authorities, or of a more or less indeterminate person acting in the face of the passivity or with the aid, declared or not, of the authorities, there has been created a general situation characterized by the fact that various persons suffer attacks against their fundamental rights, generally with an imminent risk that the harm may be extended to others." IACHR, Informe sobre el Caso 1684, at 4, Archive of the IACHR. [Author's translation]

When the case was considered at the 28th session of the Commission, the rapporteur maintained that the authority of the Commission to examine general cases was embodied in article 9 of its Statute, particularly 9(b) and (c) (articles 18(b) and (c) of the present Statute), and that the exhaustion of internal remedies was *not* a requirement applicable to general cases, but only to "individual" cases under article 9(bis)(d). *See* IACHR, REPORT ON THE WORK ACCOMPLISHED BY THE IACHR DURING ITS TWENTY-EIGHTH SESSION (Special) (1–5 May 1972), OAS Doc. OEA/Ser.L/V/II.28, doc. 24, rev. 1, at 13–20 (24 Aug. 1972). The majority of the members agreed, voting "in the sense that case 1684 was a 'general case' . . . and consequently, the Commission was not required to insist on the requirement established in Article 9(bis)(d) of its Statute relative to exhaustion of internal remedies." *Id.* at 20, para. 59.

In the Commission's REPORT ON THE STATUS OF HUMAN RIGHTS IN CHILE, the situation in that country was described as a "general case" to which was related the idea of a "systematic disregard of fundamental human rights": "During this session, the study of the present situation of human rights in Chile has taken a great part of our time. On the one hand, we have examined those individual cases, clearly determinable, in which the violation of certain fundamental rights of one or several specified persons has been denounced. But, in addition, it has been necessary to analyze separately that which we might call a 'general case,' that is, the aggregation of charges from different sources according to which there is a policy in Chile which would imply, according to the claimants, the systematic disregard of fundamental human rights." OAS Doc. OEA/Ser.L/V/II/34, doc. 21, corr. 1, at 54 (25 Oct. 1974).

11. The following are some examples of "general" petitions examined by the Commission:

Case 1641 (Nicaragua)—denouncing repeated violations of human rights affecting citizens in general and involving arbitrary detention, assassination, and torture.

Cases 1702 and 1748 (Guatemala)—denouncing the assassination of some 700 persons, the systematic violation of human rights affecting the population at large, and the suppression of individual guarantees through the declaration of a state of siege, Resolución sobre los Casos Nos. 1702 y 1748, OAS Doc. OEA/Ser.L/V/II.32, doc. 21, rev. 1 (17 April 1974).

The following are examples of "collective" petitions:

Case 1684 (Brazil)—denouncing the torture and mistreatment of political prisoners, Resolución sobre el Caso 1684, OAS Doc. OEA/Ser.L/V/II.28, doc. 14 (3 May 1972).

Case 1688 (Nicaragua)—denouncing the murder of four members of the Moncada family and violation of the integrity of the person of others, Resolution on Case 1688, OAS Doc. OEA/Ser.L/V/II.28, doc. 20, rev. 1 (5 May 1972).

Case 1773 (United States)—denouncing the violation of the right to equality before the law and the right to nationality of 333 Spanish-speaking residents of the United States, brought on behalf of the entire U.S. Spanish-speaking community, Resolución sobre el Caso 1773, OAS Doc. OEA/Ser.L/V/II.34, doc. 28 (24 Oct. 1975).

Case 1780 (Colombia)—denouncing the violation of the right to life, liberty, and integrity of the person of farmers occupying land on the border between Venezuela and Colombia, Resolución sobre el Caso 1780, OAS Doc. OEA/Ser.L/V/II.36, doc. 41, rev. 1 (23 Oct. 1975).

Case 1802 (Paraguay)—denouncing the violation of the right to life, liberty, and integrity of the person of members of the Aché tribe, Resolución sobre el Caso 1802, OAS Doc. OEA/Ser.L/V/II.41, doc. 14 (27 May 1977).

12. IACHR, Regulations, art. 34(2).

13. IACHR, Regulations, art. 34(1). Laurids Mikaelsen's discussion of the exhaustion of national remedies under the European system is applicable in many respects to the Inter-American system. L. MIKAELSEN, EUROPEAN PROTECTION OF HUMAN RIGHTS, 105–34 (1980). See also Trindade, *The Burden of Proof with*

Regard to Exhaustion of Local Remedies in International Law, 9 HUM. RTS. J. 81 (No. 1, 1976).

14. The exhaustion of *administrative* remedies may not be required in every case, however. In Case 1697, for example, the Commission refused to accept Brazil's argument that petitioners had failed to exhaust their domestic remedies before the Council for Defense of Human Rights and therefore could not appeal to the IACHR. While it avoided a decision on the larger question of whether governmental agencies which are not explicitly judicial bodies constitute a part of domestic legal remedies, the Commission's Resolution stated that "the circumstance that this case has been submitted to the Council for the Defense of Human Rights in Brazil, does not inhibit, in view of the dispositions of its Statute, its examination by the Commission." OAS Doc. OEA/Ser.L/V/II.28, doc. 11 (2 May 1972). For another analysis, *see* Lebland, *The Inter-American Commission on Human Rights*, 9 HUM. RTS. J. 645 (No. 4, 1976).

15. The Commission recognized this specific exception in its 1978 ANNUAL REPORT: "It is obvious that in countries where the judiciary is not completely independent, or where its independence may be formally respected . . . [but] judges are subjected to pressures and threats from the executive authorities, there can be no effective domestic defense of human rights. Legal remedies such as 'habeas corpus' or the writ of *amparo* are useless if judges are not independent and live in a climate of insecurity and terror, which inhibits them from acting. To complete the picture, if, as often happens, there is no legislative branch, or if the legislators are docile instruments of the will of the executive, there is a total lack of domestic protection of human rights and fundamental liberties." OAS Doc. OEA/Ser.L/V/II.47, doc. 13, rev. 1, at 26 (29 June 1979).

16. IACHR, Regulations, art. 34(3).

17. Arts. 22–27 and 29–39 of the IACHR Regulations apply to both procedures. Those that apply only to the procedure for petitions lodged against states parties to the Convention are arts. 28 and 40–47; arts. 48–50 apply only to the procedure established for petitions against member states that have not ratified the Convention. *Also see* IACHR Statute, art. 1(2).

18. *See, e.g.*, the Commission's statements on its lack of jurisdiction to receive petitions alleging violations of human rights by terrorist groups, IACHR, REPORT ON THE SITUATION OF HUMAN RIGHTS IN ARGENTINA, OAS Doc. OEA/Ser.L/V/II.49, doc. 19, corr.1 (11 April 1980); IACHR, REPORT ON THE SITUATION OF HUMAN RIGHTS IN COLOMBIA, OAS Doc. OEA/Ser.L/V/II.53, doc. 22 (30 June 1981).

19. IACHR, Regulations, art. 35(1).

20. *Id.*, art. 35(2).

21. *Id.*, art. 36(2)(a).

22. *See* chapter 4. *See also* Tardu, *The Protocol to the United Nations Cove-*

nant on Civil and Political Rights and the Inter-American System: A Study of Co-Existing Petition Procedures, 70 AM. J. INT'L L. 778 (1976).

23. *See* chapter 4.

24. IACHR, Regulations, art. 36(2)(b).

25. *See* chapter 8.

26. IACHR, Regulations, art. 39.

27. *See, e.g.*, case 2720 (Bolivia). When the government failed to respond to allegations of torture and lack of due process, the Commission applied the presumption in article 51(1) of the previous Regulations. OAS Doc. OEA/Ser.L/V/II.46, doc. 22 (8 Mar. 1979).

28. *See, e.g.*, case 3228 (United States), in which the Commission on several occasions heard representatives of petitioners who alleged a denial of due process rights to Haitian refugees entering the United States, although the U.S. Government had objected in writing to admissibility of the petition. (Documents on file with the International Human Rights Law Group, Washington, D.C.)

29. Convention, art. 48. *See* Norris, *Observations in Loco: Practice and Procedure of the Inter-American Commission on Human Rights*, 15 TEX. INT'L L. J. 46 (1980).

30. IACHR, Regulations, art. 31(2).

31. *Id.*, art. 42(1).

32. Convention, art. 48(1)(f). For an interpretation of this language, which also is used in article 28(b) of the European Convention, see F. JACOBS, THE EUROPEAN CONVENTION ON HUMAN RIGHTS, 254–55 (1975). The friendly settlement procedure of the European Commission of Human Rights is described in Daubie, *Conciliation et protection européenne des droits de l'homme*, 9 REVUE BELGE DE DROIT INTERNATIONAL 503 (1973).

33. Convention, art. 49; IACHR, Regulations, art. 42(2).

34. *See* IACHR, Regulations, arts. 43–47.

35. *See* IACHR, Regulations, arts. 48–50.

36. *See, e.g.*, Case 3228, note 28 *supra*, in which the Commission sent a telegram to the U.S. Secretary of State requesting that "the Government of the United States cooperate with the Commission by refraining from any action which would result in the deportation of Haitian citizens seeking political asylum while the case is under study by the Commission." Cablegram from Edmundo Vargas Carreno, Executive Secretary, and Luis Demetrio Tinoco Castro, Chairman, to Cyrus R. Vance, 7 April 1980 (copy on file with the International Human Rights Law Group, Washington, D.C.).

37. This discussion excludes the Court's advisory jurisdiction under art. 64 of the Convention. The competence, jurisdiction, and procedures of the Court are set forth in arts. 61–69 of the Convention and its Statute, adopted in OAS General Assembly Res. No. 448 (1979) and reprinted in the HANDBOOK, *supra* note 4.

The Rules of the Court are available in the ANNUAL REPORT OF THE INTER-AMERICAN COURT OF HUMAN RIGHTS TO THE GENERAL ASSEMBLY, OAS Doc. OEA/Ser.G/CP/doc. 1113/80, at 26–44 (1980). [Hereinafter cited as IAC, Rules]

38. IACHR, Regulations, art. 47(2).

39. *Id.*, art. 68.

40. *Id.*, art. 69.

41. *Id.*, arts. 24(2) and 64(4).

42. *Id.*, art. 65; IAC, Rules, art. 20.

43. Convention, art. 63(1); IAC, Rules, art. 45.

8

Practice and Procedure on Individual Applications under the European Convention on Human Rights

KEVIN BOYLE

In comparison with the other international procedures for the protection of human rights discussed in the present book, the most notable feature of the system established by the European Convention on Human Rights is its maturity. The Convention, drawn up under the aegis of the Council of Europe, entered into force in 1953, and the European Commission of Human Rights registered its first individual application in 1955. Since that time, the Commission has received and registered over 9,000 applications; the number of state parties to the Convention has doubled to 21; and the right of individual petition under article 25 of the Convention now extends to over 240 million people.

Time, and the relative political stability of Western Europe, have allowed the principal organs of the Convention to grow in confidence and significance. There is now in existence a considerable body of substantive and procedural human rights law which any lawyer who considers invoking the Convention's machinery will find as essential to grasp as that existing within a domestic legal system. In addition to the basic documents relating to the Convention, decisions of the Commission and Court are published singly and in collected form on a continuing basis. Numerous scholarly commentaries, including periodical literature, are now available on the substantive rights protected under the Convention and their interpretation, and reference should be made to these materials in instances where an application appears to raise new or complex issues under the Convention.[1]

The optional individual petition procedure under article 25 of the Convention is its best known feature, and it has now been accepted by seventeen of the twenty-one state parties. It has proved a model for other treaties establishing international human rights machinery, such as the American Convention on Human Rights and the Optional Protocol to the Covenant on Civil and Political Rights. Important as the individual complaint procedure has proved, however, it would be wrong to conclude that the state parties have somehow been supplanted in significance under the Convention. The cooperation of states, especially those complained against, has been crucial to the success of the system of individual application. There is much in the functioning of the Convention machinery that reflects a concern to encourage that cooperation and to ensure that signatory states retain confidence in the Convention and its organs. The emphasis on consultation with states during the handling of complaints, the obligation to seek a friendly settlement, and the confidentiality of the proceedings are features of practice under the Convention which an applicant or lawyer needs to understand.

It should also be stressed that the Convention constitutes a forum of last resort. Its function is to provide a system of "outer protection" for the traditional range of civil rights and political freedoms which are by and large already protected under the legal systems of the participating states. While the European Commission of Human Rights may, through its interpretation of particular Convention provisions, expand rights that would otherwise be unprotected in domestic law, only rarely does the Commission face complaints of human rights violations on the scale or of the kind that are too well known elsewhere in the world.[2] Indeed, the jurisprudence of the Commission and the Court may at times seem rather technical, as they often define the edges or limits of rights following an equally close scrutiny of the issues by domestic courts.

A reflection of the view of the Commission as a forum only of last resort is the fact that less than 2 percent of all cases registered with the Commission succeed in passing the first hurdle of admissibility. The most frequent reason for the rejection of complaints is that the applicant has no grounds for invoking international remedies, given the state of protection secured for his or her rights under domestic law.

The Institutional Framework

There are three organs relevant to proceedings under the European Convention: the European Commission of Human Rights, the European Court of Human Rights, and the Committee of Ministers, each of which performs functions with respect to individual applications. All hold their regular sessions in Strasbourg, France, although the Commission has conducted hearings elsewhere.

The *Commission* is a quasi-judicial body composed of a number of jurists equal to the number of states that have ratified the Convention and who serve in their personal capacity. It meets five times per year in two-week sessions. The Commission's first task is to receive applications from individuals or states and assess their admissibility. Should an application be admitted, the Commission then has the dual function of determining the facts and attempting to achieve a friendly settlement between the parties. The Commission's decisions on admissibility are published, as are, in most cases, its opinions on whether or not there has been a breach of the Convention in cases that it has declared admissible. The Commission's opinions are not legally binding on the state parties.

The *European Court of Human Rights* consists of a number of judges equal to the number of states of the Council of Europe, all of which are currently parties to the Convention. The members of the Court must have the qualifications required for appointment to high judicial office or be jurists of recognized competence. The Court may sit in chambers of seven judges or in plenary sessions. Although it possesses limited competence under the Second Protocol to the Convention to give advisory opinions, the Court's principal function is to decide cases already heard by the Commission and referred to it either by one of the states concerned in the proceedings or the Commission itself. Acceptance of the compulsory jurisdiction of the Court is optional under article 46 of the Convention, and nineteen states have made the declarations necessary to accept the Court's jurisdiction. Only the Commission and states (not individuals) may formally appear as parties before the Court, and its decisions are legally binding.[3]

The *Committee of Ministers of the Council of Europe* is the political arm of the Convention and acts as the ultimate guarantor of human rights under the Convention. Its members serve, not as individuals, but as government representatives of the members of the Council of Europe. If a case is not referred to the Court following the adoption of a report by the

Commission, it is for the Committee of Ministers to decide whether there has been a violation of the Convention. With respect to decisions of the European Court, the Committee of Ministers is responsible for supervising the execution of the Court's judgment. It can by resolution require a state to take measures to remedy a violation, but its ultimate sanction is to suspend or expel a state from the Council of Europe.[4]

Given the very large number of complaints made to the Commission and the fact that it is only a part-time body, the role of the Commission's *Secretariat* is essential to the working of the Convention. The Secretary to the Commission is the person through whom all communications to the Commission must be addressed, and attorneys on the Secretariat staff are responsible for processing complaints, answering correspondence, and preparing cases for consideration by the Commission.

Preliminary Considerations

Figure 1 illustrates the major procedural steps in consideration of an application alleging violations of the Convention. As these procedures are by now fairly well defined and have been explored in numerous articles and books, the remainder of this chapter will offer an overview in order to present a picture of the actual workings of the procedures to an individual, NGO, or lawyer considering filing an application. A detailed analysis of all the Commission's jurisprudence is not possible in this limited format, and reference should be made to other sources for more specific information on particular points.

Substantive Requirements

Jurisdiction: The Commission's Competence to Receive Complaints
The Commission can examine individual complaints only with respect to states that have accepted the right of individual petition under article 25 of the Convention. A state may commit itself to the individual-petition procedure indefinitely or for a specific period. Although in principle the declaration made under article 25 can embrace complaints arising prior to the declaration, the terms of the declaration by the state parties usually rule this out. It is prudent therefore to check on whether a state party has accepted the right of individual petition and on the date and terms of such acceptance.

Figure 1

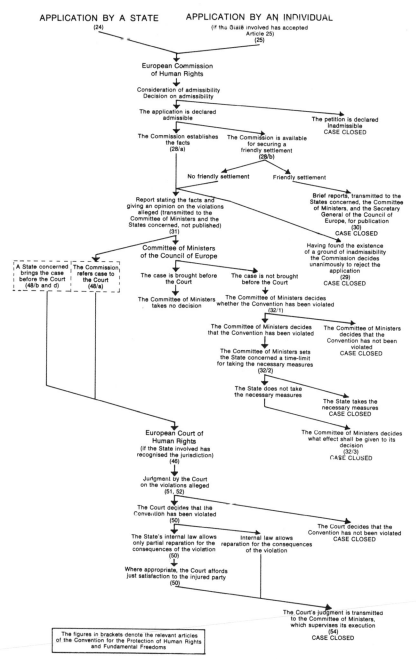

APPLICATION BY A STATE
(24)

APPLICATION BY AN INDIVIDUAL
(if the State involved has accepted
Article 25)
(25)

European Commission
of Human Rights

Consideration of admissibility
Decision on admissibility

The application is declared
admissible

The petition is declared
inadmissible
CASE CLOSED

The Commission establishes
the facts
(28/a)

The Commission is available
for securing a
friendly settlement
(28/b)

No friendly settlement

Friendly settlement

Report stating the facts and
giving an opinion on the violations
alleged (transmitted to the
Committee of Ministers and the
States concerned, not published)
(31)

Brief reports, transmitted to the
States concerned, the Committee
of Ministers, and the Secretary
General of the Council of
Europe, for publication
(30)
CASE CLOSED

Committee of Ministers
of the Council of Europe

Having found the existence
of a ground of inadmissibility
the Commission decides
unanimously to reject the
application
(29)
CASE CLOSED

A State concerned
brings the case
before the Court
(48/b and d)

The Commission
refers case to
the Court
(48/a)

The case is brought before
the Court

The case is not brought
before the Court

The Committee of Ministers
takes no decision

The Committee of Ministers decides
whether the Convention has been violated
(32/1)

The Committee of Ministers decides
that the Convention has been violated

The Committee of Ministers
decides that the
Convention has not been
violated
CASE CLOSED

The Committee of Ministers sets
the State concerned a time-limit
for taking the necessary measures
(32/2)

The State does not take
the necessary measures

The State takes the
necessary measures
CASE CLOSED

European Court of
Human Rights
(if the State involved has
recognised the jurisdiction)
(46)

The Committee of Ministers decides
what effect shall be given to its
decision
(32/3)
CASE CLOSED

Judgment by the Court
on the violations alleged
(51, 52)

The Court decides that the
Convention has been violated
(50)

The Court decides that the
Convention has not been violated
CASE CLOSED

The State's internal law allows
only partial reparation for the
consequences of the violation
(50)

Internal law allows
reparation for the consequences
of the violation

Where appropriate, the Court affords
just satisfaction to the injured party
(50)

The Court's judgment is transmitted
to the Committee of Ministers,
which supervises its execution
(54)
CASE CLOSED

The figures in brackets denote the relevant articles
of the Convention for the Protection of Human Rights
and Fundamental Freedoms

Source: Council of Europe, *What Is the Council of Europe Doing to Protect
Human Rights?* (1977), at 29.

The European Convention on Human Rights and the five Protocols that have subsequently been adopted cover a wide range of rights, most of which are in the area of civil and political rights.[5] The great majority of applications considered thus far have concerned freedom from torture or inhuman or degrading treatment or punishment (article 3), alleged unlawful detention (article 5), or the right to a fair trial (article 6). The scope of applications is expanding, however, and recent cases have included such issues as freedom of the press,[6] homosexual rights,[7] compulsory sex education,[8] and the right of access to the courts.[9]

States have ratified the Convention with varying reservations and may not have ratified some or all of the protocols. For example, Protocol No. 4 to the Convention, which secures certain additional rights (e.g., freedom of movement) to those set out in the Convention itself, has so far been ratified by only sixteen states. Most of these states have extended the right of individual petition under article 25 to include this Protocol.

The European Agreement relating to persons participating in proceedings of the European Commission and Court of Human Rights grants certain immunities to such persons and may be relevant in particular cases.

Finally, an applicant should be aware of whether the state complained against has filed a notice of derogation from any rights under the provisions of article 15, which permits such derogations "[i]n time of war and other public emergency threatening the life of the nation . . . to the extent strictly required by the exigencies of the situation."

Standing
Article 25(1) provides:

The Commission may receive petitions addressed to the Secretary-General of the Council of Europe *from any person, non-governmental organization or group of individuals claiming to be the victim* of a violation by one of the High Contracting Parties of the rights set forth in this Convention, provided that the High Contracting Party against which the complaint has been lodged has declared that it recognizes the competence of the Commission to receive such petitions. Those of the High Contracting Parties who have made such a declaration undertake not to hinder in any way the effective exercise of this right. (emphasis added)

The most important requirement is that the applicant be a "victim," and the concept of victim has been frequently considered by the Commission. The Commission has permitted both *direct* and *indirect* victims to maintain an application; the latter are generally relatives or others with a close connection to the direct victim.

Article 1 of the Convention imposes an obligation on the contracting states to secure the rights protected to all persons "within their jurisdiction," nationals or aliens. It is not necessary that an application complain of actions within the national territory. In *Cyprus* v. *Turkey*, the Commission held that "the authorised agents of the State including diplomatic or counsellor agents and armed forces not only remain under its jurisdiction when abroad, but bring any other person or property 'within the jurisdiction' of that state, to the extent that they exercise authority over such persons or property. In so far as, by their acts or omissions, they affect such persons or property the responsibility of the State is engaged."[10]

If the alleged victim is a NGO or group of individuals, the application must be made by the person or persons competent to represent the organization under its own internal rules or as provided by domestic law. If a group of individuals is not incorporated, then the application must be submitted in the names of all of them. Anonymous applications are inadmissible.

The complaint must further allege that the violation results from action or inaction *by the state*. State responsibility extends to the actions of any state employee, for example, an individual police officer, but actions by a private individual or organization do not fall within the Commission's competence.

The alleged violation must be of a right protected under the Convention, and the right should be identified in the application (although this is not required). Many individual complaints have been rejected because the Convention's scope does not extend to protect the right violated, however serious.

The Commission has been liberal in its interpretation of standing for individual applicants. However, it will not entertain an *in abstracto* application or an *actio popularis*. In one case, an Irish member of Parliament complained in general terms about the existence of certain emergency laws in Ireland and asked the Commission to examine their compatibility with the Convention. The Commission rejected the application since it did not complain of a violation of the Convention through, for example, the application of these laws to the complainant.[11]

Exhaustion of Domestic Remedies

Failure to exhaust domestic remedies as required under article 26 is the rock upon which a great number of complaints to Strasbourg founder. It is the most important preliminary consideration for the applicant, once it is determined that the alleged violation falls within the scope of the Convention. What constitutes a "remedy," when it is deemed to be exhausted, and the circumstances under which an applicant may be excused from exhaustion because a remedy is "inadequate and ineffective" have all been the subject of numerous decisions by the Commission and Court and of scholarly discussion.[12] That jurisprudence should be studied carefully before deciding to launch proceedings under the Convention, and, in normal circumstances, an applicant should expect to pursue all available domestic administrative and judicial appeals prior to bringing an application to the Commission.

Priority and Urgent Cases

The Commission ordinarily considers applications in the order in which they become ready for hearing, and it is not uncommon for a period of two years or more to pass before a report is drawn up in an admissible case. However, under rule 28 of its Rules of Procedure, the Commission can give priority to an application in circumstances of a genuine emergency or urgency. A request for precedence in the treatment of an application should be made in a covering letter that details clearly the grounds on which the request is made. Given the case load of the Commission, the decision to give precedence is not taken lightly and should be sought only in well-founded cases, for example, if the victim is the subject of continuing ill-treatment in prison or is liable to imminent deportation or expulsion from a country.

Formal Requirements

An application form is supplied on request by the Secretariat for the submission of a complaint. However, it is not necessary to use this form, and an applicant is free to submit an application in any form, provided it contains the relevant matters required by the Commission's Rules of Procedure.

Contents of an Application

Rule 38 of the Rules provides that an application shall set out:
1. the name, age, occupation, and address of the applicant;
2. the name, occupation, and address of his or her representative, if any;

3. the name of the High Contracting Party against which the application is made;
4. as far as possible, the object of the application and the provision of the Convention alleged to have been violated;
5. a statement of the facts and argument;
6. any relevant documents and, in particular, any judgments or other decisions relating to the object of the application.

In addition, rule 38 requires that an application provide information on the exhaustion of domestic remedies. In particular, all available documentation with respect to domestic judicial or other proceedings, including transcripts and decisions, should be filed with the application.

The applicant has the burden to supply all evidence on which the complaint is based, and an application should therefore be fully and carefully prepared before submission. If prepared by a lawyer, it should contain, in addition to an exposition of the facts, reasoned arguments on how the facts constitute a violation of the Convention by the respondent government. Although the Commission is not bound by precedent, where possible such arguments should be supported by references to the caselaw of the Convention. It may also be appropriate to refer to decisions of domestic courts.

Language

The official languages are English and French, but the Commission will accept applications in another language where it is the language of a state that accepts the right of individual petition, that is, the Scandinavian languages, Dutch, German, Flemish, Italian, Spanish, or Portuguese. In exceptional circumstances, the Commission may authorize the application to be submitted in a language other than these. Hearings are conducted in one of the official languages or any of the other languages mentioned, if the parties so request.

The Six Months Rule

Under article 26, the Commission may only receive a complaint "within a period of six months from the date on which the final decision [in the domestic jurisdiction] was taken." The relevant date for the purposes of the "six months rule" is normally deemed to be the date on which the Commission received the first communication about an application, even if that only sets out the complaint in a summary form, and even if the complaint is not formally registered on that date. The Commission may entertain the possibility of submitting an application prior to the final stages of exhaustion of local remedies, and this may be wise if the domestic remedy being pursued is speculative or uncertain. The "six months rule" does not apply to a complaint of a continuing violation.[13]

Damages

If monetary damages are sought, the application should so state. The specific amount claimed may be indicated, but it is not required by the Rules of Procedure.

Abuse of the Right of Petition

An application can be rejected under article 27(2) of the Convention as an abuse of the right of petition, and, as is true for other international procedures, abusive or insulting language should be avoided. In several instances, the Commission has declared inadmissible complaints that made serious and unfounded accusations against the government or against the Commission and Secretariat.[14] Any attempt to generate publicity for political ends through an application under the Convention runs the risk of being treated as an abuse of petition, particularly if the complaint is weak.

Before an application is lodged, it is legitimate to give information about it to the media, and the fact that an application has been filed may be released to the press. However, after that date the confidentiality of proceedings should be respected at all times. The Commission has been particularly sensitive to being used for publicity (although this suspicion seems to have eased somewhat in recent years), and the best rule regarding publicity is to direct all media inquiries to the Council of Europe. Regular press releases are issued on the Commission's activities through the Secretary of the Commission, and the Commission's decisions on the admissibility of an application are always published.

Power of Attorney

Written authorization or a power of attorney must be executed by the applicant in favor of the legal or other representative. This should be submitted with the application or whenever representation is arranged, and failure to provide this authorization will delay registration and consideration of an application.

Signing the Application

Article 27 provides that the Commission may not deal with any petition which is anonymous, and the Rules of Procedure require that an application be signed by the applicant or by the representative. If, however, an applicant does not wish to be identified to the respondent government, this should be communicated when the application is filed, and the request will be respected by the Commission.

Legal Representation and Legal Aid

A lawyer is not essential for proceedings at Strasbourg, and less than one-third of the petitions registered to date have been filed by lawyers. An applicant may be self-represented or may be represented by anyone of his or her choice approved by the Commission. However, after a case is registered and where it appears that it involves serious issues under the Convention, the Commission will normally advise legal representation (particularly if an applicant would have difficulty in representing his or her own interests, for example, in the case of mentally ill or imprisoned complainants). The legal or other representative should be resident in a country that has ratified the Convention, but the Commission can waive this requirement. The representative must file with the Commission a power of attorney or other authorization from the applicant.

There are no filing costs associated with an application under the Convention. Although the Commission has power to order that the applicant bear the costs of a witness the applicant has requested, this has never occurred.

One of the most innovative and, in practical terms, important features of the European machinery is the provision for legal aid that has been established for individual applications. The assistance is paid out of the general funds of the Council of Europe and is governed by an Addendum to the Rules of Procedure of the Commission. The Commission may grant free legal aid in connection with the representation of a case either at the request of an applicant lodging an application or on its own initiative. While an applicant may appoint and be represented in proceedings by a nonlawyer, as noted, fees are payable only to "a barrister-at-law, solicitor or professor at law or professionally qualified person of similar status."[15] In cases where a number of individuals are involved or where the issues are complex, the Commission may pay for representation by more than one lawyer. Alternatively, fees may be increased where one lawyer is representing a number of individuals.

Legal aid covers not only fees but traveling and subsistence expenses and "other necessary out-of-pocket expenses." It normally is available only after the application has been communicated to the respondent government, and observations are sought from the applicant on the government's response. Thereafter, legal aid will be available for preparation of all written pleadings and also for appearances at oral hearings. The fees normally authorized are not generous. They are determined by reference to the average fees paid for legal aid work within the Council of Europe, and representation of a poor applicant remains semi-volunteer work. However, the fact that necessary expenses incurred in preparation of a case are reimbursed and that travel and subsistence for all appearances at hearings are paid is extremely important, and it does ensure that a case can be adequately prepared without the actual outlay of funds by an applicant.

Pre-Admissibility Procedure

Once an application has been sent to the Commission, there are a number of stages prior to a determination of whether or not the application is admissible. These are the introduction of the application, its registration, examination by a rapporteur and consideration of his or her report by the Commission, and finally a decision on admissibility, which normally follows an oral hearing.

Introduction

The application should be addressed to the Secretary-General of the Council of Europe, in care of the Secretary of the European Commission of Human Rights. As provided in the Rules, all subsequent correspondence in the case is conducted with the Secretary of the Commission.

In practice, the handling of individual applications is largely the day-to-day responsibility of members of the Secretariat. They open a provisional file for each application, conduct correspondence with an applicant, and indicate any obvious grounds of inadmissibility, such as failure to appeal to a domestic court or alleging violation of a right not protected under the Convention. At this stage, the Secretariat has authority to discourage applications that are plainly outside the scope of the Convention or obviously inadmissible. Secretariat members may suggest or request additional information, particularly on the question of exhaustion of domestic remedies, although a well-prepared application should already include such information. A considerable period may elapse between receipt of an initial communication concerning a complaint and its actual registration.

Registration

Registration is the formal process whereby a complaint becomes an application and receives a case number. As has been noted, registration is not automatic, and the Secretariat will discourage obviously unfounded complaints. However, the Secretariat must register a complaint if the applicant insists. Registration may be refused on the authority of the President of the Commission if it is clear that the claim is totally outside the Convention or the applicant or representative has refused to provide information requested by the Secretariat. Once an application is registered, a member of the Commission is appointed as rapporteur and is charged with the responsibility of examining the admissibility of the case. The rapporteur, in conjunction with the member of the Secretariat who has been handling the case, prepares a report on admissibility and may request further information from the applicant at this stage. To complete the file, the rapporteur also may request information from the government against which the complaint has been made, and this information will be forwarded to the applicant for comment. (This does *not* constitute "communication" of an application to the government, discussed below.) On completion of the examination, the rapporteur prepares a report for the full Commission, which includes a statement of the facts, a summary of the observations of the parties, an indication of the relevant issues under the Convention, and proposals on admissibility or other action to be taken.

Preliminary Examination by the Commission

A major portion of the work of the Commission during its five plenary sessions each year concerns discussion and decision on rapporteurs' reports dealing with admissibility. The rules and practice of the Commission permit a number of possible decisions at this point,
1. to declare an application inadmissible *de plano*;
2. to strike it off the list;
3. to communicate the application to the government for observations on admissibility; or
4. to adjourn the application.

The great majority of applications are rejected under one of the first two categories; in 1981, 360 out of the 430 applications on which decisions were taken by the Commission were declared inadmissible or struck off the list *de plano* prior to communication to the government concerned. Consideration of an application may be adjourned in order to obtain additional information or because its disposition may depend on the outcome of other cases.

In practical terms, an application fails unless it is communicated to the respondent government for its written observations on admissibility. Such communication ought to be the minimum goal of any application under the Convention prepared by a lawyer. Whatever the eventual outcome of the application, communication puts the government on notice that a reasonably serious complaint has been filed, requires formal governmental participation in the process, and may lead to a resolution of the problem even prior to any formal involvement by the Commission in attempts at a friendly settlement.

Once the decision to communicate an application is made by the Commission, the respondent government is normally given eight weeks within which to submit its observations. The Commission fowards a copy of the government's observations to the applicant, who is then invited to submit observations in reply. The focus of observations from both parties at this stage will include both issues of fact (unless they are undisputed) and admissibility issues under articles 26 and 27 of the Convention. Once the exchange of observations is concluded, a new report on admissibility is prepared by the rapporteur and discussed by the full Commission. If the application is not rejected at this point, the Commission may either immediately declare the application admissible or schedule oral hearings on admissibility.

Oral Hearings on Admissibility

An oral hearing on admissibility will concern legal arguments based on the written pleadings, which will have clarified the issues of fact and law. The proceedings are relatively informal, and both parties are given the opportunity to address the Commission and to reply to each other's submission. The President of the Commission may direct the parties to particular issues which the Commission wishes addressed, and members may ask questions during or after the presentation. Hearings on admissibility are held at Strasbourg during the regular sessions of the full Commission.

It is increasingly the practice of the Commission to have only one hearing on an application; this is achieved by holding a joint hearing on admissibility and the merits. This procedure saves time and also permits the parties and the Commission to address issues that may have a bearing both on admissibility and on the merits, for example, whether or not there exists a practice of violation that would render domestic remedies ineffective.

Post-Admissibility Procedure

Assuming that the Commission decides separately the admissibility of an application, that decision will be published after the hearing. Strictly speaking, the Commission's judicial role ends at that stage. Once a case has been admitted, the Commission proceeds, under article 28, to the dual functions of conducting an investigation to establish the facts and of encouraging efforts to reach friendly settlement.

Consideration of the Merits

Both the applicant and the respondent government will be invited to submit written observations or memorials on the merits of the case. The Commission may request answers to particular questions put by it to both parties, although in many instances there may be little to add by way of legal argument to the written and oral submissions on admissibility. If the facts are in dispute at this stage, the Commission may arrange oral hearings at which evidence will be taken from witnesses for the applicant, the respondent government, and/or those requested by the Commission itself.

Witnesses normally testify under oath, and they may be cross-examined by the opposing side and asked questions by members of the Commission. There are no formal rules of evidence to guide the Commission's investigation, and the Commission is likely to admit any relevant evidence, including hearsay or other statements that might be barred in a domestic forum. It is to be expected, of course, that greater weight will be given to direct evidence as opposed to general or hearsay testimony.

The taking of evidence from witnesses by the Commission need not occur in Strasbourg, and evidence is often heard by less than the full Commission. Commission delegates may, for example, visit a prison in another country for the purpose of hearing witnesses or examining evidence. Article 28 obliges the state to furnish "all necessary facilities" for the Commission's or delegates' investigations.[16] In addition to this general obligation, the European Agreement relating to persons participating in the proceedings of the European Commission and Court of Human Rights grants certain immunities from legal process to an applicant, as well as facilities for communication with the Commission and with legal representatives in connection with proceedings before the Commission.

Friendly Settlement

Parallel to its investigation of the merits, the Commission is charged with the responsibility under article 28 "to place itself at the disposal of the parties" in order to facilitate a friendly settlement. A settlement may involve the amendment of legislation or monetary compensation, although the Commission must approve any settlement and ensure that it is consistent with general concerns for the protection of human rights. In practice, there are relatively few formal friendly settlements prior to the Commission's drafting its report on the merits.

Report of the Commission

Under article 31 of the Convention, the Commission is required to draw up a report for the Committee of Ministers if no settlement is achieved. The report states the factual conclusions of the Commission and gives its opinion as to whether there has been a breach of the Convention. Minority or separate opinions may also be included. The Commission's opinion is not directly binding on the state concerned.

The report is transmitted to the Committee of Ministers and to the state concerned, which may not publish it, but not to the applicant. The applicant is, however, informed that a report has been adopted. After a three-month interval, the Committee of Ministers decides whether a breach of the Convention has occurred and whether to publish the Commission's report. Within this three-month period, the respondent government of the commission may refer the case to the European Court of Human Rights for a final decision. It now seems to be the practice of the Commission, particularly where a breach is found, to take the initiative and refer important cases to the Court.

The European Court of Human Rights

If a case is referred to the Court, the Commission's report on the merits is made public by the Registrar. The Commission will have chosen two delegates to prepare and present the Commission's submissions to the Court; if the Commission is divided in its opinion, both majority and minority views may be represented.

Although an individual applicant cannot refer a case to the Court and has no formal standing before it, the Court's decisions are increasingly significant for individual applications. First, all but one case considered by the Court concerns individual cases referred to it by the Commission. Second, it has become the Commission's practice, sanctioned by the Court, to invite the applicant or lawyer to assist the Commission in both the preparation and presentation of its case before the Court.

The Commission and the government file written submissions or memorials with the Court, and the applicant's representative will be invited by the Commission to make written comments on the memorial prepared by the government. These will be appended to the Commission's own responses to the government's memorial and presented to the Court. At the hearing, the applicant's representative is normally given an opportunity to address the Court.

The Court invariably reserves judgment, which is later read by the President of the Court at a public session. The judgment is then published and transmitted to the Committee of Ministers, which is responsible for supervising its execution. If the Court rules that the Convention has been breached, it has power to award "just satisfaction" or compensation. The matter of compensation and costs may be left to be negotiated by the parties, but if no settlement is reached, it may be brought before the Court for decision.

Conclusion

While the relative maturity of the European Convention already has been noted, the ultimate question must be one addressed to its effectiveness. It is true that only a small number of individuals whose complaints have been admitted and vindicated have benefited directly from the Convention. At the same time, large-scale conflicts that have led to widespread human rights violations—in Greece during the junta, in Cyprus in the 1970s, and the continuing conflict in Northern Ireland—have been moderated only in limited ways, if at all, as a result of the invocation of the Convention's enforcement machinery.

But it is too limited a view to measure the Convention's achievements by reference only to the small number of cases actually admitted. The Convention and the individual petition procedure that it pioneered at the international level have achieved success in a more indirect fashion. For example, the Convention's primary aim of safeguarding human rights is achieved through the promotion of general standards directly applicable in member states. While the bulk of complaints to Strasbourg have been filed by prisoners, the scope of applications is widening to embrace other rights and freedoms under the Convention. Such issues as the right to private life, freedom of association, access to courts, and freedom of speech have an important impact on the legal systems of the signatory states and the rights of a great many individuals, in addition to those who actually file applications.

Potentially very significant is acceptance of the Convention by the European Court of Justice, the court of the European Economic Community (EEC), as relevant human rights law in the context of litigation under the EEC treaties.[17] The possibility of accession to the Convention by the community itself is also under active discussion.

The major hindrance to the effective implementation of the European Convention is its limited capacity to cope with the growing number of applications submitted to the Commission. Delay, already a serious problem, can only worsen with the recent extension of the right of individual petition to Spain, Portugal, and France. The Commission will require greatly increased administrative and financial resources to respond to this additional case load if it is to maintain its effectiveness as an international human rights body. If sufficient financial resources are provided, one can expect the European system for the protection of human rights to become even more fully integrated into European political and legal life.

Notes

1. *See* appendix A, Bibliographic Note, and for a detailed treatment of the individual petition procedure of the Convention, Kruger, *The European Commission of Human Rights*, 1 HUM. R.L.J. 66 (1980); O'Boyle, *Practice and Proce-*

dure under the European Convention on Human Rights, 20 SANTA CLARA L. REV. 697 (1980); and COUNCIL OF EUROPE, BRINGING AN APPLICATION BEFORE THE EUROPEAN COMMISSION OF HUMAN RIGHTS (1972). The author acknowledges his indebtedness to these three works in the preparation of the present chapter.

2. The exceptions to this statement are the interstate complaints brought under article 24 of the Convention, which are not considered in this chapter. These complaints have raised serious questions of widespread human rights violations in Italy (Austria v. Italy, [1961] Y.B. EUR. CONV. ON HUMAN RIGHTS 172 [Eur. Comm'n on Human Rights], hereinafter cited as YEARBOOK), Cyprus (Cyprus v. Turkey) (Nos. 1 & 2), decisions on admissibility, 2 DECISIONS & REPORTS 125 (1975); *id.* (No. 3), 13 DECISIONS & REPORTS 85 (1979); and pre-independence complaints in Greece v. United Kingdom, (1959) YEARBOOK 182 (Eur. Comm'n on Human Rights); Greece under the junta ("Greek" Case, [1969] YEARBOOK 1 [Eur. Comm'n on Human Rights]); Northern Ireland ("Irish" Case, [1976] YEARBOOK 512 [Eur. Comm'n on Human Rights]; and [1978] YEARBOOK 602 [Eur. Court of Human Rights]); and Turkey (applications concerning martial law in Turkey were filed in 1982 by Denmark, France, Netherlands, Norway, and Sweden against Turkey, Apps. Nos. 9940–9943/82).

This approach might be contrasted with that of the Inter-American Commission on Human Rights, which in recent years has adopted detailed reports on the human rights situations in Argentina, Bolivia, Chile, Colombia, Cuba, El Salvador, Guatemala, Haiti, Nicaragua, Panama, Paraguay, and Uruguay. *See* chapter 7.

3. The Court was seized with only two cases during the first seven years of its existence, but it has become increasingly active and important since the mid-1970s. See O'Boyle, *supra* note 1, at 722 n. 125.

4. This has never occurred, although the Greek Government denounced the Statute of the Council of Europe when it was apparent that it would be found in violation of the Convention in 1969. For a compilation of the Committee's resolutions, see COUNCIL OF EUROPE, COLLECTION OF RESOLUTIONS ADOPTED BY THE COMMITTEE OF MINISTERS IN APPLICATION OF ARTICLE 32 OF THE EUROPEAN CONVENTION FOR THE PROTECTION OF HUMAN RIGHTS AND FUNDAMENTAL FREEDOMS 1959–1979 (1979), Council of Europe Doc. H(79)7.

5. A sixth Protocol, abolishing capital punishment in peacetime, was opened for signature in April 1983.

6. "The Sunday Times" Case, Eur. Court H.R., Judgment of 26 April 1979, Ser. A No. 30.

7. Dudgeon v. United Kingdom, App. No. 7525/76, Report of the Commission of 13 Mar. 1980; Eur. Court H.R., Judgment of 22 Oct. 1981.

8. "Kjeldsen, Busk Madsen and Pedersen" Case, [1976] YEARBOOK 502 (Eur. Court of Human Rights).

9. "Airey" Case, Eur. Court H.R., Judgment of 9 Oct. 1979, Ser. A No. 32.

10. Cyprus v. Turkey (No. 3), *supra* note 2.

11. App. No. 867/60, [1960] YEARBOOK 270 (Eur. Comm. on Human Rights).

12. The leading cases on the question of exhaustion of domestic remedies are probably the "Irish" Case, *supra* note 2; Donnelly et al. v. United Kingdom (No. 1), partial decision on admissibility, 43 COLLECTION OF DECISIONS 149 (1973), and *id.* (No. 2), final decision on admissibility, 4 DECISIONS & REPORTS 4 (1976); and the "Greek" Case, *supra* note 2. *See* O'Boyle, *supra* note 2 at 712–15; O'Boyle, *Torture and Emergency Powers under the European Convention on Human Rights: Ireland v. United Kingdom*, 71 AM. J. INT'L L. 674, 688–701 (1977); Boyle & Hannum, *The Donnelly Case, Administrative Practice and Domestic Remedies under the European Convention: One Step Forward and Two Steps Back*, 71 AM. J. INT'L L. 316 (1977); and Hannum & Boyle, *Individual Applications under the European Convention on Human Rights and the Concept of Administrative Practice: The Donnelly Case*, 68 AM. J. INT'L L. 440 (1974).

13. *See* McFeeley and others v. United Kingdom, partial decision on admissibility, 20 DECISIONS & REPORTS 44 (1980).

14. *See, e.g.,* some of the early applications filed concerning the Northern Irish situation, which are summarized in COUNCIL OF EUROPE, STOCK-TAKING ON THE EUROPEAN CONVENTION ON HUMAN RIGHTS 85 (1979).

15. Rule 4, Addendum to the Commission's Rules of Procedure, *reprinted in* COUNCIL OF EUROPE, COLLECTED TEXTS 315 (1978).

16. Query what sanctions are available should a government refuse to supply certain information or facilities on security grounds? See O'Boyle (1977), *supra* note 12 at 684 n. 45, 705–06.

17. *See* Nold v. Commission of the European Communities, [1974] EUROPEAN COURT REPORTS 491; *The Protection of Fundamental Rights in the European Community*, In BULLETIN OF THE EUROPEAN COMMUNITIES (supplemented May 1976); A. TOTH, PROTECTION OF INDIVIDUALS IN THE EUROPEAN COMMUNITIES (1978).

9

The African Commission on Human and Peoples' Rights: Prospects and Procedures

RICHARD GITTLEMAN

Eleven African states have ratified one or both of the International Covenants on human rights,[1] and five have also accepted the Optional Protocol to the Covenant on Civil and Political Rights.[2] Despite many conferences and much interest, however, no regional intergovernmental human rights institution had been established, either within or outside the framework of the Organization of African Unity (OAU), until the 1981 adoption of the "African Charter" which is the subject of the present chapter.[3]

On 27 June 1981, the Eighteenth Assembly of Heads of State and Government of the OAU, convening in Nairobi, Kenya, adopted the African Charter on Human and Peoples' Rights (hereinafter cited as the African Charter or the Charter).[4] The Charter provides for the establishment within the OAU of an African Commission on Human and Peoples' Rights, whose members will be elected by the OAU Assembly of Heads of State and Government at the first ordinary session of the Assembly following the Charter's entry into force.[5]

This chapter offers an overview of the Charter provisions relating to the Commission and its procedure. The first section describes the Commission's mandate, the second section sets out the procedure for initiating a communication, and the final section briefly considers the Charter's substantive provisions and notes some of the problems a practitioner is likely to face in filing a complaint under the Charter.

A major caveat is warranted at the outset. It is unlikely that the Charter will enter into force in the near future, and this overview of the procedures cannot be more than a preliminary effort.[6] In addition, the Commission is empowered to write its own rules of procedure, and those rules may affect substantially the Commission's functioning and effectiveness. At the same time, current ambiguities contained in the Charter may be remedied by appropriate procedural clarifications.

Mandate of the Commission

The functions of the Commission, as set forth in article 45, should properly be divided into two categories: promotional functions and protective functions. African and non-African nongovernmental organizations may play an important role in each area.

The basic promotional functions of the Commission are to collect documents, to undertake studies, to organize seminars, to disseminate information, and to encourage national and local institutions concerned with human and peoples' rights. Other promotional activities include the formulation of "principles and rules aimed at solving legal problems relating to human and peoples' rights and fundamental freedoms upon which African Governments may base their legislation."[7]

The human rights movement in Africa is in a nascent state of development. While the Commission is given great latitude in constructing a human rights education program, the real burden will fall on national and local institutions. Given the meager public resources currently available for such educational or promotional efforts, NGOs can assist in ameliorating the situation by contributing manpower and resources in any of the areas within the Commission's promotional mandate.

Perhaps the greatest need at this stage is for better dissemination of information to the people regarding their rights. The All African Conference of Churches, for example, has stated that "due to the high rate of illiteracy, people are unaware of their rights, and when they are aware of them, they see them as a favor from the politician."[8] In a 1980 study on regional African promotion of human rights, the Commission to Study the Organization of Peace cites a commentator for "advanc[ing] the interesting proposition that the educational process is only just now appropriate because of the recent emergence of Africa from colonial situations. . . . [H]uman rights become relevant in legal and social terms only when the primary political relationship is between the individual and the state. . . . Now that independent sovereign entities have been created, it becomes appropriate . . . to educate largely tribal and rural populations in the fundamentals of the relationship between the individual and the state."[9]

The effective promotion of human rights, however, invariably results in rising expectations that these rights will be granted in fact and, if violated, that sanctions may be available. Unfortunately, the international framework for enforcing the rights set forth in the Charter does not yet exist, nor do many governments seem particularly anxious to establish effective domestic institutions. The challenge of the African Commission and interested NGOs and governments will be to build the institutions required to enforce human rights while concurrently disseminating information to the grass-roots level of society. The balance is a delicate one, yet it is essential if local governments are to accept human rights institution-building as a positive advance rather than a step toward political instability.

Midway between the Commission's promotional tasks and the mechanisms envisaged to consider complaints of human rights violations is the Commission's competence under article 45(3) to "interpret all the provisions of the present Charter at the request of a State Party, an institution of the OAU or an African organization recognized by the OAU." The last category, NGOs "recognized by the OAU," is an extremely limited one, but this authority to issue what would appear to be advisory opinions might enable general human rights issues to be brought before the Commission in such a way that direct conflict or accusations could be avoided without totally ignoring areas of human rights concern.

Finally, the Charter empowers the Commission to "ensure the protection of human and peoples' rights" under the conditions and procedures set forth in the other Charter provisions. The next section considers the Commission's role in protecting human rights through its consideration of interstate and "other" communications.

Procedures for Considering Communications

Communications from States

The procedure for consideration of a communication by one state party that another state party has violated the terms of the Charter (articles 47–

54) makes it clear that the primary objective is to encourage the states concerned to reach a friendly settlement without formally involving the investigatory or conciliatory mechanisms of the Commission. This desire to promote friendly settlements, whether interstate or in the context of an individual communication, may also be found in, for example, article 28 of the European Convention on Human Rights and article 48 of the American Convention on Human Rights. However, the direct contact between states prior to the formal involvement of the African Commission is unique to the African Charter.

Under article 47, a party that has "good reasons" to believe that another party has violated the provisions of the Charter may raise the matter in writing with the allegedly violating state, also notifying the Chairman of the Commission and the Secretary-General of the OAU. The accused state has three months to respond with an explanation or statement, which "should include as much as possible relevant information relating to the laws and rules of procedure applied and applicable and the redress already given or course of action available."[10] If within the three-month period the issue remains unresolved, either state may submit the matter to the Commission.

Although bilateral negotiations are the preferred method of dispute resolution, a state party may submit a communication directly to the Commission under article 49, bypassing the negotiation process. The Chairman of the Commission, the Secretary-General of the OAU, and the accused state are all to receive a copy of the communication.

In keeping with the common international rule, no communication will be considered by the Commission until all local remedies have been exhausted, unless the Commission determines that exhaustion of remedies is unduly prolonged.

The Commission is given extremely broad investigative powers under article 46: "The Commission may resort to any appropriate method of investigation; it may hear from the Secretary-General of the Organization of African Unity or any other person capable of enlightening it." It may be anticipated that the Commission's rules of procedure will provide in greater detail the methods for selecting and hearing witnesses or receiving information. It might be noted that article 42(5) permits the Secretary-General of the OAU to attend meetings of the Commission, although he or she has no right to participate in the deliberations or vote.

Once the Commission has obtained all the information "it deems necessary" and has determined that an amicable solution is impossible, it prepares a report stating "the facts and its findings."[11] The report is submitted to the states concerned and to the OAU Assembly. Article 53 states,

"While transmitting its report, the Commission may make to the Assembly of Heads of State and Government such recommendations as it deems useful." Although it is not clear, it would seem that the recommendations of the Commission are to be made directly to the Assembly rather than incorporated into the report. It appears that a report may only be published with the approval of the Assembly.[12]

Other Communications

Under article 55 there is no restriction as to who may file a communication with the Commission, and individuals, groups of individuals, and NGOs, whether or not they themselves are victims of the illegal violation, may file a communication. The criteria for consideration of communications are set out in article 56: they must be compatible with the Charter of the OAU and the African Charter; they may not be anonymous, written in disparaging or insulting language, or based exclusively on news media reports; they must be submitted within a reasonable time after exhaustion of local remedies; and they should not be cases "which have been settled" by the states concerned in accordance with various international instruments.

As noted above, a state need only have "good reasons" to believe that another state has violated a provision of the Charter in order to submit a communication. Presumably, nonstate communications will be judged on similar grounds, although it appears that any communication may be considered if it receives the support of a majority of the Commission and meets the criteria of article 56.[13]

The exception to this vague standard is where the Commission considers that one or more communications "apparently relate to special cases which reveal the existence of a series of serious or massive violations" of rights.[14] In such a case, the Commission must notify the Assembly of the situation and may proceed with an "in-depth study" and "factual report, accompanied by its findings and recommendations," only upon the request of the Assembly.[15] In an emergency so designated by the Commission, the Chairman of the Assembly has the authority to request an in-depth study.

It is not at all clear whether this interpretation of the Charter as establishing a dual procedure for "other communications" is correct. It may be that it is intended that the Commission will consider *only* "special cases," the study of which requires the prior approval of the Assembly. If this is the case, it would be unfortunate, for it seems to reduce the Commission to merely a functional sub-committee of the Assembly with no independent authority of its own. Certainly the interpretation offered here—that the Commission has sufficient authority under articles 45(2), 46, and 55(2) to investigate "other communications" which do *not* contain allegations of "serious or massive violations"—is consistent with the Commission's independent status as well as with the ultimate institutional sovereignty of the OAU Assembly.

If the Commission does have the authority to proceed with an investigation of a communication that is not a "special case," that procedure is clearly less cumbersome than the "special case" one. Unless the situation is obviously egregious and the complainant relatively certain of political victory in the Assembly, it therefore would seem prudent to couch communications in such a way as to avoid labeling as a "special case."

Interpretation of the Charter's Substantive Provisions

The substantive provisions of the African Charter contain "clawback" clauses that permit a state to restrict rights to the extent permitted by domestic law.[16] Such extremely vague standards appear to place no external restraint upon government actions, although that is arguably the purpose of human rights instruments. Article 6, the right to liberty, provides an example. It states that "every individual shall have the right to liberty and to the security of his person. No one may be deprived of his freedom *except for reasons and conditions previously laid down by law*" (emphasis added). The Charter does not define or limit such "reasons and conditions previously laid down by law" or similar phrases such as "within the law" (article 9) or "provided that he abides by the law" (article 10).

Admittedly, a provision that purports to protect the individual but actually does so only to the extent that he or she is protected under national law is of very little value, especially in cases where national law does not provide effective redress for violations. Assuming that the Charter *is* intended to provide substantive international rights of its own, the problem becomes one of defining the presently undefined limits of the clawback clauses.

The African Charter is a dynamic political document as well as a legal instrument. Article 45(3) empowers the Commission to interpret the provisions of the Charter. In interpreting the Charter, the Commission

shall draw inspiration from international law on human and peoples' rights, particularly from the provisions of various African instruments on human and peoples' rights, the Charter of the United Nations, the Charter of the Organization of African Unity, the Universal Declaration of Human Rights, and other instruments adopted by the United Nations and by African countries in the field of human and peoples' rights as well as from the provisions of various instruments adopted within the Specialized Agencies of the United Nations of which the parties to the present Charter are members.[17]

If the substantive provisions of the Charter lack sufficient clarity to be readily definable, then it is not unreasonable to turn to other, more precise standards that are equally binding upon states. Under the principle of international law known as *pacta sunt servanda*, treaties are binding upon states that enter into them. When a party to the African Charter is also a party, for example, to the International Covenant on Civil and Political Rights, a complainant might be well advised to cite the law and practice under the Covenant as well as the relevant Charter provision. The right to liberty under the Covenant, for example, seems to provide more detailed protections than articles 6 (quoted above) and 7 of the Charter:

1. Everyone has the right to liberty and security of person. No one shall be subjected to arbitrary arrest or detention. No one shall be deprived of his liberty except on such grounds and in accordance with such procedures as are established by law.
2. Anyone who is arrested shall be informed, at the time of arrest, of the reasons for his arrest, and shall be promptly informed of any charges against him.
3. Anyone arrested or detained on a criminal charge shall be brought promptly before a judge or other officer authorized by law to exercise judicial power and shall be entitled to trial within a reasonable time or to release. It shall not be the general rule that persons awaiting trial shall be detained in custody, but release may be subject to guarantees to appear for trial, at any other stage of the judicial proceedings, and, should occasion arise, for execution of the judgment.
4. Anyone who is deprived of his liberty by arrest or detention shall be entitled to take proceedings before a court, in order that such court may decide without delay on the lawfulness of his detention and order his release if the detention is not lawful.
5. Anyone who has been the victim of unlawful arrest or detention shall have an enforceable right to compensation.[18]

The standard of article 9 of the Covenant may influence the interpretation of articles 6 and 7 of the Charter, thus providing a somewhat greater objective restraint on state activity than that contained in the African formulation, "except for reasons and conditions previously laid down by law." This influence should apply equally to African states whether or not they are themselves parties to the International Covenant; otherwise, the Commission would be forced to create one standard where the accused state was a party to the Covenant (under which the African Charter would be interpreted as consistent with the Covenant insofar as possible) and a different standard if the accused state were not a party to the Covenant (in which case the Covenant might be considered to have no effect on interpretation of the Charter). In any event, it would seem that reference to relevant provisions and jurisprudence of other international human rights instruments may be helpful in guiding the Commission's interpretation of the Charter under article 45(3).

Another area in which the Covenant on Civil and Political Rights may supplement the protections of the African Charter is the suspension or derogation from guarantees during times of emergency. The African Charter contains no provision permitting the suspension of rights; on the other hand, the "clawback" clauses of many articles seem to permit the de facto suspension of rights merely through the enactment of national legislation. In interpreting such legislative restrictions, the African Commission could refer to the Covenant provision that limits derogations to situations in which there exists an officially proclaimed "public emergency which threatens the life of the nation."[19] The absolute, nonderogable nature of freedom of conscience under the Covenant, for example, is more protective than article 8 of the Charter, which permits restrictions on freedom of conscience and religion "subject to law and order."

Given the preliminary nature of the observations contained in this chapter, it remains to be seen what influence other human rights documents will have on the eventual interpretive role of the Commission. Nevertheless, the Charter's directive that the commission is to "draw inspiration" from the Universal Declaration of Human Rights and other international human rights instruments, combined with the general obligation of states to conform to their international obligations, does offer the opportunity for the commission to look to other sources to interpret provisions of the African Charter which may be unclear or of first impression.

Final Observations

Despite the likelihood that it will be some time before the African Charter on Human and Peoples' Rights enters into force, its adoption is a milestone in the promotion and protection of human rights in Africa. If ratifications are unduly delayed, perhaps consideration could be given by the OAU to establishing an interim African Commission on Human and Peoples' Rights which could begin some of its important promotional tasks even prior to formal entry into force of the Charter (similar to the status for many years of the Inter-American Commission of Human Rights).

Nongovernmental organizations can be particularly helpful in disseminating information concerning the Charter—and human rights in general—at the grass-roots level, thus complementing the OAU's educational efforts in this area. As national institutions, both governmental and private, are developed and strengthened, they can assist in promoting the objectives of the Charter prior to the functioning of the Commission.

In the area of protection of human rights, the Charter reflects a strong preference for mediation, conciliation, and consensus as opposed to confrontational or adversarial procedures. Actions taken under the Charter remain confidential until the (normally annual) OAU Assembly of Heads of State and Government decides otherwise, and the Assembly usually acts by consensus. In an area as sensitive as human rights, there is no reason to expect that the Assembly will abandon its consensus approach or will even make public recommendations to states except in unusual circumstances.

At this very early stage, one cannot predict whether the relatively broad standards of the Charter, the confidentiality of all proceedings, and the Commission's dependence on the Assembly will lead to more effective protection of human rights in Africa. As is the case in every other region of the world and under other international procedures, the ultimate success of the Charter will rest with the African states themselves, and one can only hope that they are, in the words of the Charter's Preamble, "firmly convinced of their duty to promote and protect human and peoples' rights and freedoms taking into account the importance traditionally attached to these rights and freedoms in Africa."

Notes

1. Central African Republic, Gambia, Guinea, Kenya, Madagascar, Mali, Mauritius, Rwanda, Senegal, Tanzania, and Zaire.

2. Central African Republic, Madagascar, Mauritius, Senegal, and Zaire.

3. *See* Ramcharan, *Human Rights in Africa: Whither Now?* 12 U. GHANA L.J.

88 (1975) for a history of movements for an African Commission of Human Rights from 1967 to 1975; for reference to more recent African interest, *see*, *e.g.*, INTERNATIONAL COMMISSION OF JURISTS, HUMAN RIGHTS IN A ONE PARTY STATE (1978); Hannum, *The Butare Colloquium on Human Rights and Economic Development in Francophone Africa*, 1 UNIVERSAL HUMAN RIGHTS 63 (No. 2, 1979).

4. African Charter on Human and Peoples' Rights, *adopted* 20 June 1981, OAU Doc. CAB/LEG/67/3, *reprinted in* INT'L LEGAL MATERIALS 58 (1982).

5. Article 63(3) of the Charter provides that it will enter into force three months after being ratified by a majority of the member states of the OAU, which currently number fifty. According to available information, six states had ratified the Charter as of February 1983: Congo, Guinea, Liberia, Mali, Senegal, and Togo. Eleven additional states have signed but not yet ratified the charter: Egypt, Gabon, Gambia, Mauritania, Nigeria, Rwanda, Sierra Leone, Somalia, Sudan, Tanzania, and Zambia.

6. A fuller analysis of the Charter may be found in Gittleman, *The African Charter on Human and Peoples' Rights: A Legal Analysis*, 22 VA. J. INT'L L. 667 (1982).

7. African Charter, *supra* note 4, art. 45(1)(b).

8. All African Conference of Churches, *Due Process and the Rule of Law*, STRUCTURES OF INJUSTICE 10 (1975), cited in COMMISSION TO STUDY THE ORGANIZATION OF PEACE, REGIONAL PROTECTION AND PROMOTION OF HUMAN RIGHTS IN AFRICA 21 (1980).

9. COMMISSION TO STUDY THE ORGANIZATION OF PEACE, note 8 *supra*.

10. African Charter, art. 47.

11. *Id.*, art. 52.

12. *Id.*, art. 59(2).

13. *See id.*, art. 55(2).

14. *Id.*, art. 58.

15. The Assembly normally requires a two-thirds vote prior to any action and often acts only by consensus. *See* Charter of the Organization of African Unity, arts. IX, X, XII, XXV, and XXVII.

16. For a discussion of "clawback" clauses, see Norris, *The Suspension of Guarantees*, 30 AM. U.L. REV. 189, 193 n. 24 (1980). *See also* Higgins, *Derogations Under Human Rights Treaties*, 48 BRIT. Y.B. INT'L L. 281 (1978).

17. African Charter, art. 60.

18. International Covenant on Civil and Political Rights, art. 9.

19. *Id.*, art. 4(1).

PART III

Other Techniques and Forums
for Protecting Rights

10
International Reporting Procedures

DANA D. FISCHER

As a potential restraint on the conduct of states, a reporting system is the weakest in the range of implementation techniques.[1] It generally imposes on states the duty to report compliance but not the duty to remedy violations. An examining body is typically mandated to "study" or "consider" the reports, but efforts to judge or even comment specifically on the compliance of individual states is fiercely resisted. A particularly weak link in most reporting systems is the absence of an independent fact-finding capacity on the part of the examining organ.

Despite these seemingly debilitating weaknesses, the practice of several bodies charged with receiving human rights compliance reports suggests that a reporting system *can* have more influence on many governments than the interstate and individual complaint procedures whose theoretical powers of investigation and judgment remain little-used or ignored. As a means of effecting change and highlighting discrepancies between a government's words and deeds, individuals and NGOs can and should seek ways of increasing their influence on the examination process and ensuring that state reports are not just an empty public relations exercise.

Since reporting procedures rarely provide for the formal participation of individuals or NGOs, knowledge of each system and how it works is essential. This chapter will first outline the reporting procedures established for four major human rights treaties; the International Convention on the Elimination of All Forms of Racial Discrimination; the International Covenant on Civil and Political Rights; the International Covenant on Economic, Social and Cultural Rights; and the International Convention on the Suppression and Punishment of the Crime of Apartheid. We will then suggest specific avenues that individuals and NGOs can explore in order to monitor and influence these reporting procedures.

The International Convention on the Elimination of All Forms of Racial Discrimination

The International Convention on the Elimination of All Forms of Racial Discrimination entered into force in 1969, and, as of July 1982, there were 115 state parties. It was the first international instrument on human rights adopted by the United Nations to establish its own implementation system, based on the Committee on the Elimination of Racial Discrimination (CERD). Eighteen experts comprise the Committee and they must be individuals of "high moral standing and acknowledged impartiality" who "serve in their personal capacity." The experts must be nationals of states that are parties to the Convention; they are elected by parties for four-year terms and may be reelected.[2]

Article 9(2) of the Convention requires each state to submit to the Secretary-General, for consideration by the committee, a report on the legislative, judicial, administrative, or other measures that the state has adopted to give effect to the provisions of the Convention. The initial report is due within one year after the entry into force of the Convention for the state concerned, and subsequent reports must be filed every two years or at the request of the Committee. A number of states have been late in submitting either initial or periodic reports. The status of all reports is listed in CERD's Annual Report to the General Assembly, although many countries seem to be willing to accept the negative publicity that accompanies designation as a noncomplying state in a UN document.[3]

CERD has adopted guidelines, most recently revised in April 1980, concerning the form and content of state reports. In affirming the Committee's interest in "the actual situation as regards the practical implementation of the provisions of the Convention and the progress achieved," the 1980 revisions should, according to one Committee member, encourage the committee "to look into what was hidden underneath the legal camouflage behind which governments frequently sheltered to hide reality."[4]

The Committee meets twice a year, with most sessions thus far at the UN Office at Geneva or at UN Headquarters in New York (one has been held in Vienna). It has been suggested that holding sessions in different regions of the world would increase awareness of and interest in the Convention and the activities of CERD, but the expense involved is likely to prevent the adoption of such proposals. The dates and location of future meetings can be found in CERD's Annual Report to the General Assembly.

CERD's practice in examining reports is still evolving after a decade of experimentation. The basic directive is set forth in Rule 66A of the Provisional Rules of Procedure:

1. When considering a report submitted by a State Party under article 9, the Committee shall first determine whether the report provides the information referred to in the relevant communications of the Committee.
2. If a report of the State Party to the Convention, in the opinion of the Committee, does not contain sufficient information, the Committee may request that State to furnish additional information.
3. If, on the basis of its examination of the reports and information supplied by the State Party, the Committee determines that some of the obligations of that State under the Convention have not been discharged, it may make suggestions and general recommendations in accordance with article 9, paragraph 2, of the Convention.

Thus far, CERD has never made a formal determination of noncompliance as envisaged under rule 66A(3). In its early years, the Commmittee judged reports against the standard requirements of rule 66A(1) and classified them as "satisfactory" or "unsatisfactory" as a means of indicating the relative completeness of information contained in the report. This was *not* a determination of compliance or noncompliance with the substantive provisions of the Convention, but only a comment on the procedural acceptability or completeness of the report as filed. By 1974, the reports being received by the Committee generally fulfilled the requirements of article 9, and the Committee discontinued the satisfactory/unsatisfactory classification because it "had outlived its earlier usefulness."[5] Since 1974, the Committee has prepared a summary of its examination of each state report, including views expressed by the Committee and its members. These summaries are public and may be found in the Committee's Annual Report.

The Committee's failure thus far to apply rule 66A(3) should be viewed in the context of an important procedural innovation introduced in 1972, which provides for the presence of a state's representative during the Committee's consideration of that state's report. This presence enables the Committee to address direct criticisms of the state's compliance without adopting a formal ruling to that effect. The procedure enables the state in question to remedy the default without having incurred the stigma of a formal adverse determination, and, in the long run, may prove to be more effective in promoting implementation of the Convention than formal determinations of noncompliance. However, such formal condemnation must remain as an ultimate sanction if states are to be encouraged to comply with the Committee's informal criticisms and recommendations.[6]

In order to examine effectively a state's report, CERD (or any other such body) must have access to independent information with which to verify or contradict state claims. Although the Committee has not adopted a formal rule of procedure on the subject of outside information, in practice, members are allowed to use any information they may receive as experts. Thus, "suggestions and general recommendations" under article 9(2) of the Convention and Article 66A(3) of the Rules can be based not only on reports submitted but also on supplemental private or governmental information.

The International Covenant on Civil and Political Rights

The complaint machinery of the Optional Protocol to the International Covenant on Civil and Political Rights is discussed in chapter 4. Only twenty-seven states have accepted the Optional Protocol and fourteen states the interstate complaint mechanism under article 41 of the Covenant, but all seventy parties (July 1982) are bound by the reporting requirements of article 40.

While these reporting procedures resemble those of the Racial Discrimination Convention, the Covenant protects a much wider range of substantive human rights. Therefore, it is likely that many more individuals and NGOs will have an interest in monitoring and influencing implementation of the Covenant and its examining organ, the Human Rights Committee.

The Human Rights Committee is composed of eighteen nationals of states parties elected by secret ballot from persons nominated by states parties.[7] Like CERD, Committee members are to be persons of "high moral character and recognized competence in the field of human rights," and they serve in their personal capacities. As is the case in most international bodies, consideration is given to geographical balance among the members and to representation of "different forms of civilization and of the principal legal systems." The members are elected for four-year terms and may be reelected. The Committee now meets three times a year instead of the originally planned two. Although there has been some variation, the fall and summer sessions usually take place at the UN Office in Geneva and the spring session at UN Headquarters in New York. The schedule of the Committee's sessions a year in advance can be found in its Annual Report to the General Assembly.[8]

Under article 40 of the Covenant, the parties are required to submit reports on the measures they have adopted "which give effect to the rights recognized [in the Covenant] . . . and on the progress made in the enjoyment of those rights . . . [including] factors and difficulties, if any, affecting the implementation of the present Covenant." The initial report is due one year after the Covenant enters into force for a country and thereafter at the Committee's request. The Committee is charged to "study" the reports and "transmit its [the Committee's] reports and such general comments as it may consider appropriate, to the states parties."

During its first four years of practice, the Committee has been refining the "study" stage of its reporting procedure. Some members point out that, despite improvements and the formulation of general guidelines, "study" by the Committee remains haphazard and uncoordinated. Nevertheless, members have repeatedly expressed interest in information on actual practice in addition to the formal legal protections that may exist within a given country, indicating a welcome willingness to look beyond form to substance that may presage an increasingly activist Committee in the future.

At its inception, the Committee adopted CERD's practice of inviting a representative of the reporting state to introduce the report and answer questions put by members of the committee. Thus far no state has failed to send a representative. After an introductory statement, the representative listens to questions and comments by Committee members. He may reply immediately or by way of a later supplementary report. As of August 1981, forty-four states had undergone the initial examination, and, in response to requests for more detailed information, nine supplementary reports had been submitted to and examined by the Committee.

The great majority of states parties to the Covenant have formally fulfilled their reporting obligations. However, a number of countries have either failed to submit an initial report or have not yet submitted the additional information they promised during consideration of their initial reports. Since 1980, the Committee's Annual Report has noted those countries that have failed to fulfill their reporting obligations under article 40.

The Committee has experimented with a different method of work in examining supplemental state reports than that used when an initial report is examined. The practice for the "second round" has been for members to ask questions, and for the state representative to respond, on a topic-by-topic basis, thus focusing on areas of particular concern. The second appearance of a state before the Committee gives members an opportunity to refer to information provided during the initial examination and to repeat questions to which unsatisfactory answers have been received. This procedure is far from cross-examination, but it does result in a public record that exposes more clearly a country's efforts to evade or ignore uncomfortable issues. Although this "second round" procedure has been applied at least in part in every examination of supplementary information, the Eastern European members declined to participate in these examinations between the eighth and tenth sessions. This posture can be traced to differences within the Committee as to its responsibilities with regard to the reporting procedure. The implementation of a compromise reached by the Committee in October 1980 (discussed below) has eased at least some of these differences.

The question of whether the members may avail themselves of information other than that provided by the states parties has prompted much discussion. One possible source of other, perhaps critical, information is the specialized agencies. Article 40(3) authorizes the Secretary-General, after consultation with the Committee, to "transmit to the specialized agencies concerned, copies of such parts of the reports as fall within their fields of competence," and provisions for cooperation with the specialized agencies have been included in the Provisional Rules of Procedure.[9] Although the agencies, most particularly the International Labor Organization (ILO), have been eager to assist the Committee in its work, the Committee has proceeded very cautiously in developing any relationship. At the beginning of the eighth session, the Committee decided that, "information, mainly on the specialized agencies' interpretation of and practice in relation to the corresponding provisions of their instruments, should be made available to the members of the committee on a regular basis, and that information can be made available to them on request during meetings."[10] The specialized agencies may comment on state reports only if requested to do so by the Committee, and no such request has ever been made.

Although no formal role has been assigned NGOs under the Covenant, it has been suggested that ECOSOC could provide a limited role for NGOs in consultative status with the Council on the pattern laid down in 1962 in relation to the examination of the (now discontinued) Periodic Reports on Human Rights. Under ECOSOC Resolution 888(XXIV), NGOs enjoying consultative status were invited by the Council to submit "comments and observations of an objective character on the situation in the field of hu-

man rights" to assist the Commission on Human Rights in its consideration of the summaries of periodic reports.

While the "study" of reports has been criticized by many observers as
incomplete, probing questions by individual Committee members have
kept the process from becoming a purely formal exercise. Until recently,
however, efforts to move beyond the study stage have been thwarted by
seemingly irreconcilable differences among the Committee members.

Due to very different conceptions of the proper role of the Committee,
its members have been divided from the beginning on the meaning of its
"reports" and "general comments." At one extreme, it has been argued
that article 40(4) requires the Committee to prepare a report on each report
submitted by a state party. Under this view, the state reports are intended
to enable the Committee to determine whether states are, in fact, guaranteeing the rights recognized in the Covenant. At the other extreme is the
view that the Committee reports are no different from the annual report
required by article 45. Thus, the Committee would not be called upon or
even permitted to appraise or judge the compliance of a country with its
substantive obligations under the Covenant.

Similarly, there are disagreements over the nature of the "general comments" and "recommendations" the Committee is permitted to offer. One
view holds that the Committee may make comments directed to a particular state, provided that they are general in character, that is, not relating
to named individuals or specific cases. The more conservative position
contends that the "general comments" provision precludes recommendations addressed to particular states.[11]

The positions outlined above were developed by, respectively, Western
and Eastern European members; the former favored an expansive view of
the Committee's competence, whereas the latter wished to interpret the
Covenant restrictively. In a lengthy discussion of the issue at the tenth
(1980) session, members from developing countries expressed their positions, and, for the first time, it became clear that the Eastern European
members were isolated in their restrictive interpretation.[12]

A major compromise on how to proceed beyond the "study" stage of
state reports was reached at the next session.[13] In exchange for an agreement to proceed with the adoption of non-country-specific "general comments," the Eastern European members left open the possibility of further
consideration of the issue of separate Committee reports on each state
report. They also agreed to agree on a procedure for periodically examining state reports as provided for under article 40(1)(b), thus helping to
defuse conflict over the "second round" procedure.

In the future, the Committee will request the Secretariat to prepare an "analysis" of the examination of the report, which "should set out system-atically both the questions asked and the responses given." Although not a substitute for working groups or a permanent Committee staff, this assistance by the Secretariat will help the members to organize an increasingly cumbersome collection of material.

In an effort to rationalize the review process, the Committee also agreed that, prior to the meeting with the representative of the reporting state, a working group of three members will meet to review the information so far received by the Committee "in order to identify those matters which it would seem most helpful to discuss with the reporting state."

The Committee began implementing the consensus agreement in July 1981 with a decision on periodicity or frequency of future reports, the formulation of new guidelines for subsequent reports, and the first "general comments" under article 40(4).

In accordance with article 40(1)(b), the Committee essentially agreed to request that governments submit subsequent reports at five-year intervals from the date their initial report was due or considered. This decision does not affect the power of the Committee to request an additional report whenever it deems such a course appropriate.[14]

The periodic reports are to concentrate especially on, inter alia, responses to questions raised by the Committee, including additional information as to questions not previously answered or not fully answered; changes made or proposed to be made in the laws and practices relevant to the Covenant; and factors affecting and difficulties experienced in implementation of the Covenant.[15]

Based on its early experience in examining initial and supplementary reports, the Committee drafted several sets of general comments that it felt would assist the states parties in implementing the Covenant. The first three comments offer specific suggestions on procedural aspects of the reporting practices of the state parties, such as punctuality in fulfilling the reporting obligation within the time limit prescribed by article 40(1); completeness of reports according to Committee's guidelines; paying attention to factors and difficulties affecting the implementation of the Covenant; and ways to ensure that individuals know what their rights under the Covenant are and also that all administrative and judicial authorities are aware of obligations which the state has assumed under the Covenant. The last two comments suggest improvements in reporting compliance with broad rights to equality and of nondiscrimination, contained in articles 2(1), 3, 4, and 26.[16]

On balance, the compromise reached on article 40(4) during the eleventh session amounts to one step backward and two steps forward. The

Committee is no closer than it was four years ago to making specific recommendations on the law and practice of the states parties. Any effort on
the part of what was then clearly a majority of the Committee to force the
issue by a vote would have imperiled the informal working atmosphere of
the Committee. By agreeing to the phrase "without prejudice to the further
consideration of the Committee's duties under article 40(4)," the members
from the Eastern European states merely refrained from insisting on a
formal interpretation of the only action they are willing to take anyway,
that is, cooperation in the formulation of non-country-specific general
comments.

The efforts to implement the compromise underline both the strengths
and weaknesses of consensus as a method of decision making.[17] On the
one hand, the members recognized that the development of the Committee
would suffer if no compromise were reached. In this case, the choices
were either to do nothing or to proceed on the basis of the lowest common
denominator of consensus. On the other hand, a consensus with which the
vast majority of the Committee is dissatisfied is bound to wobble when
attempts are made to implement it. The theoretical debate on the meaning
of article 40(4) continues to brew and intrudes constantly into efforts at
implementation.[18]

The issue of the Committee's "reports" has, in effect, been shelved for
the time being. As a result, those members favoring reports on particular
states are likely to insert much more comment on a state's compliance
with the provisions of the Covenant into the questioning process; those
comments will then be reflected in the summary records of the Committee's public sessions.

Although some will doubt the possible efficacy of merely "general"
comments, the Committee would have lost its impressive momentum if
no compromise could have been reached. Nevertheless, the retention of
consensus through inaction can hardly be counted a victory for human
rights. The Committee's future work should be closely scrutinized, and its
attempts to institute meaningful review of state reports supported.

The International Covenant on Economic, Social and Cultural Rights

The International Covenant on Economic, Social and Cultural Rights
entered into force in 1976, and it had seventy-three state parties as of 1

July 1982. The parties are required to report to ECOSOC on the measures that they have adopted and the progress made in achieving the rights recognized in the Covenant.

Copies of relevant parts of the reports are to be transmitted by the Secretary-General to the UN's specialized agencies. ECOSOC is empowered to ask the specialized agencies to report on implementation of provisions of the Covenant that fall within the scope of their activities, including decisions and recommendations to promote such implementation which the specialized agencies have adopted.[19]

Unlike the International Covenant on Civil and Political Rights, the Covenant on Economic, Social and Cultural Rights makes no provision for the examination of reports by a new body composed of independent experts. This lack of specificity may reflect the fact that the Covenant itself requires only that countries achieve "progressively" the rights set forth, unlike the immediately binding nature of many of the provisions of the Covenant on Civil and Political Rights. Rather, ECOSOC as a whole is assigned this responsibility. To assist it in the consideration of reports, ECOSOC decided to establish a sessional working group whenever reports on the implementation of the Covenant were due for consideration.[20] The working group consists of fifteen members that are members of the Council and parties to the Covenant, as well as observers from other states and the specialized agencies. It was decided that reports will be submitted in three stages at two-year intervals: stage 1 covers articles 6–9 (right to work, to fair working conditions, and to social security, and rights of trade unions); stage 2 covers articles 10–12 (family rights and rights to an adequate standard of living and health); and stage 3 covers articles 13–15 (rights to education and culture). The resolution also calls upon the specialized agencies to submit reports as provided for in article 18 of the Covenant.

The working group met for the first time in early 1979. The primary issues discussed were the procedures for consideration of the state reports and whether attention should be confined to the state reports themselves or whether the group could also take into consideration reports from the specialized agencies. It was decided to follow the practice of CERD and the Human Rights Committee and consider the state reports individually, including the possibility of oral presentations by representatives of the countries concerned.

The role of the specialized agencies has been a matter of controversy from the beginning. Although their right to participate in the proceedings of the working group is clear, there were repeated efforts to exclude them.

Finally, an informal agreement was reached allowing reference to the reports of the specialized agencies by any member.

During its second session (April 1980), the working group began to examine reports submitted under the first stage (articles 6–9) of the reporting program established by ECOSOC. Participation by the specialized agencies in the examination process was immediately raised, when the representative from the ILO sought to be recognized by the chairman during consideration of the report submitted by Ecuador. The representatives of the USSR and Romania objected, but it was ultimately decided that the specialized agencies might make a general statement after members of the working group had spoken.

The first examination of reports left a great deal to be desired. The Soviet representative seemed determined to prevent any questioning of the parties' performance under the Covenant. As a result, the working group's report is a mere description of the work carried out and contains no conclusions or recommendation.

After a review of the working group in 1981, ECOSOC, inter alia, urged states that were members of the working group to include in their delegations experts in the matters dealt with in the Covenant. At the third meeting of the working group in April 1981, it was clear that this appeal had gone largely unheeded. With the exception of the USSR and Norway, all states were represented by members of their permanent missions who had not previously taken part in the work of the group. Members' technical preparation was poor, and the questions asked were superficial. The members were unable to submit proposals for conclusions or recommendations on the reports considered by the group. Therefore, for the second year in succession, the working group's discussion of individual reports have taken the form of questions and answers in the group, without any action that could assist ECOSOC in exercising the functions entrusted to it in the implementation of the Covenant.[21]

Even if more time could be allowed for the examination of reports, and governments agree to appoint representatives with greater expertise to the working group, representatives with technical competence would still be subject to instructions from their governments. This fact and the absence of meaningful NGO participation seem to preclude balanced and objective evaluation of the reports submitted.

Even if the working group were able to present ECOSOC with a more complete report on which to base decisions, the latitude of ECOSOC under articles 19, 21, and 22 of the Covenant is extremely limited. ECOSOC may refer the state reports and those of the specialized agencies to the

Commission on Human Rights for study and *general* recommendations or, as appropriate, for information (article 19). It also may submit to the General Assembly reports and recommendations of a *general* nature and a summary of information received from state parties and specialized agencies (article 21). It may bring to the attention of other UN organs and specialized agencies any matters arising out of the reports that may assist such bodies in developing international measures likely to contribute to the implementation of the Covenant (article 22).

In contrast to the general nature of any recommendations that maybe made by ECOSOC, the specialized agencies' reports are to indicate the "progress made in achieving the observance of the Covenant including particulars of decisions and recommendations on such implementation adopted by their competent organs." This language suggests that the agencies should report in precise terms on at least their own activities, thereby providing technical information that may support the general recommendations of other UN bodies.

Although the ILO, World Health Organization, and Food and Agriculture Organization have submitted reports to the working group, only the ILO has actually tried to participate in the examinations conducted by the working group. With the exception of the ILO, other UN specialized agencies are intergovernmental structures ultimately subject to the wishes of their constituent governments, so it is perhaps not surprising that they have not yet contributed to implementation of the Covenant's reporting system. Officials of the agencies know there would be strong resistance if they tried to force the issue.

This review of the first two years' efforts to implement the Covenant leads to the rather dismal conclusion that the reporting procedure is seriously and probably irreparably flawed. Short of the unlikely prospect of amending the Covenant, it seems to be left to the NGOs to squeeze any effectiveness out of these weak procedures.

The International Convention on the Suppression and Punishment of the Crime of Apartheid

The International Convention on the Suppression and Punishment of the Crime of Apartheid entered into force in 1976 and had sixty-seven state parties as of July 1982. The Convention declares apartheid to be a crime against humanity and subjects all acts resulting from the policies and practices of apartheid and similar policies and practices of racial segregation and discrimination, as defined in article 2 of the Convention, to international criminal responsibility irrespective of motive. Article 5 of the Convention provides that persons accused of the crime of apartheid may be tried by a competent tribunal in any state party to the Convention, which automatically acquires jurisdiction over the accused; alternatively, they could be tried by an international criminal tribunal, the formation of which the states parties are still discussing.[22]

The Convention authorizes the Chairman of the UN Commission on Human Rights to appoint a group consisting of three members of the Commission (the "Group of Three"), who also represent parties to the Convention. The Group of Three, which meets for not more than five days either just before or after the Commission's annual session, considers reports submitted periodically by the parties to the Convention on the legislative, judicial, administrative, or other measures that they have adopted pursuant to the Convention.

The Group of Three adopted general guidelines for the form and content of the state reports, and states are to submit their first report not later than two years after becoming parties to the Convention and their periodic reports biennially thereafter.[23] When the Group of Three considers a state's report, it invites that state to send a representative to be present. There are no published summary records of the meetings, although the Group of Three makes an annual report to the Commission on Human Rights.

The Convention only mandates the Group of Three to "consider" the reports submitted by states in accordance with article 7, and sixteen initial reports and four periodic reports were considered at the Group's first three meetings. In its third report, the Group of Three decided "to study the reports of the states parties in depth and to make recommendations which would cover broader aspects of the implementation of the Convention than those reflected in the reports. . . . [The] Group, as the only body which consists exclusively of representatives of the states parties to the Convention, considers itself duty-bound to express opinions on the situation in connection with the implementation of the Convention."[24] This willingness on the part of the Group of Three to expand its competence in the area of apartheid contrasts sharply with the restrictive views of many governments on implementation of the two Covenants.

Article 10(b) of the Convention empowers the Commission on Human Rights to "prepare, on the basis of reports from competent organs of the United Nations and periodic reports from states parties to the present Convention, a list of individuals, organizations, institutions and representatives of States which are alleged to be responsible for the crimes enumerated in article II of the Convention, as well as those against whom legal proceedings have been undertaken by States Parties to the Convention." In its general guidelines for the preparation of state reports, the Group of Three has asked the states parties to identify in their periodic reports such individuals, institutions, and representatives of states. The first such list was published on 31 January 1980 and is based in part on the Group's own mission of inquiry to London in 1979, at which time the Group received written and oral evidence.[25]

The directness and specificity of the report is startling for a UN document. Eighteen cases of death and nineteen cases of torture and deprivation of freedom and fundamental rights are set forth, including identification of the victim and the alleged perpetrators of the crimes, analysis of the facts, and presentation of conclusions and "legal findings." The Human Rights Commission instructed the Secretariat to give the list the widest possible publication, but the Secretary-General has been very cautious about implementing this directive. This may be due, in part, to the Convention's provision in article XI that acts of apartheid within the meaning of the Convention "shall not be considered political crimes for the purpose of extradition . . . [and that] States Parties to the present Convention undertake in such cases to grant extradition in accordance with their legislation and with the treaties in force." The reluctance may also be traced to the fact that not a single Western industrialized nation is a party to the Convention. Thus far, implementation of the Commission's directive has been limited to publication of the list in a press release and in the UN's *Bulletin of Human Rights*.[26]

Strategies for NGO Participation

None of the four reporting procedures analyzed above makes formal provision for the participation of NGOs. Therefore, NGO activities designed to influence and promote human rights through these procedures must be both selective and creative.

As with every activity, a NGO must first decide whether its resources permit extensive support of what will be, in most cases, only an indirect means of advancing specific human rights causes. In addition to the considerations set forth in chapter 2, there are fairly severe geographical constraints on informal NGO influence on reporting procedures: with rare exceptions (such as the Group of Three's mission of inquiry in London), those bodies charged with examining state reports meet in Geneva or New York, and trips to either of these cities place a considerable strain on most budgets. On the other hand, knowledge of the schedules of the various groups might enable a NGO to combine "lobbying" on state reports with other UN activities. Of course, information may also be provided to individual members by mail.

There are three primary areas in which NGOs can play an important role: checking formal compliance by states with the various reporting requirements; contributing to the substantive examination of reports; and commenting on and publicizing the results of such examinations.

Compliance with Reporting Requirements

The Annual Reports of CERD and the Human Rights Committee note those countries that have not fulfilled the reporting requirements. Whether the failure to comply is due to bureaucratic inefficiency or less benign motives, NGOs should ensure that noncompliance will not pass unnoticed by either the examining body or the country concerned. Domestic pressures, where possible, to live up to international obligations might encourage greater attention to human rights issues generally as well as with respect to country-specific items of concern. Failure to comply with reporting requirements should certainly be raised, where appropriate, in other human rights forums.

State reports under all the reporting procedures discussed should be public, and requests for copies should be addressed directly to the appropriate government departments. The refusal of governments to provide domestic or international NGOs with reports might, in itself, constitute grounds for questioning the government's good faith in human rights matters.

Examination of Reports

Even though formal NGO submissions are not provided for in any of the reporting procedures, preparation of substantive critiques of state reports is undoubtedly the most fruitful area for NGO participation in the reporting process. Owing to the absence of any independent fact-finding capacity on the part of the examining bodies, NGO-provided information is essential to any meaningful analysis of the reports submitted. Depending on the expertise and resources of the NGO, the information provided might range from suggestions for questions to state representatives, to detailed legal analyses, to informal submission of an entire "counter-report" where it is felt that the governmental report is broadly inaccurate and misleading.

The state reports are publicly available as UN documents well before they are due to be examined by the various oversight bodies, although candor requires one to recognize that UN documents are not always easy to obtain. Requests for the reports should be made both to the appropriate UN body (when in doubt, correspondence can be addressed in care of the Human Rights Centre in Geneva) and directly to the government concerned.

The *Human Rights Committee*, which examines reports under the Covenant on Civil and Political Rights, is the forum with the most potential for meaningful NGO participation. The volume of material received by the Committee members and the limited time in which to consider it has already led many members to welcome NGO input as preliminary organizers and evaluators of the information received from governments.

The most helpful NGO input is probably that which refers specifically to the factual and legal situation in the particular country under review. NGOs whose mandates are more issue-oriented, such as abolition of the death penalty or protection of trade union rights, could highlight treatment of those issues in the state reports.

NGOs should prepare supplemental information for members of the Committee as far in advance as possible. When the consensus agreement on implementing article 40(4) (discussed above) is fully implemented, particular attention should be paid to contacting the Committee's working group of three members, which will meet prior to each Committee session "in order to identify those matters which it would seem most helpful to discuss with the reporting state."[27] While formal meetings of the working group will be private, the names of the members will be public. They can be contacted directly, on an informal basis, with relevant information. If a state's report and NGO resources make preparation of a "counterreport" possible, such a report should be distributed to all eighteen members of the Committee. As with all materials submitted to the UN or similar international bodies, NGO information should be as factual and nonpolitical as possible.

Most of the above observations concerning the Human Rights Committee also apply to the *Committee on the Elimination of Racial Discrimination*. Although CERD members have perhaps not been as forthcoming in their appreciation of NGO activity as members of the Human Rights Committee, the style and procedures of the two bodies are similar. Again, factual information responsive to issues raised in the periodic reports submitted to CERD should be informally submitted to individual members for their consideration. When a state makes specific undertakings in the course of oral consideration of its report by CERD, NGOs can perform a valuable function by monitoring subsequent compliance. Clear cases of noncompliance or unresponsiveness that are brought to CERD's attention may encourage the state concerned to alter its practices or, failing that, might create pressure on CERD to adopt a formal finding of noncompliance with the Convention under article 66A(3) of the Rules.

Apart from the unlikely amendment of the Covenant on Economic, Social and Cultural Rights, the potential for meaningful NGO participation in reviews by *ECOSOC* or its *Sessional Working Group* is slight (except for comments on the relevant ECOSOC agenda item by NGOs with consultative status).[28] While there are no restrictions on the informal distribution of material by NGOs to ECOSOC or Sessional Working Group delegations, the fact that members of these bodies are governmental representatives renders it less likely, in most instances, that NGOs will be able to influence politically motivated decisions of those delegations. New avenues might open as the ECOSOC procedures develop, but it is not possible at this time to offer more than very general encouragement.

The best route presently open to NGOs may be to work through the UN's specialized agencies in the formulation of their reports on the Convention. The Committee of Experts of the ILO makes full use of information from workers' and employers' organizations, and other NGO material could also be submitted on issues within the ILO's mandate. UNESCO's Committee on Conventions and Recommendations is the appropriate body to receive human rights information submitted by NGOs in the educational, scientific, and cultural spheres. Neither the Food and Agricultural Organization nor the World Health Organization has established channels for receipt of NGO information, although NGO inquiries about the possibility of submitting information concerning implementation of the Convention could conceivably result in the establishment of such channels.

In any event, reality forces one to recognize that working through the specialized agencies is, at best, a rather indirect way of contributing to a serious discussion of the many issues raised in state reports under the Covenant. Future developments may give rise to greater optimism.

The political nature of the *Group of Three* established under the *Apartheid Convention* makes NGO participation problematic. Certainly, NGOs that focus on apartheid and southern Africa should not hesitate to contribute to an analysis of the periodic reports required under the Convention or, if they possess specific information, to assist in compilation by the Human Rights Commission of lists of those allegedly responsible for the crime of apartheid. At the same time, however, the highly political under-pinnings of the whole issue of apartheid should be acknowledged. NGOs should not only contribute to the work of bodies under the Convention, but they should also monitor the examination process itself and publicize any abuses that may detract from the objective, universal condemnation of apartheid that should be the foundation of activity in this area.

Finally, it is essential that NGOs have regular observers present at the public meetings of the examining bodies. First, a NGO presence ensures a degree of publicity for the proceedings, which may encourage greater veracity in state representatives' answers to questions. Second, much of the influence a NGO can exert is through personal contacts with the members, and these relationships are best cultivated before and after the public meetings. Third, although there are summary records of the proceedings of three of the bodies, there are many important developments that take place in open session but off the public record. Where there are no summary records, as in the case of the Group of Three, having a representative present is the only way a NGO will know what has occurred.

Postexamination Publicity

No reporting procedure will be effective in promoting human rights if it is ignored, and one of the easiest and most positive measures NGOs can take with respect to state reports is to publicize them. Summary records of discussions of the state reports are available within days, and the often critical comments and questions of members of the examining bodies (particularly in the cases of CERD and the Human Rights Committee) can certainly be quoted by NGOs or raised in subsequent talks with government officials.

With sufficient investment of time and resources, the larger NGOs are in a position to take postexamination publicity a step further. Drawing on state reports and summary records, they could evaluate a country's performance under *all* human rights treaties to which it has adhered. If the countries were chosen carefully and the evaluations objective, such an effort would publicize information that is available but sometimes difficult to obtain and might well encourage pro human rights forces in the country concerned. Given the rather esoteric nature of many UN documents, it must be the responsibility of local human rights NGOs to assure the national government that its noncompliance or evasiveness in the face of international obligations which it has freely accepted has not gone unnoticed.

In cases where a government has undertaken to alter domestic law or practice in response to its international obligations, NGOs should also take care to give credit to such developments.[30] By publicizing the positive aspects of compliance with international human rights norms, NGOs can play an important role in removing the stigma that many states continue to feel is attached to any international oversight of domestic human rights practices.

Final Observations

Requiring government reports on human rights does not per se constitute an effective means of implementing or enforcing human rights standards. None of the four treaties examined in this chapter, for example, requires a reporting state to taken any action as a result of the examination process (although a formal finding of noncompliance would imply a breach of an international legal obligation).

However, a reporting process that includes an informed, public, critical appraisal of the performance of states under these treaties *can* contribute to the promotion of human rights, by either assisting those states that wish to conform or by pressuring (however marginally) those states that refuse to conform. Such an appraisal is absolutely dependent on the availability of reliable, independent information to supplement that supplied by the reporting state. The fact that NGO participation in the process is informal rather than official does not detract from either the need or the opportunity for such participation.

Leaving the implementation of reporting systems to the quiet diplomacy of infrequent, little-known meetings will ensure that reporting systems remain ineffective and may contribute to their abuse by states which loudly proclaim their adherence to human rights treaties and then ignore their implementation. NGO attention to these procedures at least raises the possibility of strengthening them, and it will certainly raise the cost of noncompliance to those governments which now hope that the procedures will be largely forgotten.

Notes

1. The highly developed reporting system of the ILO is of a qualitatively different nature and is treated in chapter 5.

2. *See* appendix F for the names of the current Committee members.

3. Requests for reports should be addressed to Director, Human Rights Centre, UN Office at Geneva, Palais des Nations, Geneva, Switzerland. The official citation for the 1980 annual report is REPORT OF THE COMMITTEE ON THE ELIMINATION OF RACIAL DISCRIMINATION, 35 UN GAOR, Supp. (No. 18), UN Doc. A/35/18 (1980).

4. 1980 REPORT, *id.* at 6.

5. UN Doc. CERD/C/R.12 (1970), *reproduced in* 25 UN GAOR, Supp. (No. 27) 32, UN Doc. A/8027 (1970).

6. *See* Buergenthal, *Implementing the UN Racial Convention*, 12 TEXAS INT'L L.J. 187 (1977).

7. A list of members is contained in appendix F.

8. *E.g.*, REPORT OF THE HUMAN RIGHTS COMMITTEE, 35 UN GAOR, Supp. (No. 40), UN Doc. A/35/40 (1980).

9. The Committee's Provisional Rules of Procedure may be found in UN Doc. CCPR/C/3/Rev.1 (1979).

10. *Supra* note 8 at 94–95.

11. *See* UN Docs. CCPR/C/SR.48, 49, 50, 55, 73 (1978).

12. *See* UN Docs. CCPR/C/SR.231, 232 (1980).

13. The agreement is set forth as Statement on the Duties of the Human Rights Committee under Article 40 of the Covenant, UN Doc. CCPR/C/18 (1981) (adopted on 30 Oct. 1980).

14. *See* REPORT OF THE HUMAN RIGHTS COMMITTEE, 36 UN GAOR, Supp. (No. 40) Annex IV, UN Doc. A/36/40 (1981).

15. *Id.* at Annex V.

16. *Id.* at Annex VII.

17. Under article 39(2)(b) of the Covenant, decisions of the Committee are to be made by majority vote of the members present. However, when the Committee adopted its Provisional Rules of Procedure, there was considerable discussion as to whether decisions would be taken by majority vote or consensus. *See* UN Docs. CCPR/C/SR.3, 4, 6, 7, 14 (1977). The compromise is reflected in Rule 51, which provides that the decisions of the Committee shall be made by a majority of the members present but with a footnoted qualification: "The members of the Committee generally expressed the view that its method of work normally should allow for attempts to reach decisions by consensus before voting." *Supra*

note 9 at 10. The Committee had conducted its business by consensus through the thirteenth session.

18. *See, e.g.*, UN Docs. CCPR/C/SR.304, 306, 309 (1981).

19. *See* Alston, *The United Nation's Specialized Agencies and Documentation of the International Covenant on Economic, Social and Cultural Rights*, 18 COL. J. TRANSNAT'L L. 79 (1979) for the role of the specialized agencies in shaping the content and form of the rights that were included in the Covenant as well as their effective lobbying against application of the procedures of the Human Rights Committee to the Covenant. The technical competence and expertise of the specialized agencies was a prime consideration when the implementation procedure for this treaty was drafted.

It had been argued before the Commission on Human Rights in 1951 "that a special committee, along the lines of the Human Rights Committee, might involve itself in technical questions in which it would have only limited expertise and might attempt to fix standards of its own in the specialized fields that were the concern of the agencies." Commission on Human Rights, REPORT OF THE SEVENTH SESS., 13 UN ESCOR, Supp. (No. 9) 87, UN Doc. E/1992, E/CN.4/ 640 (1951).

21. *See* E.S.C. Res. 1988(LX), 60 UN ESCOR, Supp. (No. 1) 11, UN Doc. E/5850 (1976).

22. REPORT OF THE SESSIONAL WORKING GROUP ON THE IMPLEMENTATION OF THE INTERNATIONAL COVENANT ON ECONOMIC, SOCIAL AND CULTURAL RIGHTS, UN Doc. E/1981/64 (1981).

23. *See* Bassiouni & Derby, *Final Report on the Establishment of an International Criminal Court for the Implementation of the Apartheid Convention and Other Relevant International Instruments*, 9 HOFSTRA L. REV. 523 (1981).

24. The guidelines are annexed to the Group's first annual report, UN Doc. F/ CN.4/1286 (1978).

25. UN Doc. E/CN.4/1326 (1979) at 6.

26. UN Doc. E/CN.4/1366 (1980).

27. UN DIVISION OF HUMAN RIGHTS, BULLETIN OF HUMAN RIGHTS (No. 28, 1980).

28. UN Doc. CCPR/C/SR.260 (1980).

29. *Cf.* the discussion in chapter 10 of NGO interventions before the Human Rights Commission and Sub-Commission.

30. Specific improvements have occurred, for example, in Sweden, which repealed a law concerning antisocial behavior, and in Senegal, which amended certain legislation limiting the number of political parties to four and imposing an obligation on Senegalese citizens to obtain an exit visa in order to leave the country. *See* UN Docs. CCPR/C/SR.52 and 53 (1978), 188 and 189 (1979), 263 and 295 (1981).

11

Direct Intervention at the UN: NGO Participation in the Commission on Human Rights and Its Sub-Commission

MENNO KAMMINGA
AND NIGEL S. RODLEY

If the UN has not been as effective as it might be in securing universal support for human rights, it is not owing to lack of procedures. A case of alleged torture of a prisoner in Uruguay, for example, can be raised in at least three ways. It can be submitted as an individual complaint to the Human Rights Committee set up under the International Covenant on Civil and Political Rights. It also can be submitted to the United Nations under ECOSOC Resolution 1503 (XLVIII) as a case that forms part of a "consistent pattern of gross violations" of human rights. And, finally, it can be raised orally or in writing under the appropriate agenda item during a session of the UN Commission on Human Rights (hereinafter, the Commission) or its Sub-Commission on Prevention of Discrimination and Protection of Minorities (hereinafter, the Sub-Commission).

The present chapter is concerned only with the third, rather specific

The authors are staff members of the International Secretariat of Amnesty International, but the views expressed herein are solely those of the authors and not necessarily those of Amnesty International.

alternative: interventions at the Commission and the Sub-Commission. Two primary characteristics distinguish such interventions from other UN and international procedures: first, the rules governing interventions are generally less technically restrictive than more well defined procedures, and, second, such interventions are highly visible components of the already public and often newsworthy meetings of the Commission and Sub-Commission.

This high visibility often means that a NGO will have a greater impact, either positively or negatively, on discussions in the Commission or Sub-Commission than it might under confidential or less publicized procedures. It may also be more difficult for governmental delegates or Sub-Commission members to avoid confrontation with politically sensitive issues.

On the other hand, a negative impression created by an ill-founded or politically motivated NGO statement may constitute a more serious setback than such a statement made in private. For example, an abusive petition under the Optional Protocol will simply be dismissed by the Human Rights Committee. An unfounded submission under the 1503 procedure will not be investigated. But an inappropriate intervention at the Commission or the Sub-Commission may result not only in political damage to the cause being espoused but also in damage to the reputation of the organization in question, including possible withdrawal of consultative status. It may also contribute to increased restrictions on the activities of nongovernmental organizations at the UN, thereby indirectly limiting access to the Commission and Sub-Commission for others. Accordingly, any intervention at the Commission or the Sub-Commission should be very carefully planned and executed.

Who May Intervene?

Direct intervention at the Commission and Sub-Commission is possible only for representatives of NGOs that have been granted consultative status with the Economic and Social Council (ECOSOC) and who have been officially accredited by the NGO to the UN's NGO Liaison Officer in Geneva (presently the site of all meetings of both the Commission and the Sub-Commission).[1] Other NGOs can work only indirectly and in concert with an accredited NGO at the Commission or Sub-Commission, and even such informal joint action may raise questions. Nevertheless, some six hundred NGOs currently enjoy consultative status (in category I or II) with

ECOSOC or have been placed on the NGO Roster (a status more or less equivalent to that of category II consultative status). Unfortunately, only a very few NGOs can be considered to be active participants in the work of the Commission and Sub-Commission.

The conditions and procedures for granting consultative status are set out in ECOSOC Resolution 1296 (XLIV) (1968).[2] According to this resolution, the aims and purposes of the organization must conform to the spirit, purposes, and principles of the Charter of the United Nations. The organization must undertake to support the work of the United Nations and to promote knowledge of its principles and activities. It must be representative of a broadly based constituency and have recognized international standing, although a broad interpretation of these requirements is often accepted.

Resolution 1296 distinguishes among NGOs in three different categories: organizations that are concerned with most of the activities of ECOSOC (category I), organizations which are concerned with only a few of the fields of activity covered by ECOSOC (category II), and more specialized organizations that may be placed on ECOSOC's "Roster." NGOs in category I enjoy slightly greater privileges than those in category II, whereas there is little difference between category II and Roster status. Presently, 236 organizations have acquired consultative status and 368 organizations have been granted Roster status.

The purpose of this system of consultative status is to enable ECOSOC or any of its subsidiary bodies to secure expert competence in the subject under discussion and "to enable organizations which represent important elements of public opinion in a large number of countries to express their views."[3] At the same time, it enables ECOSOC to limit participation to organizations with such competence.

ECOSOC decides which NGOs will be granted consultative or roster status based on the advice of its Committee on Nongovernmental Organizations. This committee normally meets only once every two years, so the process of obtaining consultative status is a relatively lengthy one. Information about the purposes, membership, and funding of an organization must be provided, as well as some evidence that the organization has expertise in the broad areas of ECOSOC's concerns or within specific areas such as human rights. Although not formally a consideration, the general political orientation of an organization may become a factor in the determination of status, and it is not unknown for groups of members of the committee (and ECOSOC) informally to condition the granting of status to one organization with an orientation from one geographic or political background to the granting of the same status to a NGO from a different background in a "package deal."

Paragraph 36 of Resolution 1296 specifies the circumstances under which consultative status may be suspended or withdrawn. Of particular relevance to NGOs interested in human rights is subparagraph (b), which provides that consultative status shall be withdrawn or suspended "if the organization clearly abuses its consultative status by systematically engaging in unsubstantiated or politically motivated acts against States Members of the United Nations contrary to and incompatible with the principles of the Charter." This provision is sometimes invoked by governments that have been accused by a NGO in a UN forum of serious human rights violations, and it should be borne in mind when interventions are contemplated. In practice, however, we are not aware of use of this provision to withdraw consultative status from any NGO.

The Commission on Human Rights and Its Sub-Commission

The *Commission on Human Rights* is the principal UN body responsible for the promotion and protection of human rights. The Commission consists of forty-three member states of the United Nations, elected by ECOSOC, and meets in Geneva once a year for a period of six weeks (usually in February/March).

The work of the Commission on Human Rights covers the whole range of human rights topics, including economic, social, and cultural rights; the right of self-determination; rights of children and migrant workers; conscientious objection against military service; religious intolerance; racial discrimination; and others. If a NGO is interested in only one or a small number of topics, it is usually difficult to plan to be in Geneva exactly at the time this item is under discussion. Although an agenda and timetable are established at the beginning of each session, in practice the Commission sometimes runs well behind schedule, and agenda items may often be rearranged. The basic document essential to an understanding of the work of the Commission (and Sub-Commission) is the annotated provisional agenda issued a few weeks prior to each session.

Most of the Commission's deliberations are open to the public. The only agenda item which is normally discussed in private or confidential session is that concerning "situations which appear to reveal a consistent pattern of gross violations of human rights" raised in communications under the procedures of ECOSOC Resolution 1503.[4] The Commission's work can roughly be divided into two areas: drafting international human rights standards and reviewing the implementation of those standards. Working groups are often established to assist in these tasks, and most of these working groups can also be attended by NGO representatives.

The *Sub-Commission on Prevention of Discrimination and Protection of Minorities* is a suborgan of the Commission. Its name is a relic of the past, for it is not merely concerned with discrimination and minority rights but reports to the Commission on the same wide range of human rights issues with which the Commission itself is involved. In 1980, it requested that its name be changed to the Sub-Commission of the Commission on Human Rights to reflect its expanded competence, although the request has not been acted upon by the Commission.

The Sub-Commission's four-week annual sessions are held in Geneva, usually in August-September. The Sub-Commission is composed of twenty-six independent experts elected by the Commission for three-year terms, the most recent election having occurred in 1981.[5] Since the members of the Sub-Commission are not government delegates or representatives, their deliberations are often less influenced by the broad political concerns of individual governments than are those of the Commission. This slightly less political atmosphere also contributes to a greater appreciation of NGO interventions and activities than at the Commission.

Several different categories of observers may attend sessions of the Commission and the Sub-Commission, including member states and non-member states of the United Nations, UN bodies, UN specialized agencies, regional intergovernmental organizations, national liberation movements recognized by the General Assembly, and nongovernmental organizations in consultative status with ECOSOC. Only members of the Commission or Sub-Commission and observers in one of these categories are allowed to intervene at the Commission or the Sub-Commission. Other individuals are merely admitted to the public gallery as spectators and may not participate in the proceedings.

Written Statements

A NGO in consultative status with ECOSOC and interested in human rights will receive throughout the year several requests from the UN Secretariat to provide written information on particular subjects or particular countries These are subjects or countries concerning which ECOSOC, the Commission, or the Sub-Commission have asked the Secretariat to prepare a report in one form or another. It is important to comply with these requests insofar as possible, since the Secretariat relies heavily on information provided by NGOs for its reports. The reports, in turn, provide the basis for subsequent UN actions and may therefore constitute a valuable contribution by NGOs to the decision-making process. In some cases, the information will be summarized in a synopsis prepared by the Secretariat, while in others, the submission will be reproduced verbatim as an official UN document circulated to the Commission or the Sub-Commission.

In addition to written statements requested by the Secretariat, NGOs in consultative status with ECOSOC also may submit, on their own initiative, written statements relating to specific agenda items. In accordance with paragraph 20 of Resolution 1296, such statements may not exceed two thousand words for NGOs in category I or fifteen hundred words for NGOs in category II or on the Roster. Statements should be submitted in one of the official languages of the United Nations (Chinese, English, French, Russian, and Spanish) and, whenever possible, should be submitted four to six weeks before the beginning of the session in order to allow time for translations and for consultations between the Secretariat and the NGO.

The Secretariat decides whether to circulate the statement, and its judgment is final. Thus, consultations between the Secretariat and the NGO are often helpful, even when statements meet the formal requirements of length, language, deadline, and topicality. NGOs are expected to give "due consideration" to the Secretariat's comments.

What criteria does the Secretary-General employ to decide whether or not to circulate a statement? First, it is obvious that the language used in the statement may not be abusive and should be factual and precise. Furthermore, there are generally no problems with statements relating to countries that are named on the public agenda of the Commission or Sub-Commission. This applies to countries that have been on the agenda for many years, such as Chile, Israel (occupied territories), and South Africa, and also to countries that have come under scrutiny more recently, such as Democratic Kampuchea, El Salvador, Equatorial Guinea, and Guatemala. These countries will be noted on the agenda.

Reference to specific countries is often made under a general agenda item, for example, "violations of human rights in any part of the world," which are considered annually by the Commission pursuant to ECOSOC

Resolution 1235 (XLII) (1967) and Commission Resolution 8 (XXIII) (1967). In such cases, it may be necessary to consult the full annotated agenda issued a few weeks before each session of the Commission or Sub-Commission, which may refer to earlier discussions of a specific country by the Commission, the Sub-Commission, or other UN organs.

The situation is more complicated with respect to a country not specifically named on the agenda or annotated agenda. The basic rule is that a NGO may not systematically engage in unsubstantiated or politically motivated acts against member states. Further, ECOSOC Resolution 728F (XXVIII) (1959) provides that the Commission (and, by implication, the Sub-Commission) can take no action on "complaints" concerning human rights. Therefore, written statements that are considered to constitute a "complaint" about specific human rights violations are likely to be merely sent to the government concerned and listed on a confidential summary circulated to Commission members.

For many years the Secretariat interpreted these restrictions as prohibiting any mention by NGOs in their written statements of the names of specific countries accused of human rights violations. The result of this practice was a large number of statements set in terms so general that one often wondered which country was being described. In recent years, this "rule" has been relaxed somewhat, although it is still a good idea to allow sufficient time for consultation with the UN Secretariat in order to determine how specific a statement can be.[6] If possible, written statements should be sent to the Director of the UN Human Rights Centre in Geneva. One option that may be acceptable is reference to countries in footnotes or as examples only and mentioning, where appropriate, countries of different political systems.

Oral Statements

Unlike written statements, oral statements are almost always made at the initiative of the NGO concerned. The procedures for requesting to speak are simple: A NGO representative merely walks up to the Secretary of the Commission or Sub-Commission and asks, by means of a brief note giving the name of the organization and the person wishing to speak, to be put on the speakers' list. NGOs are normally allowed to speak at the end of debate on an agenda item, but, occasionally, if country representatives or members are hesitant to take the floor early in the debate, NGOs may speak first. It is wise to distribute the text of your statement to the interpreters in advance, so that the simultaneous translation is as accurate as possible. You may also want to notify the delegations from the countries you are going to speak about, particularly if they are not Commission or Sub-Commission members, so that you can be certain that they note your statement. In other cases, such forewarning may be avoided in order to decrease the likelihood of an objection to the statement.

If an organization is not very well known or has only recently received consultative status, its representative may want to explain the purposes of the NGO in one or two sentences at the beginning of the statement. If the statement is newsworthy, copies may be distributed to press correspondents at the UN newsroom.

Although oral statements are generally allowed to be more specific than written statements, making such statements is considerably more delicate. It is possible that the Chair will cut off a speaker if he or she considers the statement inappropriate, or representatives of countries against which a statement is directed may interrupt the statement in order to obtain such a ruling from the Chair. It should be noted that NGOs have no right to challenge a ruling from the Chair and speak only at the invitation of the Commission and Sub-Commission. Nor do NGOs have a formal right of reply if they are attacked by another participant. However, as occurred at the 1980 session of the Sub-Commission, the Chair may give a NGO representative a chance to make a further statement. If a NGO representative fears that a statement may be challenged, it may be advisable to discuss it with one or more sympathetic members of the body. Then the member(s) will be in a position to "defend" the interests of the NGO.

There are no clear guidelines as to what is permissible in an oral NGO statement. As a general rule, it is reasonable to assume that any intervention that the Secretary-General would circulate if it were submitted as a written statement can safely be delivered orally. In addition, a 1952 opinion of the Legal Office of the UN Secretariat is also instructive. In reply to questions from members of the Sub-Commission concerning limits on remarks critical of governments by NGOs with consultative status, the Secretariat stated that, except for the fact that NGOs should restrict their remarks to items on the agenda, "the consultative arrangements did not place any restriction on the contents of statements made by the representatives of NGOs. In particular, there was no rule or precedent whereby such representatives were required to refrain from criticizing the governments of Member States or from taking issue with statements made by members of the Sub-Commission."[7]

Although this opinion is now 30 years old, its interpretation is not obsolete. In June 1980, while addressing the World Forum of International Associations in Brussels, the Deputy Secretary-General and Legal Adviser of the UN repeated this statement verbatim.[8] Unfortunately, the precedents in this area remain confusing and, to some extent, contradictory.

Some examples from recent years demonstrate the difficulties faced by NGOs in preparing oral statements critical of particular countries. During the 1973 session of the Commission, the representative of the Anti-Slavery Society spoke about the near extermination of aboriginal tribes "in one of the smaller countries of South America." The delegate of Chile interrupted on a point of order to request the name of the country to which he was referring. The representative of the Anti-Slavery Society replied that he had been led to believe that it was the Commission's custom not to permit NGOs to mention countries by name except by way of congratulation. He welcomed the opportunity to inform the Commission that the state to which he was referring was Paraguay.[9] At the following session of the Commission (in 1974), the representative of the World Conference on Religion and Peace spoke extensively of human rights violations in the Republic of Korea, Spain, Paraguay, and the Republic of Vietnam. His statement was apparently not interrupted or challenged in any way.[10] However, when the same NGO representative made a similar intervention in 1975 and named South Africa, the Philippines, Pakistan, Syria, Cyprus, Egypt, Czechoslovakia, USSR, and Zaire, several representatives "deplored that his organization had seen fit to make unfounded and slanderous accusations against member States and expressed the view that such statements constituted an abuse of the privilege accorded to nongovernmental organizations to participate in the deliberations of the Commmission."[11] However, no similar reaction had been elicited by a more nuanced statement delivered during the same session by the Amnesty International representative and which referred to "mass violations" of human rights in southern Africa, Chile, Brazil, and Indonesia.[12]

When ECOSOC discussed these matters in 1976, it radically amended a proposed restrictive resolution (drafted by the Commission) so that the ultimate effect amounted to little more than a reaffirmation of Resolution 1296 (no systematic, unsubstantiated, or politically motivated attacks).[13] In sum, the rules of the game, such as they were, were not modified; NGOs were merely reminded that they had to be careful.

In 1977, ECOSOC was again the forum for a discussion of the limits on NGO participation. Argentina asserted that certain NGOs had used their position to make political attacks on individual member states during the preceding Commission session. It also complained that NGOs were sometimes represented by persons who move from one organization to another without any clear evidence that they belong to the organization in question, citing the example of a person who had first addressed the Sub-Commission on behalf of the International Commission of Jurists and subsequently was allowed to do the same at the Commission on behalf of Pax Romana. According to the Argentine government, the person in question was a member of the Argentine branch of an international "terrorist" movement. Argentina concluded that it should be determined whether these organizations had made their consultative status subject to suspension or withdrawal.[14]

A radically different view was expressed by the Netherlands government. The Netherlands stated that firm and specific evidence was required before expressions of concern by NGOs could be labelled "unsubstantiated" or "politically motivated" in accordance with paragraph 36(b) of Resolution 1296. The reference in paragraph 36(b) to the "principles of the Charter" should not be understood to imply that statements are unacceptable because they allegedly relate to matters that are within the domestic jurisdiction of states under article 2, paragraph 7, of the Charter.[15]

At the end of the 1977 debate, ECOSOC did "appeal" to NGOs "to exercise particular care" in the selection of their representatives. ECOSOC clearly had in mind specially accredited representatives who might be personally involved in the situation of the country being denounced in an oral intervention. In light of this appeal, it may be unwise for a NGO to permit its consultative status to be used as a means of allowing individuals to address the Commission or Sub-Commission or of facilitating direct testimony from "witnesses" who otherwise would not represent the NGO. Thus, there may be an understandable reluctance on the part of NGOs with consultative status to serve merely as a conduit for an oral or written intervention by another organization no matter how compelling the subject matter. On the other hand, approaching NGOs with consultative status in advance of a Commission or Sub-Commission session with a request to present relevant information to one of those bodies may be fruitful for those NGOs that lack the expertise or international character to obtain consultative status in their own right.

In 1978, an informal agreement was reached among members of the Commission that no public reference to situations which had already been considered behind closed doors under the 1503 procedure should be allowed. Several NGO representatives were interrupted during their oral statements and asked to identify the countries to which they were referring. If it was a country that had already been considered under the 1503 procedure, the NGO was prohibited from continuing its statement. The agreement applied only to that session, however, and in 1980 the Commission resorted to its earlier practice of scheduling the public discussion of country situations before the 1503 procedure, thus avoiding the problem. In 1981, the Commission again had its confidential session first, but this time the Chair correctly followed the rule that no reference was to be made to decisions taken under the confidential procedure "and confidential materials relating thereto." In other words, NGOs were free to raise human rights concerns in countries already considered under the 1503 procedure as long as they did not refer to confidential decisions and materials (of which they are in theory not aware).

At the 1980 session of the Commission, the representatives of Amnesty International presented testimony concerning persons who had "disappeared" in Argentina. The representative of Argentina, supported by Uruguay and Ethiopia, interrupted to say that this represented a political attack on a member of the Commission. The Chair ruled that Amnesty International could continue, stating that, although NGOs had no right to attack a country, they were entitled to provide information. This could only be done meaningfully if they were allowed to mention names and details.[16]

It would be premature to take this most recent ruling as the final word on what NGOs are allowed to present at the Commission or Sub-Commission. In fact, this may depend not so much on the contents of the statement itself as on the attitude of the Chair, the general atmosphere of the meeting, and on the political influence of the country against which the statement is directed. A statement that contains a general argument, for example, the importance of the UN's establishing an effective mechanism for dealing with the problem of "disappearances," and then illustrates the argument with examples from a number of specific countries may well be less likely to be challenged than one which attacks a country—especially if that country is a member of the Commission. However, the precedents for specific references to countries do exist, and in the Sub-Commission they can now be considered fairly well settled. It is nevertheless a good idea to consult beforehand with knowledgeable NGOs or members of the UN Secretariat before embarking upon an oral statement in either body.

Finally, selection of the most appropriate agenda item may increase the chances of a statement being accepted. Generally, the widest latitude seems to be allowed under the broad item concerning "violations of human rights in any part of the world," discussed under the provisions of ECOSOC Resolution 1235. A statement referring to the situation of the Korean minority in Japan, for example, was ruled out of order at the 1980 session of the Sub-Commission when it was presented under the agenda item dealing with minority rights. Prior consultation with the Chair or the Secretariat would doubtlessly have been helpful, and the statement would probably have been permitted during the more general debate on violations.

In general, there are fewer restrictions on NGO participation in working groups than in the plenary sessions of the Commission and the Sub-Commission. For example, in the slavery working group of the Sub-Commission, NGOs and members of the Sub-Commission often speak in an informal atmosphere of near equality. The same is true in the Commission's working group on the draft convention against torture. The freedom accorded to NGOs in working group debates depends on the expertise and reputation of the NGO itself, the style of the Chair, and, in some cases, even the physical arrangement of the room in which the meeting is held.

Other Techniques

In addition to oral and written interventions, several other techniques can be used to influence the Commission or the Sub-Commission or to supply them with information. Perhaps the most successful is to engage in informal talks with delegates outside the conference room, in the corridors, or in the delegates' lounge. Sub-Commission members, who serve in their personal capacity, usually welcome discussions with NGOs about specific situations (except those considered confidentially under the 1503 procedure) or general topics. Although most speak English, knowledge of French or Spanish is most helpful at this informal level.

It is also possible, of course, to mail relevant information to members prior to the session, and addresses of governmental delegations to the Commission and individual members of the Sub-Commission may be obtained from the UN Secretariat. Distributing papers by putting copies in the pigeonholes of delegates or simply on the conference table is not recommended, except with the approval of the Secretariat. Another possibility is to organize a press conference in one of the rooms designated for this purpose in the Palais des Nations at Geneva. Approval of the appropriate officials of the UN Secretariat must be obtained, and such conferences should only be arranged for particularly newsworthy events.

Final Remarks

Interventions by NGOs at the Commission and the Sub-Commission are important because they confront delegates directly with issues of public concern. Without these interventions, UN consideration of human rights matters might remain a sterile diplomatic game played by persons with little knowledge of the facts. Nevertheless, intervening at sessions of the Commission and the Sub-Commission requires careful preparation and a rather specialized knowledge of the proceedings. Even then, there is always a risk that an initiative may run into difficulties or become counterproductive if it is seen as pressuring the delegates. There is a constant need to strike a balance between statements that are bland and without impact, on the one hand, and interventions that are explicit but overly combative, on the other. An ill-conceived intervention can, as has been noted, lead to a reaction that might restrict the rights of all NGOs in the future.

Some mention should also be made of the value *to NGOs* of participating in UN meetings. At a mundane level, presence in Geneva makes it much easier to obtain otherwise hard-to-find UN documents. Well-prepared interventions will contribute to the general reputation of a NGO and, therefore, to its effectiveness. Informal contacts established with delegates may prove useful, as many delegates are involved with human rights issues in other governmental or private capacities.

In recent years, interventions by NGOs have usually been of high quality in terms of accuracy and impartiality. As a consequence of this, the input of NGOs is taken seriously by many delegations. A continuing problem, however, is that the most active NGOs tend to be organizations which have all or most of their membership in the industrialized world. This has led to understandable charges that the NGO community is unrepresentative of the world as a whole. It is hoped that this chapter will provide some of the tools necessary to encourage wider participation by NGOs based in the Third World. That participation is badly needed.

Notes

1. The only exception to this rule appears to be the practice established thus far by the Sub-Commission's Working Group on Indigenous Populations, which has permitted representatives of indigenous peoples to participate in its work even though they may not have formal consultative status.

2. E.S.C. Res. 1296(XLIV), 44 UN ESCOR, Supp. (No. 1) 21, UN Doc. E/4548 (1968).

3. *Id.*, para. 14.

4. *See* chapter 4.

5. A list of those members elected in 1981 is included in appendix E.

6. Even greater specificity in written statements was allowed at the 1981 Sub-Commission session. For example, statements under agenda items concerning detention and the independence of the judiciary referred in critical terms to the situations in Sri Lanka, Philippines, United States, Chile, and South Korea. UN Docs. E/CN.4/Sub.2/NGO/96 and 102 (1981). [ed. note]

7. UN Doc. E/CN.4/Sub.2/SR.95 (1952).

8. *See* E. Suy, *De l'International au Transnational, in* INTERNATIONAL ASSOCIATIONS 350–51 (No. 8, 1980).

9. UN Doc. E/CN.4/SR.1232 at 259 (1973).

10. UN Doc. E/CN.4/SR.1274 at 113 (1974).

11. UN Doc. E/CN.4/1179 at para. 66 (1975).

12. UN Doc. E/CN.4/SR.1300 at para. 97 (1975).

13. E.S.C. Res. 1919(LVIII), 58 UN ECSOR, Supp. (No. 1) 8, UN Doc. E/5683 (1976).

14. *See* UN Doc. E/C.2/771/Add.2 (1977).

15. UN Doc. E/C.2/771/Add.3 (1977).

16. UN Doc. E/CN.4/SR.1552 (1980).

12

Quasi-Legal Standards and Guidelines for Protecting Human Rights of Detained Persons

JIRI TOMAN

Among the great number of international human rights instruments, special place should be reserved for the standards and guidelines elaborated by the United Nations in the form of models for national legislation. While these instruments are not directly legally binding, they constitute not only recommendations to unify national legislation, but also interpretations of human rights principles which may eventually be integrated into international law. The standards and guidelines adopted by UN organs are, of course, internally binding, insofar as future declarations and resolutions on the same subjects are concerned.

Owing to their international standard-setting character, these rules, primarily in the field of crime prevention and control and administration of criminal justice, are more appropriately considered to be quasi-legal rather than nonlegal in their effect. The most important of these instruments are the UN Standard Minimum Rules for the Treatment of Prisoners, and the Code of Conduct for Law Enforcement Officials; these will be the main subjects of this chapter. Other instruments are in preparation, including a Code of Medical Ethics relevant to the protection of detainees, and Principles for the Protection of All Persons under any Form of Detention and Imprisonment.

The United Nations Standard Minimum Rules for the Treatment of Prisoners[1]

Historical Development of the Rules

The idea of formulating minimal "rights" for all "deprived of their liberty by a judicial decision" was first presented to the meeting of the International Penal and Penitentiary Commission at Bern, Switzerland, in July 1926. This led to the elaboration of fifty-five rules, which were eventually endorsed by the League of Nations of 1934.

After the Second World War, the revised rules were submitted to the United Nations, circulated to member states and the specialized agencies, and adopted at the First United Nations Congress on the Prevention of Crime and Treatment of Offenders [hereinafter cited as UN Congress], held at Geneva in 1955. The ninety-four rules adopted by the UN Congress were approved by the Economic and Social Council (ECOSOC) in Resolution 663C (XXIV) of 31 July 1957 which, inter alia, invited governments to consider the adoption and application of the Standard Minimum Rules for the Treatment of Prisoners (hereinafter, the Rules) in the administration of penal institutions and to arrange for the widest possible publicity for the Rules. The resolution also requested the Secretary-General to review, every five years, the progress made in applying the Rules.

While this ECOSOC resolution may be seen as an interpretation of the general provisions of the Universal Declaration of Human Rights, the legal value and implementation of the Rules depends on individual countries and their incorporation of the Rules into domestic laws and regulations. The Fourth UN Congress in 1970 expressed its dissatisfaction with the fact that the Rules had not attained the status of an international convention, but it appears doubtful that such a convention on the treatment of detainees will ever by adopted by many members of the international community.

The desire for more effective implementation of the Rules resulted in the adoption by the UN General Assembly of Resolution 2858 (XXVI) of 20 December 1971. The General Assembly drew the attention of member states to the Rules and recommended that they should be implemented in the administration of penal and correctional institutions and that favorable consideration should be given to their incorporation into national legislation. These recommendations were essentially repeated in General Assembly Resolution 3144B (XXVIII), adopted unanimously on 14 December 1973.

The United Nations has recognized that "the humanitarian principles enunciated in the Standard Minimum Rules are, in fact, embodied in the Universal Declaration."[2] However, the application and implementation of the Rules depends very much on the general atmosphere of human rights in the country concerned.

Content of the Rules

The Rules do not describe a model system of penal institutions. Rather, they establish minimum guidelines, which may be adapted to the political, economic, social, and legal circumstances of individual countries. The Rules do, however, reflect the modern approach of reform-minded penologists who believe in rehabilitation and restraint of a prisoner rather than emphasizing retribution and deterrence.

According to the Rules, the purpose of imprisonment is to cut off an offender from the outside world by depriving him or her of "the right of self-determination by depriving him of his liberty. Therefore, the prison system shall not, except as incidental to justifiable segregation or the maintenance of discipline, aggravate the suffering inherent in such a situation."[3] The Rules are not concerned with the reasons for or manner of detention, but are addressed solely to the conditions of detention. This attitude is similar to that adopted by NGOs such as the International Committee of the Red Cross and may produce more tangible results for detainees than questioning the reasons for their detention. The Rules thus are complementary to the substantive protections against arbitrary detention that are provided in other human rights instruments.

As a final general observation, we should bear in mind that the Rules must be considered within the framework of the criminal justice system and with reference to protection of the victims of crime, as well. Criminal justice and detention are intended to protect society against crime, but also to reeducate and rehabilitate those who commit crimes and to "ensure, as far as possible, that upon his return to society the offender is not only willing but able to lead a law-abiding and self-supporting life."[4] This reintegration of the released prisoner into normal life is considered by the Rules as a duty of society.

The Rules do not specifically address the treatment of juvenile offenders, and this gap led the Sixth UN Congress in 1980 to recommend the development of Standard Minimum Rules for the administration of juvenile justice and the care of juveniles.[5]

The Rules are divided into two main parts, "Rules of General Application" and "Rules Applicable to Special Categories." Two additional recommendations, the first on the selection and training of personnel, and the second on open penal and correctional institutions, also are included.

Part I (rules 6–55) contains the basic minimum conditions for the detention of "all categories of prisoners, criminal or civil, untried or convicted, including prisoners subject to 'security measures' or corrective measures ordered by the judge"[6] The "basic principle" of the rules is that they are to be applied impartially, without discrimination on grounds of "race, color, sex, language, religion, political or other opinion, national or social origin, property, birth or other status," but with due respect for religious and moral beliefs.[7]

Subsequent Rules deal with the formalities of registration (Rule 7); separation of different categories of prisoners (Rule 8); and regulation of a prisoner's daily life, including accommodation, personal hygiene, clothing, bedding, food, exercise, and sport (Rules 9–21). Detailed consideration is given to the provision of medical services (Rules 22–26), and the Rules recommend that a prison medical officer should have at least some knowledge of psychiatry. The Rules also recommend that every prisoner be seen and examined by a medical officer "as soon as possible after his admission and thereafter as necessary."[8]

The provisions on discipline and punishment (Rules 27–34) include an absolute prohibition on the use of corporal punishment; punishment by placing a prisoner in a dark cell; cruel, inhuman, or degrading punishment; and the use of instruments of restraint, such as handcuffs, as punishment.

Other provisions offer guidelines, inter alia, for contacts between prisoners and the outside world, rights to receive information, the right to practice a religion, and the right to make requests or complaints to the prison administration (Rules 35–45).

Rules 46–54 deal with institutional personnel and include restrictions on the use of force, which must be "no more than is strictly necessary" and which must be immediately reported to the director of the institution.[9] Rule 55 recommends the regular inspection of penal institutions.

The "special categories" of prisoners dealt with in Part II of the Rules consist of prisoners under sentence (Part A), insane and mentally abnormal prisoners (Part B), prisoners under arrest or awaiting trial (Part C), civil prisoners (Part D), and persons arrested or imprisoned without charge (Part E). The Rules contained in Part A (Rules 56–81) are the most complete, and they are equally applicable to category B, C, and D prisoners, "provided they do not conflict with the rules governing those categories and are for their benefit."[10]

While recognizing that the purpose of depriving a person of liberty "is ultimately to protect society against crime," the Rules emphasize rehabilitation and education and contain detailed recommendations with respect to prison work, which is to be required of all prisoners under sentence "subject to their physical and mental fitness."[11]

The provisions concerning mentally abnormal prisoners are cursory and only require that such persons be specially treated and be under the care of a medical officer (Rules 82–83). They do *not* consider the standards under which a person may be determined to be mentally ill and are, therefore, not relevant to the possible abuse of psychiatry in order to detain persons for political purposes.[12]

Untried prisoners are to be segregated from convicted prisoners and, in general, are to be treated in a manner which reflects the presumption of innocence that they enjoy (Part C, Rules 84–93).

Rule 94 (Part D), which concerns those imprisoned for debt or pursuant to a court order under any other noncriminal process, may be rendered moot in part by the provision of article 11 of the International Covenant on Civil and Political Rights, which prohibits imprisonment "merely on the ground of inability to fulfil a contractural obligation."

Part E, which pertains to persons arrested or detained without charge, consists of a single rule and was added to the Standard Minimum Rules by ECOSOC Resolution 2076 (LXII) in 1977, perhaps reflecting the increasing use of detention without trial by governments and the concommitant increase in human rights violations during such detention. The new rule provides that, "without prejudice to the provisions of article 9 of the International Covenant on Civil and Political Rights, persons arrested or imprisoned without charge shall be accorded the same protection" as that accorded under part I of the Rules (rules of general application), Part II, section C (prisoners under arrest or awaiting trial), and also under the relevant provisions of Part II, section A (prisoners under sentence), "provided that no measures shall be taken implying that re-education or rehabilitation is in any way appropriate to persons not convicted of any criminal offense."

Finally, the 1977 ECOSOC resolution also attached two recommendations to the Standard Minimum Rules, concerning the selection and training of penal and correctional personnel and the establishment of open penal and correctional institutions. As none of the UN surveys on implementation of the Rules has included reference to these recommendations, it is not possible to estimate their practical influence and value at this time.

Implementation of the Rules

On the Domestic or National Level

The Standard Minimum Rules can be implemented at the national level either by their direct incorporation into national legislation or, indirectly, by using the standards recommended by the Rules as norms in a system of national supervision of penal and correctional institutions.

Incorporation into domestic legislation or regulation has been recommended in the various ECOSOC resolutions concerning the Rules and is undoubtedly the most effective form of implementation. Unfortunately, the results have been rather disappointing. The UN conducted two surveys on the application of the Standard Minimum Rules, in 1967 and 1974. The first survey received only forty-three answers from UN members; fifteen of the responding states indicated that prison laws and regulations adopted subsequent to the Rules had been influenced by them, but only a few countries could demonstrate substantial incorporation. The 1974 survey did not substantially modify this image, although sixty-two states responded to the request for information, the majority reaffirming some influence of the Rules on national penal legislation.

In a 1975 study, the survey responses indicated that more than 70 percent of the total replies were in the "fully implemented" area. "These full implementation figures are, indeed, probably overstated since based on the self-reported assessment of responding prison authorities rather than empirical observations of the actual conditions in prisons irrespective of announced law, regulation and policy of the central administration."[13] In the United States there was a tendency to cite the Rules as having influenced legislation even where it was clear that there was no direct influence in the enactment of correctional codes. A third of the states reported such a legislative connection when "it was evident that in many instances there was ignorance of the content (or even existence) of the Rules."[14]

There is, however, an indirect influence of the Rules on national legislation and practice. In the United States, for example, principles of the Rules are embodied in documents such as the American Law Institute's 1962 Model Penal Code, the American Correctional Association's 1970 Declaration of Principles of Prison Discipline, and the correctional standards developed in 1973 by the National Advisory Commission on Criminal Justice Standards and Goals.

At least six states in the United States have administratively adopted the Standard Minimum Rules, generally by Executive Orders.[15] While some of the orders contain exceptions or limitations to the full application of the Rules, this is consistent with the spirit of the Rules and the provision that "not all of the rules are capable of application in all places and at all times."[16] These administrative mechanisms for incorporating the Rules into domestic practice appear to be more realistic than legislative adoption, especially at the federal level.

The United Nations Social Defense Research Institute has proposed several prerequisites for the effective protection of prisoners' rights within the framework of national prison systems. These include development of a detailed formal statement describing prisoner interests worthy of protection; ensuring that legal procedures are readily accessible to prisoners; constituting independent judicial and administrative authorities to implement the established procedures; and truly enforcing decisions despite the traditional resistance of affected correctional agencies and prevailing divisions of governmental powers and authorities.[17]

Supervision and scrutiny of the prisons and institutions responsible for the treatment of detainees may be organized in many different ways. Some countries do not even have a central authority responsible for prison administration. Where such bodies do exist, however, they will be the most appropriate agents to oversee application of the Standard Minimum Rules. These bodies will be also the best intermediaries for promoting and disseminating knowledge of the Rules within the national prison system.

Legislative Supervision

In some countries supervision of prisoners' rights and the correctional system is carried out by legislative bodies. The most common vehicle for such supervision is, perhaps, the system of a parliamentary ombudsman often associated with the Scandinavian countries of Sweden, Denmark, Norway, and Finland, but which has also been established in other countries, including Australia, Great Britain, Canada, Guyana, and Israel. The ombudsman system is used in the United States to supervise the correctional systems in Minnesota, Ohio, Connecticut, South Carolina, Oregon, and Indiana.[18]

Executive Supervision

If there is no central national authority responsible for prison administration in a country, the supervisory responsibility is diffused at different levels of government. An administrative body is often powerless to take action except in institutions under its direct control and its authority to alter regulations or procedures may be limited to recommendations to higher administrative levels or even to legislative bodies. In other cases, administrative measures may be subject to change by local authorities or even by individual prison administrators.

In Japan, for example, the Civil Liberties Bureau is an organ of the Ministry of Justice empowered to investigate and offer advice on all types of infringements of human rights, including those that may occur in correctional institutions. In other countries, treatment of prisoners may be supervised by visiting judges or other official visitors, by local magistrates, or by administrative officials (e.g., in Australia, Israel, Kenya, Singapore). In Great Britain, these functions are exercised by boards of visitors appointed by the Home Secretary, while different kinds of "supervisory boards" or "administrative committees" exist in Austria, Belgium, the Netherlands, Norway, Sweden, and Switzerland. These visiting or supervisory bodies are essentially advisory, but their powers may include the right to visit prisons, interview prisoners, or even impose certain disciplinary or emergency measures.

Judicial Supervision[19]

Judicial oversight of prison conditions may be the responsibility of courts of general competence or of special courts. The latter exist, for example, in Poland ("courts for the enforcement of punishment") and in Portugal ("courts for the execution of sentences"). Specific powers to supervise prison conditions, are granted to judges in, for example, the Federal Republic of Germany, Mexico, and Yugoslavia, and specially designated judges exist in France *(juge d'application des peines)* and Italy *(guidice de sorveglianza)*.

In the United States, the courts play a very important role in the protection of prisoners' rights at both the state and federal levels.[20] This judicial interest is expressed primarily through the application of federal constitutional guarantees (particularly the First,[21] Eighth,[22] and Fourteenth Amendments[23]) and represents an abandonment of the previous judicial doctrine of noninterference with the administrative decisions of correctional officials.[24]

More relevant for our purposes are the numerous instances in which U.S. courts have cited the Standard Minimum Rules as supportive or dispositive of their decisions on prisoners' rights and prison conditions.[25]

Apart from Connecticut's administrative adoption of the United Nations Standard Minimum Rules for the Treatment of Prisoners, those standards may be significant as expressions of the obligations to the international community of the member states of the United Nations, cf. *Filartiga v. Pena-Irala*, 630 F. 2d 876 (2d Cir.

1980), and as part of the body of international law (including customary international law) concerning human rights which has been built upon the foundation of the United Nations Charter. . . . The United Nations Charter is, of course, a treaty ratified by the United States. . . . Although not self-executing, . . . the Charter's provisions on human rights are evidence of principles of customary international law recognized as part of the law of the United States. . . . [UN adoption of the Rules] constitutes an authoritative international statement of basic norms of human dignity and of certain practices which are repugnant to the conscience of mankind. The Standards embodied in this statement are relevant to the canons of decency and fairness which express the notions of justice embodied in the Due Process Clause.[26]

Whether the Rules are cited as direct authority (in those states that have adopted them administratively) or as support for a decision on constitutional grounds, there is no doubt that the content of the Rules has had an impact on judicial decisions in several U.S. jurisdictions.

In some countries, judicial responsibility for supervision of prisons and protection of prisoners' rights rests with the public prosecutor, as an officer of the court. This is the case in, for example, the Soviet Union (where there also may be special public commissions) and France (where the administrative jurisdiction of the *Conseil d'Etat* includes oversight of prison administration and conditions).

On the Regional Level

The Council of Europe updated and adapted the Standard Minimum Rules to European conditions and needs through rules adopted by the Council's Committee of Ministers in 1973.[27] While the European rules retain the basic wording and format of the Standard Minimum Rules, a few new provisions were added: affirmation of respect for human dignity as a basic principle of confinement (Rule 6); prohibition of injurious medical and scientific experimentation on prisoners (Rule 22); elimination of "collective punishment" (Rule 27); a suggestion for more communication and cooperation between categories of staff in the treatment of prisoners (Rule 51); and a call for the involvement of prisoners in drawing up individual treatment programs (Rule 67). The European rules also introduce control outside the prison administration by a judicial authority or other duly constituted visiting body, expanding the provisions of original Rule 55.

The procedures of the European Convention on Human Rights play an important role in this field, as more than half of the individual applications under the Convention are filed by prisoners. Many complaints concern prison conditions, and, while the European rules are not directly binding, the standards they set may be expected to influence the interpretation of the Convention by the European Commission and Court of Human Rights.

Conditions of detention and the protection of detainees are also an important facet of the work of the Inter-American Commission on Human Rights, although there is no regional set of standards equivalent to the European Standard Minimum Rules.

On the International Level

The summary of the historical development of the Rules at the beginning of this chapter outlines the major developments in implementation of the Rules since their adoption by ECOSOC in 1957. The UN surveys in 1967 and 1974 and the General Assembly resolutions adopted in 1971 and 1973 have contributed to an increasing awareness of the standards set forth in the Rules.

The goal of present international efforts to implement the Rules does not seem to be to recodify or expand the texts (with the exception of the addition of Rule 95 in 1977), but rather to improve the dissemination and application of the present text. At the same time, however, concern with the conditions of prisoners and detainees has led to the adoption of several international instruments that focus on specific problems rather than general guidelines applicable to inmates and officials of all correctional or penal institutions. It is with these new developments that the remainder of this chapter will deal.

Code of Conduct for Law Enforcement Officials[28]

Following a recommendation by the Commission on Human Rights, General Assembly Resolution 3218 (XXIX) of 6 November 1974 requested the Fifth UN Congress "to give urgent attention to the question of development of an international code of ethics for police and related law enforcement agencies." The Congress discussed several drafts that had been transmitted to it by professional law enforcement associations, experts, and the Government of the Netherlands, prepared guidelines, and recommended that the General Assembly establish a committee of experts to prepare an international code of police ethics. The question was referred by the General Assembly to the Committee on Crime Prevention and Control in 1975.

Although the Congress agreed on the feasibility of the international code, it stressed the need to ensure that law enforcement officials fulfill their duties without resorting to torture and other cruel, inhuman, or degrading treatment or punishment. The urgency of the situation led the Congress unanimously to propose to the General Assembly a declaration on this subject, and such a declaration was adopted by acclamation by the General Assembly as Resolution 3452 (XXX) of 9 December 1975.[29]

The draft adopted by the Committee on Crime Prevention and Control was amended and ultimately adopted without a vote by the General Assembly as Resolution 34/169 of 17 December 1979. The resolution provides, inter alia, that the actions of law enforcement officials should be subject to public scrutiny, although it does not prescribe the kind of reviewing agency, and it underscores the fact that the standards set forth in the Code can have practical value only if they are included in the training, education, and monitoring of the law enforcement system. The General Assembly subsequently called upon states to use the Code within the framework of national legislation and practice and to make the text available in national languages.[30]

Enforcement and implementation of the Code face much the same difficulties as the Standard Minimum Rules, although formal adoption of the Code by the full General Assembly may give it a somewhat more authoritative character than that originally enjoyed by the Rules. In any event, the recent date of the Code's adoption makes it impossible to judge its impact at this time; it is, at least, further evidence of growing UN interest in conditions of detention and treatment of detainees in recent years.

The final version of the Code contains eight articles with commentaries which are intended to facilitate domestic implementation.

The commentary to article 1 defines the term "law enforcement officials" as "all officers of the law whether appointed or elected, who exercise police powers, especially the powers of arrest or detention," and it clearly includes military authorities and other security forces.

Article 2 requires law enforcement officials to respect and protect human dignity and to maintain and uphold the human rights of all persons. "Human rights" are not specifically defined, but they certainly include those rights guaranteed under other international instruments, such as the Universal Declaration of Human Rights, the two International Covenants, and (perhaps) the Standard Minimum Rules.

Article 3 imposes relatively stringent restrictions on the use of force by law enforcement officials in the performance of their duties. Force is authorized "only when strictly necessary and to the extent required," and the commentary underlines the exceptional character of these measures and the principle of proportionality. The use of firearms is to be considered an extreme measure, and in general, "firearms should not be used except when a suspected offender offers armed resistance or otherwise jeopardizes the lives of others, and less extreme measures are not sufficient to restrain or apprehend the suspect offender. In every instance in which a firearm is discharged, a report should be made promptly to the competent authorities."

Article 4 sets forth the confidential character of information obtained by law enforcement officials.

Article 5 essentially repeats the universal prohibition against torture and inhuman or degrading treatment. It reiterates that no superior order or exceptional circumstance (such as a state or threat of war, a threat to national security, or internal political instability) can be invoked as a justification for torture.

Article 6 ensures protection of the health of persons in custody and requires immediate action to secure medical attention whenever required. Article 7 prohibits acts of corruption, such as bribery.

Article 8, in addition to the requirement that "law enforcement officials shall respect the law and the present Code," also states a positive obligation to prevent and report any violation of the law and Code. An interesting provision states that violations should be reported "within the chain of command *or outside of it*, if no other remedies are available or effective" (emphasis added). In this respect, the commentary mentions that "the mass media may be regarded as performing complaint review functions similar to [governmental agencies]. . . . Law enforcement officials may, therefore, be justified if, as a last resort and in accordance with the laws and customs of their own countries and with the provisions of Article 4 of the present Code [confidentiality] they bring violations to the attention of public opinion through the mass media."

The commentary to the final article states that it "seeks to preserve the balance between the need for internal discipline of the agency on which public safety on the one hand is largely dependent, and the need for dealing with violations of basic human rights." The fact that standards for striking this balance are being established by the United Nations must be seen as an important step forward and a recognition that the conduct of law enforcement officials in a purely domestic situation is a proper subject for international concern.

Declaration on the Protection of All Persons from Being Subjected to Torture and Other Cruel, Inhuman or Degrading Treatment or Punishment

The above-entitled declaration ("Declaration against Torture") was adopted in General Assembly Resolution 3452 (XXX) of 9 December 1975 and is a landmark in UN efforts to protect the rights of prisoners and detainess.[31] It should be noted that decisions to develop a Code of Conduct for Law Enforcement Officials and a Code of Medical Ethics were contained in the resolution adopted immediately after the Declaration, and these codes were specifically intended to implement the principles of the Declaration.[32]

As was the case for the Universal Declaration of Human Rights when it was adopted in 1948, the Declaration against Torture has no directly binding legal effect. However, it may be seen as an authoritative interpretation of article 5 of the Universal Declaration ("No one shall be subjected to torture or to cruel, inhuman or degrading treatment or punishment.") and, given the universal condemnation of torture in national and international instruments, it may express customary international law on the subject.

Use of the Declaration either as persuasive commentary on the meaning of the international prohibition against torture or as direct evidence of customary international law is a prime example of the "quasi-legal" effect of all of the instruments discussed in the present chapter, although it is unlikely that any of the other codes or declarations presently constitute customary law. The Declaration was cited, for example, by a U.S. Court of Appeals in the case of *Filartiga* v. *Pena-Irala*, in which the court stated that "U.N. declarations are significant because they specify with great precision the obligations of member nations under the Charter."[33]

Principles of Medical Ethics Relevant to the Protection of Persons in Detention and Imprisonment

Unlike the previous instruments discussed, the Code of Medical Ethics is still in the process of elaboration and has not yet been formally adopted by ECOSOC or the General Assembly. Reflecting the concern for detainees that became particularly evident in UN forums in the mid-1970s, in 1974 the General Assembly asked the World Health Organization (WHO) to draft an outline of principles of medical ethics relevant to the protection of detainees from torture and other ill-treatment. Such a draft body of principles, based on a study by the Council for International Organizations of Medical Sciences[34] and the 1974 Declaration of Tokyo by the World Medical Association,[35] was adopted by WHO and circulated for governmental and specialized agency comments.[36]

In 1982, the General Assembly adopted by resolution a final set of Principles of Medical Ethics.[37] The six Principles are designed essentially to remove the physician from any participation in the process of detention or interrogation, except for such participation as is normally required to protect health or treat disease. Principles II–IV establish that the only appropriate involvement of a physician with a prisoner or detainee is that appropriate to a person outside a prison environment, that is, one involving the protection or improvement of the health of the detainee. Specifically prohibited is the active or passive participation by doctors in any form of torture, including assisting in interrogation or certifying detainees as fit for any form of punishment which could adversely effect their physical or mental health.

Principle VI deals with situations in which physicians may be compelled under duress to violate the other Principles (e.g., by treating a detainee so that he will be fit for further torture) and again emphasizes that the role of the physician should be to minimize harm to the detainee or prisoner.

While the strictly "legal" effect of the Principles of Medical Ethics may be debatable, it is hoped that their impact as a set of professional ethical standards (largely based on norms developed by doctors themselves at the 1975 Tokyo meeting) will both influence physicians who might presently be participating routinely in interrogations and also provide meaningful international support for those who refuse to participate in such situations.

Draft Body of Principles for the Protection of All Persons under Any Form of Detention and Imprisonment

Another section of General Assembly Resolution 3453 requested the UN Commission on Human Rights to study the question of torture and to take the necessary steps to draft a body of principles to protect the rights of detainees. The Commission delegated this task to its Sub-Commission on Prevention of Discrimination and Protection of Minorities, which completed its work on the draft principles in 1978.[38] The General Assembly is currently scheduled to complete its own work on the Draft Body of Principles during its 1983 session.

The Principles may be viewed as a supplement to the general protections contained in the Standard Minimum Rules, directed more specifically towards safeguarding the physical safety of detainees and prisoners. Unlike the other codes and rules discussed herein, the Draft Body of Principles has been developed primarily by UN human rights experts, NGOs, and governments rather than by the professional bodies directly concerned. On the other hand, the principles have been derived primarily from existing instruments, such as the International Covenant on Civil and Political Rights, the Standard Minimum Rules, the Code of Conduct for Law Enforcement Officials, the Vienna Convention on Consular Relations, and, in particular, the Draft Principles on Freedom from Arbitrary Arrest and Detention set forth in a 1962 Sub-Commission study.[39]

Among the more interesting provisions of the Draft Body of Principles are: states are to prohibit by law acts contrary to the principles (article 6); a record is to be kept and made available to a detainee and his or her counsel of the names of all law enforcement personnel involved in arrest and/or interrogation (articles 11, 30); immediately after arrest and after transfer to another place of detention, a detainee's family is to be notified of the detainee's whereabouts (article 14); detainees are to be medically examined promptly after their admission and also have the right to be examined by their own physician (articles 21, 22); and evidence obtained in violation of the Principles is to be inadmissible in any proceeding against a detainee or prisoner (article 23).

Other Proposals

The form of model rules exemplified by the Standard Minimum Rules and the Code of Conduct for Law Enforcement Officials seems now to be a well-accepted method of promoting human rights standards in the area of criminal justice and its administration. In addition to those instruments currently in the process of being drafted, the Sixth (1980) UN Congress on the Prevention of Crime and the Treatment of Offenders invited the Committee on Crime Prevention and Control to develop a set of standard minimum rules for the administration of juvenile justice. The Committee itself has recommended the elaboration of standards in several different areas, including:

— the selection and training of judges and prosecutors and the establishment of safeguards against abuse of discretion in sentencing;
— standard minimum rules for the treatment of offenders in the community;
— strengthening of inmate grievance procedures;
— facilitating the return of persons convicted of crime abroad to their own country to serve their sentences; and
— improving the situation of persons in pretrial custody.[40]

Conclusions

Criminal justice and administration are areas that have been traditionally considered to be exclusively within the domestic jurisdiction of states, but the UN seems to have discovered a reasonably effective method of encouraging the unification of national legislation and practice in these areas. Because of the nonbinding nature of the codes, declarations, and other instruments discussed herein, governments may feel that they constitute less of a threat to their sovereignty. While the quasi-legal effect of such instruments is less formally binding on states, the effect of the Standard Minimum Rules, for example—at least where they are widely disseminated—is not insubstantial when compared, for example, to the effect of the provisions of a binding treaty such as the International Covenant on Economic, Social and Cultural Rights.

The quasi-legal nature of these international norms should not obscure the fact that they often interpret and implement fundamental human rights— the right to be free from torture, to receive a fair trial, to have the assistance of legal counsel, and other rights. In this sense, they might be viewed as the international equivalent of administrative regulations, whose implementation will ensure that basic rights are effectively guaranteed.

The value of international standard-setting instruments varies in direct proportion to the extent they are publicized, utilized, and taken seriously by those affected by them. Much of human rights practice consists of

persuasion rather than coercion, and the existence of agreed-upon international norms can assist that process of persuasion while avoiding (where
appropriate) the adversary situation created where "violations" of human
rights are alleged.

Notes

1. The Rules were adopted in 1957 in E.S.C. Res. 663C (XXIV), 24 UN
ESCOR, Supp. (No. 1) 11, UN Doc. E/3048 (1957) and are *reprinted in* HUMAN
RIGHTS. A COMPILATION OF INTERNATIONAL INSTRUMENTS, UN Doc. ST/HR/1/
Rev. 1., UN sales no. E.78.XIV.2, at 65–72 (1978).
2. UN Doc. ST/SOA/SD/CG.2/WP.3 at 8 (1968).
3. Minimum Rules, *supra* note 1, Rule 57.
4. *Id.*, Rule 58.
5. UN Doc. A/CONF.87/14 at 11 (1980).
6. Minimum Rules, Rule 4(1).
7. *Id.*, Rule 6.
8. *Id.*, Rule 24.
9. *Id.*, Rule 54(1).
10. *Id.*, Rule 4(2).
11. *Id.*, Rule 71(2).
12. The UN Sub-Commission on Prevention of Discrimination and Protection
of Minorities is presently engaged in the preparation of draft guidelines and principles for the protection of persons detained on the grounds of mental ill-health,
including guidelines for determining whether adequate grounds exist for such detention. The rapporteur's report is contained in UN Doc. E/CN.4/Sub.2/1982/16
(1982) and the observations of a Sub-Commission working group in UN Doc. E/
CN.4/Sub.2/1982/17 (1982); *cf.* GA Res. 37/118 of 17 Dec. 1982; Res. 33/53,
33 UN GAOR, Supp. (No. 45) 144, UN Doc. A/33/45 (1978); Comm. on Human
Rights Res. 10A(XXXIII), 62 UN ESCOR, Supp. (No. 6) 84, UN Doc. E/5927,
E/CN.4/1257 (1977). [ed. note]
13. Skoler, *World Implementation of the UN Standard Minimum Rules for the
Treatment of Prisoners*, 10 J. INT'L L. & ECON. 453, 466 (1975). Much of the
information in this section is drawn from the Skoler survey.
14. *Id.* at 461.
15. Connecticut, Illinois, Minnesota, Ohio, Pennsylvania, and South Carolina.
16. Minimum Rules, Rule 2.

17. UN Social Defense Research Institute, Interim Report on Prisoners Rights, Their Enforcibility and Supervisory Mechanism, 310 (1974).

18. May, *Prison Ombudsman in America*, CORRECTIONS MAGAZINE (No. 3, 1975).

19. The author wishes to express his thanks to Connie A. Koch, from the University of Santa Clara School of Law, for the survey of recent U.S. judicial practice utilized herein.

20. For example, the U.S. Supreme Court has addressed prisoner rights issues in the following decisions: Wolff v. McDonnell, 418 U.S. 539 (1974) (rights in disciplinary proceedings); Richardson v. Ramirez, 418 U.S. 24 (1974) (voting rights); Pell v. Procunier, 417 U.S. 817 (1974), and Washington Post Co. v. Saxbe, 417 U.S. 843 (1974) (prisoner communication with press media); Procunier v. Martinez, 416 U.S. 396 (1974) (censorship of outgoing prisoner correspondence); McGinnis v. Royster, 410 U.S. 263 (1973) (prisoner rights to good time allowance); Morissey v. Brewer, 408 U.S. 471 (1972) (rights in revocation of parole and return to prison); Younger v. Gilmore, 404 U.S. 15 (1971) (prisoner access to legal materials); Johnson v. Avery, 393 U.S. 483 (1968) (prisoner access to legal assistance from fellow inmates); and Lee v. Washington, 390 U.S. 333 (1968) (racial segregation).

21. Through application of the First and Fourteenth Amendments, courts have enforced prisoner rights to freedom from discrimination on grounds of race, religion, or other unreasonable classification; freedom to correspondence and expression; to have access to the press; and to practice their religion.

22. Under the Eighth Amendment, courts have provided relief from "cruel and unusual" conditions of imprisonment, and recent cases have held that this provision proscribes more than only physically barbaric treatment. The Eighth Amendment embodies "broad and idealistic concepts of dignity, civilized standards, humanity and decency" against which we must evaluate penal measures. Thus, the Supreme Court has held "repugnant to the 8th Amendment punishments which are incompatible with the evolving standards of decency that mark the progress of a maturing society, or which involve the unnecessary and wanton infliction of pain." Estelle v. Gamble, 429 U.S. 97, 102–3 (1976). *See, e.g.*, Holt v. Sarver, 442 F.2d 304 (8th Cir. 1968) (overall prison conditions as cruel punishment); Sostre v. McGinnins, 442 F.2d 178 (2nd Cir. 1971) (extended solitary confinement); Jackson v. Bishop, 404 F.2d 571 (8th Cir. 1968) (flogging); Wright v. McMann, 387 F.2d 519 (2d Cir. 1967), and Jordan v. Fitzharris, 257 F. Supp. 674 (N.D. Cal. 1966) (strip cell cases).

23. Under the Fourteenth Amendment, courts have enforced prisoner rights of access to courts, counsel, and legal materials, as well as to due process involving procedural regularity and fairness in disciplinary, classification, and other proceedings affecting prisoner liberty. Included under this guarantee are decisions

prohibiting punishment of pretrial detainees. *See* Bell v. Wolfish, 441 U.S. 520 (1979), and Lareau v. Manson, 507 F. Supp. 1177 (D.C. Conn. 1980).

24. *See, e.g.*, Jordan v. Arnold, 408 F. Supp. 869, 875 (1978), in which the court held that although "courts should ordinarily defer in matters of security and prison administration to expertise of corrections officials, they should not abdicate Constitutional responsibility to delineate and protect fundamental liberties."

25. Among the many U.S. cases that have specifically cited the Rules, one might mention Lareau v. Manson, *supra* note 23; Detainees of Brooklyn House of Detention for Men v. Malcom, 520 F.2d 392 (2d Cir. 1975); Wolfish v. Levi, 439 F. Supp. 114 (S.D.N.Y. 1977); Morgan v. Lavalee, 526 F.2d 221 (2d Cir. 1975); Jordan v. Arnold, 408 F. Supp. 869 (1978); Jones v. Wittenberg, 440 F. Supp. 60 (1977); Estelle v. Gamble, *supra* note 22; Avant v. Clifford, 67 N.J. 496, 341 A.2d 629 (1975).

However, a federal district court recently refused to order prison authorities to provide every inmate with a personal copy of the Rules, stating that "the Federal courts will not interfere in the administration of a prison when there is evidence of facilities sufficient to provide prisoners with meaningful access to the court." Bottom v. Mondale, 657 F.2d 262 (2d Cir. 1981).

26. Lareau v. Manson, *supra* note 23 at 36–38.

27. Council of Europe, European Committee on Crime Problems, *Standard Minimum Rules for the Treatment of Prisoners*, adopted by Council of Ministers Res.73 (5) of 19 Jan. 1973, at the 217th meeting of the Ministers' Deputies.

28. The Code is set forth as an annex to G.A. Res. 34/169, 34 UN GAOR, Supp. (No. 46) 185, UN Doc. A/34/46(1979).

29. *See* discussion *infra*, at 212.

30. G.A. Res. 35/170, 35 UN GAOR, Supp. (No. 48) 193, UN Doc. A/35/48 (1981).

31. GA Res. 3452(XXX), 30 UN GAOR, Supp. (No. 34) 91, UN Doc. A/ 10034 (1976).

32. GA Res. 3453(XXX), 30 UN GAOR, Supp. (No. 34) 92, UN Doc. A/ 10034 (1976).

33. 630 F.2d 876, 880 (2d Cir. 1980). *See* discussion in chapter 12.

34. UN Doc. CIOMS/HE/P.1.

35. The Declaration is reprinted in UN Doc. A/34/273, Annex, at 8 (1979).

36. The Draft Code of Medical Ethics is contained in UN Doc. A/35/140 (1981); comments on the draft may be found in UN Docs. A/35/372 & Adds. 1–3 (1980).

37. GA Res. 37/194 of 18 Dec. 1982.

38. The Principles are contained in UN Doc. A/34/146 (1979) and the 1978 Report of the Sub-Commission, UN Doc. E/CN.4/1296, E/CN.4/Sub.2/417 at para. 109 (1978).

39. *Study of the Right of Everyone to be Free from Arbitrary Arrest, Detention and Exile*, (rev.), UN Doc. E/CN.4/826 & Corr. 1 & 2, UN sales no. 65.XIV.2 (1965).

40. *See* UN Doc. C/CN.5/536, chap. I, sec. B.

PART IV

Domestic or National Remedies

13

The Role of Domestic Courts in Enforcing International Human Rights Law

RICHARD B. LILLICH

With domestic courts increasingly taking international human rights law into account in reaching their decisions, international human rights lawyers, many of whom in the past have concentrated exclusively upon the development and utilization of international procedures, no longer can ignore the enforcement possibilities afforded by domestic courts. This chapter will discuss in fairly straightforward fashion the role of domestic courts in enforcing international human rights law, both conventional and customary, and both directly and indirectly. The focus will be on the principles and rules governing cases in federal and state courts of the United States, since the problems raised in these cases are generally representative of the problems courts face in other countries. Moreover, U.S. courts in recent years have been in the forefront of developments in this area.

The original version of this chapter, which the editor has condensed to its present form, was written during the spring of 1981 while the writer was a Sesquicentennial Associate of the Center for Advanced Studies of the University of Virginia and Thomas Jefferson Visiting Fellow, Downing College, Cambridge. Grateful acknowledgment also should be made to the Ford Foundation for its support of the writer's work through a grant to the Procedural Aspects of International Law Institute to study "The Treatment of Aliens in International Law."

A Brief Overview

Article VI, section 2, of the U.S. Constitution provides that "all Treaties made, or which shall be made, under the Authority of the United States, shall be the supreme Law of the Land; and the Judges in every State shall be bound thereby, any Thing in the Constitution or Laws of any State to the Contrary notwithstanding." Under this provision, the only one in the Constitution that speaks to the relation of international law to municipal law in U.S. courts, a self-executing treaty (or a non-self-executing treaty when implemented by Congress) supersedes all inconsistent state and local laws.[1] Additionally, under the "last-in-time" rule, a self-executing treaty supersedes earlier inconsistent federal laws.

The other major source of international law—customary international law—is not mentioned in the Constitution, but the Supreme Court has ruled that it is "part of our law, and must be ascertained and administered by the courts of justice of appropriate jurisdiction, as often as questions of right depending upon it are duly presented for their determination."[2] Having the same status as treaty law, it also supersedes all inconsistent state and local laws and, at least in principle, all earlier inconsistent federal laws.[3]

Under the dualist approach to international law, however, subsequent federal laws will prevail domestically over both conventional and customary international law when a conflict arises.[4] Thus, the United States may breach an international obligation and become responsible internationally—as it did when Congress enacted the Byrd Amendment which, pursuant to the "last-in-time" rule, required the President to violate United Nations sanctions against Rhodesia—and yet not be answerable for such a breach in U.S. courts.[5]

The UN Charter in U.S. Law

The UN Charter, having been ratified by the United States, is the supreme law of the land. Article 1(3) lists among the UN's main purposes the achievement of international cooperation "in promoting and encouraging respect for human rights and for fundamental freedoms for all without distinction as to race, sex, language, or religion." Similarly, under article 55(c) the United Nations has the duty to promote "universal respect for, and observance of, human rights and fundamental freedoms for all without distinction as to race, sex, language, or religion." Finally, under article 56 all members of the United Nations "pledge themselves to take joint and separate action in cooperation with the Organization for the achievement of the purposes set forth in Article 55."

Under the principles first enunciated in *Foster* v. *Nielson*,[6] the status of the human rights clauses of the UN Charter in U.S. law turns upon whether or not they are self-executing, since "[i]t is only when a treaty is self-executing, when it prescribes rules by which private rights may be determined, that it may be relied upon for the enforcement of such rights."[7] Going beyond the words of the human rights clauses of the UN Charter and looking for the "intent of the parties" here has proved a futile effort. "Nothing in the documents of the [San Francisco] conference," one commentator has concluded,"indicates that the framers even considered the direct legal impact of the human rights clauses on the domestic law of the members."[8] With relatively few countries having adopted the doctrine of self-executing treaties,[9] this state of affairs is not surprising. For this and other reasons, the "intent of the parties" really is irrelevant to the question of self-execution, a fact acknowledged by the *Restatement of the Foreign Relations Law of the United States (Revised)*, which acknowledges that "[i]n the absence of special agreement, how the United States carries out its international obligations is ordinarily for it to decide. Accordingly, *the intentions of the United States determines whether an agreement is to be self-executing in the United States* or should await implementing legislation."[10]

In any event, U.S. courts have held repeatedly that the human rights clauses of the UN Charter are non-self-executing and hence vest no enforceable rights in individuals. The leading case is *Sei Fujii* v. *California*,[11] in which an intermediary appellate court in California struck down a provision of the state's Alien Land Law, under which land transferred to an alien not eligible for citizenship escheated to California, on the ground that the racially motivated statute was contrary to the nondiscrimination provisions found in article 55(c) of the UN Charter. The California Supreme Court, while affirming the judgment, did so exclusively on the ground that the statute violated the equal protection clause of the fourteenth amendment. It specifically rejected the lower court's reasoning, observing that there was nothing in articles 55 and 56

to indicate that these provisions were intended to become rules of law for the courts of this country upon the ratification of the charter. . . . [Articles 55 and

56] lack the mandatory quality and definiteness which would indicate an intent to create justiciable rights in private persons immediately upon ratification. . . .

The charter represents a moral commitment of foremost importance, and we must not permit the spirit of our pledge to be compromised or disparaged in either our domestic or foreign affairs. We are satisfied, however, that the charter provisions relied on by plaintiff were not intended to supersede existing domestic legislation, and we cannot hold that they operate to invalidate the alien land law. . . .[12]

The notion that even the norm of nondiscrimination found in article 55(c) does not provide a rule of law for U.S. courts has been followed uniformly in subsequent cases. It was echoed recently in *Diggs* v. *Dent*, where a federal district court ruled that, while the Charter imposed "definite" international obligations on the United States,

treaties do not generally confer upon citizens rights which they may enforce in the courts. It is only when a treaty is "self-executing" that individuals derive enforceable rights from the treaty, without further legislative or executive action. . . . The provisions of the Charter of the United Nations are not self-executing and do not vest any of the plaintiffs with any legal rights which they may assert in this court.[13]

The court of appeals affirmed, stating that even if the Charter imposed a binding international obligation on the United States, "that obligation does not confer rights on the citizens of the United States that are enforceable in court in the absence of implementing legislation."[14]

The above approach to the human rights clauses of the UN Charter, while early on receiving some support in academic writings, has been roundly critized by most commentators. It should be noted too that the decision in *Fujii* was not appealed to the U.S. Supreme Court, so the point has not been decided for the country as a whole. Thus, while the writer believes it extremely doubtful that the present Supeme Court would hold the human rights clauses to be self-executing, other observers believe that it is unlikely that *Fujii* would be decided the same way today. Such assertions have been supported by combinations of the following arguments.

First, an expansive reading of the Charter's human rights clauses, analogous to the Court's application of the "self-executing" due process or equal protection clauses of the fourteenth amendment, finds support in the principle enunciated by the Supreme Court in *Asakura* v. *Seattle* that "[t]reaties are to be construed in a broad and liberal spirit and when two constructions are possible, one restrictive of rights which may be claimed under it, and the other favorable to them, the latter is preferred."[15]

Second, it is doubtful whether it can be maintained today—as it was argued successfully in *Fujii*—that the Charter's human rights clauses are too vague and indefinite to establish binding legal obligations enforceable in U.S. courts. Any vagueness which may have characterized articles 55 and 56 in 1945 or even 1952 "has been eliminated in large measure through subsequent adoption by the United Nations of various international human rights instruments that give juridical content to [these articles]."[16] Specifically, the Universal Declaration of Human Rights, now widely regarded as containing a universally recognized catalog of the human rights that members of the United Nations deem fundamental, may be considered to provide an authoritative interpretation of the Charter.[17] Since the human rights guaranteed in the Charter are in any event "no vaguer than any number of well-known constitutional and statutory expressions which have been left to the Courts to apply,"[18] it is not unreasonable to suggest that the *Fujii* determination that articles 55 and 56 are non-self-executing may be ripe for overruling.

Third, even if one acknowledges that the language in these articles is too general to be self-executing as to all the rights guaranteed by the Universal Declaration and the International Covenants on Civil and Political Rights and Economic, Social and Cultural Rights, the "all or nothing" approach to the interpretation of the Charter taken in *Fujii* must be rejected. For example, the universal acceptance of the nondiscrimination norm contained in article 55(c) may be evidence of a consensus supporting a rule of law prohibiting discrimination even if other human rights with less universal support cannot be protected solely on the basis of the Charter.[19] This argument finds support in the fact that the International Court of Justice, in its Advisory Opinion in the *Namibia Case*, noted that signatories of the Charter had pledged themselves "to observe and respect, in . . . [territories] having an international status, human rights and fundamental freedoms for all without distinction as to race," and that to deny human rights on the basis of race was "a flagrant violation of the purposes and principles of the Charter."[20] Many jurists believe, reasoning from this Advisory Opinion, that the basic nondiscrimination norm contained in the Charter is general in nature and binding on all states.

Fourth, it seems clear that whatever human rights norms are generated by the Charter must be given effect domestically by member states, including the United States, if they are to fulfill their legal obligations under the treaty.[21] Almost 150 years ago, Secretary of State Livingston stated that

[t]he Government of the United States presumes that whenever a treaty has been duly concluded and ratified by the acknowledged authorities competent for that

purpose, an obligation is thereby imposed upon *each and every department of the government*, to carry it into complete effect, according to its terms, and that on the performance of this obligation consists the due observance of good faith among nations.[22]

Thus, U.S. courts, being one of the "departments" of government, are obliged to construe articles 55 and 56 so as to render them effective, i.e., to regard them as self-executing.

Finally, at least one relatively recent federal court decision concerning the enforceability of international law in U.S. courts may pave the way for an eventual rejection of the *Fujii* rationale by the Supreme Court. In 1974, in *People of Saipan ex rel. Guerrero* v. *United States Department of Interior*, the U.S. Court of Appeals for the Ninth Circuit adopted a more enlightened test for determining whether a treaty is self-executing. In holding that the UN Trusteeship Agreement over Micronesia provided the plaintiffs with "direct, affirmative, and judicially enforceable rights" to challenge the execution of a lease purportedly in violation of that agreement, the court of appeals noted that

[t]he extent to which an international agreement establishes affirmative and judicially enforceable obligations without implementing legislation must be determined in each case by reference to many contextual factors: the purposes of the treaty and the objectives of its creators, the existence of domestic procedures and institutions appropriate for direct implementation, the availability and feasibility of alternative enforcement methods, and the immediate and long-range social consequences of self- or non-self-execution.[23]

Under this test, a strong case can be made that articles 55 and 56 are self-executing. While, as noted above, it appears impossible to ascertain the "intent of the parties" to the UN Charter in this regard, it is clear that, under article 1(3), one of the major "purposes" of the Charter is to "[promote] and [encourage] respect for human rights and fundamental freedoms for all without distinction as to race, sex, language, or religion." Since "alternative enforcement methods" to protect these rights generally are not available on the international level or, if available, generally lack effectiveness, continuing to construe the UN Charter's human rights clauses as non-self-executing on the domestic level seriously weakens enforcement of internationally recognized human rights. Therefore, under the *Saipan* test, an enlightened court someday may reject *Fujii* and conclude that the Charter grants individuals at least a hard core of judicially enforceable human rights.

Despite the optimism created by the above case, here as elsewhere in the law one must beware of the wish becoming the parent of the thought. True, the human rights clauses of the UN Charter—at least insofar as the basic nondiscrimination norm contained in article 55(c) is concerned—certainly would seem to be self-executing under either the traditional or more recent *Saipan* test. Moreover, support for such an interpretation may be found in article 131 of the *Restatement of the Foreign Relations Law of the United States (Revised)*, which can be read as suggesting a presumption that most treaties are self-executing. Yet, unlike some of his more activist colleagues, the writer does not believe it an opportune time to orchestrate a test case, given the present composition of the Supreme Court. Furthermore, in view of the hesitant attitude most lower court judges display toward international law in general, there are serious doubts whether one of them will take the lead and hold that the human rights clauses of the UN Charter are self-executing, even with respect to the basic nondiscrimination norm contained in article 55(c).[24] Such arguments are being made—and should be made—in appropriate cases today, but in all likelihood the judiciary will have to experience much more international human rights law consciousness-raising before the rationale behind *Fujii* is rejected.

Other Human Rights Treaties in U.S. Law

The United States has an exceptionally poor record of ratifying international human rights treaties. The Genocide Convention has languished in the Senate for over three decades, and no action is contemplated in the near future on the four human rights treaties (the International Covenant on Civil and Political Rights; the International Covenant on Economic, Social and Cultural Rights; the International Convention on the Elimination of All Forms of Racial Discrimination; and the American Convention on Human Rights) submitted to the Senate by President Carter in 1978. The United States is, however, a party to eleven international human rights agreements other than the UN Charter, at least two of which have been invoked in U.S. courts on the ground that they contain self-executing provisions.

Most litigation has centered around the Protocol Relating to the Status of Refugees, which the United States ratified in 1968 and which incorporates by reference the provisions of the Refugee Conventon of 1951. This treaty offers the refugee seeking asylum considerably more protection than that afforded him by the parallel provisions found in pre-1980 U.S. statute law.[25] Moreover, being "last-in-time" it would prevail over the statute to the benefit of the refugee if it were considered self-executing. Yet, despite its apparent self-executing character, the Immigration and Naturalization Service (INS) stoutly maintained "that the Protocol does not require a change in the standards under which claims of persecution are to be decided."[26]

Counsel for numerous (mainly Haitian) refugees challenged the INS view in a series of cases.[27] In *Sannon* v. *United States*,[28] for instance, they argued—and the U.S. District Court for the Southern District of Florida held—that a regulation issued by the Attorney General regarding the procedure a refugee must follow to obtain asylum either had been misconstrued or was invalid under the protocol. The district court, without explicitly deciding whether or not the protocol was self-executing, ruled that the interpretation of the regulation urged by the Attorney General found "no justification in the Protocol, in logic or in fairness," and in so ruling noted that "were it not for the Protocol, petitioners would have no ground for objecting to their exclusion."[29] Similarly, in *Pierre* v. *United States* the U.S. Court of Appeals for the Fifth Circuit held that a statutory provision which prohibited certain aliens from entering the United States was not applicable to appellants, stating that "application of [the statutory provision] would render the [Protocol] meaningless as a practical matter."[30] Many other cases, none of which explicitly held the protocol to be self-executing, saw U.S. courts either applying the protocol in "last-in-time" fashion or otherwise assuming *sub silentio* that it was self-executing.[31]

The upshot of these cases was that Congress, in the Refugee Act of 1980, rewrote the statutory provisions in question to bring them into conformity with the United States' international obligations under the Protocol.[32] Assuming it has achieved this objective, refugees in future can rely upon the revised statute and no longer need argue that the protocol is self-executing. If any discrepancies remain, however, the protocol surely will be invoked once again to the extent that it accords refugees greater protection than the statute. In any event, significant progress already has been made in upgrading the law applied by U.S. courts in refugee matters, progress achieved largely by astute counsel using international human rights law contained in an arguably self-executing treaty.

The second treaty that was argued to contain self-executing provisions was the Protocol of Buenos Aires,[33] which amended the Charter of the Organization of American states. In *Doe* v. *Plyler*,[34] where the lower fed-

eral courts and ultimately the Supreme Court struck down as violative of
the equal protection clause a Texas statute effectively used to deny free
elementary school education to the children of undocumented aliens,
plaintiffs contended that the statute also ran afoul of article 47 of the Protocol. This article provides, inter alia, that:

> The Member States will exert the greatest efforts, in accordance with their
> constitutional processes, to ensure the effective exercise of the right to education,
> on the following bases:
> a. Elementary education, compulsory for children of school age, shall also be
> afforded to all others who can benefit from it. When provided by the State it shall
> be without charge.

Faced with this innovative argument, the district court side-stepped deciding whether the above provision was self-executing; rather, it used article 47(a) as support for its alternative holding that the Texas statute
infringed upon an area that had been preempted by federal laws regulating
immigration and the education of disadvantaged children.[35] The U.S. Court
of Appeals for the Fifth Circuit not only ignored the argument that article
47(a) was self-executing, but, after noting in dictum that the Protocol "has
never been considered self-executing,"[36] reversed the district court's alternative federal preemption holding on the ground that article 47(a) "does
not indicate a clear commitment to educating children illegally in the
country."[37] As mentioned above, the Supreme Court decided the case on
constitutional grounds.

In the related case of *In re Alien Children Education Litigation*,[38] con-
solidated with *Doe* v. *Plyer*, the U.S. District Court for the Southern District of Texas held squarely that article 47(a) was not self-executing. The
district court did note that "[a]rticle 47(a) is no doubt sufficiently direct to
imply the intention to create affirmative and judicially enforceable rights."[39]
However, after purporting to consider the article "as a whole,"[40] it found
language which it thought pointed in the opposite direction and ultimately
reached a conclusion contrary to its initial impression and certainly at odds
with the plain meaning of the article.[41]

Aside from the Refugee Protocol and the Protocol of Buenos Aires, the
international human rights treaties ratified by the United States have not
been the subject of interpretation as to their self-executing nature. On the
distant horizon, of course, are the four human rights treaties that President
Carter submitted to the Senate in 1978. Unhappily, with each treaty came
a recommendation that the Senate, in giving its advice and consent, adopt

a declaration stating that the treaty's substantive provisions are non-self-executing.[42] As many of the provisions in the treaties appear to be self-executing in nature, to emasculate their potential domestic impact in this fashion is most unfortunate. While the legal effect of such declarations is debatable, in all likelihood they would be followed by U.S. courts. Thus, international human rights lawyers anxious to use U.S. courts to enforce to the fullest the rights guaranteed in the treaties should help mobilize public and congressional support against these self-defeating declarations.

Customary International Human Rights Law in U.S. Law

Unlike many areas of international law, treaties rather than custom have been the principal source of international human rights law. Today, however, the customary international law of human rights is becoming increasingly important, especially since it binds all states rather than only those parties to a particular treaty. As noted above, customary international law forms part of U.S. law and is determined and applied by the courts whenever appropriate in making a decision.

The starting point in defining the contemporary content of customary international human rights law is the Universal Declaration of Human Rights. At the time of its adoption, the United States, a strong supporter of the instrument, nevertheless made it clear that the Declaration was not a treaty and gave rise to no binding legal obligations.[43] In the thirty-five years since its adoption, however, "the Declaration has been invoked so many times both within and without the United Nations that lawyers now are saying that, whatever the intention of its authors may have been, the Declaration is now part of the customary law of nations and therefore is binding on all states."[44] This view, first advanced solely by legal scholars but subsequently supported by resolutions of international conferences, state practice, and even court decisions, now appears to have achieved widespread acceptance.[45] Indeed, the suggestion has even been made that the Declaration has the attributes of *jus cogens*, certainly an overly enthusiastic assertion if it is intended to imply that *all* the rights enumerated in the Declaration now constitute peremptory norms of international law.

Perhaps the most explicit recognition by the United States that at least parts of the Declaration now reflect customary international law is found in the U.S. memorial to the International Court of Justice in the *Hostages Case*.[46] After marshaling traditional international law precedents to demonstrate "that States have an international legal obligation to observe certain minimum standards in their treatment of aliens," the memorial added the following passage:

It has been argued that no such standard can or should exist, but such force as that position may have had has gradually diminished as *recognition of the existence of certain fundamental human rights has spread throughout the international community*. The existence of such fundamental human rights for all human beings, nationals and aliens alike, and the existence of *a corresponding duty on every state to respect and observe them, are now reflected,* inter alia, *in the Charter of the United Nations, the Universal Declaration of Human Rights, and corresponding portions of the International Covenant on Civil and Political Rights. . . .*[47]

As evidence of the fundamental human rights to which all individuals are entitled and which all states must guarantee, the memorial cited articles 3, 5, 7, 9, 12, and 13 of the Declaration, plus articles 7, 9, 10, and 11 of the International Covenant on Civil and Political Rights.

Since the United States, as well as Iran, has an international obligation to comply with the above provisions, the question next becomes whether this obligation can be enforced both domestically and internationally. The answer does not turn upon the self- or non-self-executing nature of the Declaration, since it is not a treaty, but upon whether the Declaration or parts thereof, as evidence of customary international law, can be used in U.S. courts either to supplement or invalidate state or federal statutes.

A major breakthrough in the use of customary international human rights law occurred in 1980 when the U.S. Court of Appeals for the Second Circuit handed down its eloquent and far-reaching decision in *Filartiga* v. *Pena-Iralu*,[48] a decision that should do as much to assist the development of this body of international law as *Fujii* did to retard it. In *Filartiga*, two Paraguayan plaintiffs brought an action in the U.S. District Court for the Eastern District of New York against another citizen of Paraguay for the torture and death of their son and brother, basing their claim on the Alien Tort Claims Act, a federal statute dating back to the original Judiciary Act of 1789, which provides that "the district courts shall have original jurisdiction of any civil action by an alien for a tort only, committed in violation of the law of nations or a treaty of the United States."[49] Since the plaintiffs did not argue that their action arose directly under a treaty to which the United States is a party, jurisdiction under the statute turned upon whether or not torture now violates "the law of nations," i.e., customary international law. The district court held that it did not.

On appeal, however, the court of appeals held that "an act of torture committed by a state official against one held in detention violates established norms of the international law of human rights, and hence the law of nations."[50] The right to be free from torture, said the court, "has become part of customary law, as *evidenced and defined by the Universal Declaration* . . . which states, in the plainest of terms, 'no one shall be subjected to torture.'"[51] The court also cited the UN's 1975 Declaration on Torture, stating that "U.N. declarations are significant because they specify with great precision the obligations of member nations under the Charter."[52] On the basis of an extensive examination of the sources from which customary international law is derived, the court had no difficulty in concluding that "official torture is now prohibited by the law of nations. The prohibition is clear and unambiguous, and admits of no distinction between treatment by aliens and citizens."[53]

Important as *Filartiga* is in establishing that torture violates customary international law, the case is even more significant in demonstrating to lawyers the growing importance of international human rights law and graphically illustrating how they should go about proving it in cases before U.S. courts. However, as the author of the *Filartiga* opinion cautioned in a subsequent magazine article, the case's holding that torture is a violation of customary international law for federal question purposes is a relatively narrow one; it should not be misread or exaggerated to support sweeping assertions that all (or even most) international human rights norms found in the Universal Declaration or elsewhere have ripened into customary international law enforceable in U.S. courts.[54]

Two subsequent cases indicate the possibilities and pitfalls of invoking customary international human rights law post-*Filartiga* and hence warrant mention. The first, *Fernandez* v. *Wilkinson*,[55] involved a Cuban refugee from the "freedom flotilla" who the INS had determined was ineligible for admission into the United States because he had been convicted of a crime involving moral turpitude. When he sought a writ of *habeas corpus*, arguing that his confinement pending possible return to Cuba violated his constitutional rights, the U.S. District Court for the District of Kansas, after surveying the cases interpreting constitutional and statutory provisions, observed that, although Fernandez's confinement constituted "arbitrary detention," "[d]ue to the unique legal status of excluded aliens in this country, it is an evil from which our Constitution and statutory laws afforded no protection."[56] The district court, however, then proceeded to break new ground by holding that "[customary] international law secures to petitioner the right to be free of arbitrary detention and that his right is being violated."[57]

Our review of the sources from which customary international law is derived clearly demonstrates that arbitrary detention is prohibited by customary international law. *Therefore, even though the indeterminate detention of an excluded alien cannot be said to violate the United States Constitution or our statutory laws, it is judicially remedial as a violation of international law.*[58]

Accordingly, the United States was ordered to terminate petitioner's arbitrary detention within ninety days.

On appeal, the Court of Appeals for the Tenth Circuit did not directly address the district court's holding, instead determining that U.S. statutory law afforded a remedy on due process grounds for Fernandez's continued detention. Noting that "[d]ue process is not a static concept," the court thought it proper "to consider international law principles for notions of fairness as to propriety of holding aliens in detention. No principle of international law is more fundamental than the concept that human beings should be free from arbitrary imprisonment."[59] The court, citing the Universal Declaration and the American Convention on Human Rights in support of this observation, noted that its construction of the statute in question "is consistent with accepted international law principles that individuals are entitled to be free of arbitrary imprisonment."[60] Thus, while it did not apply customary international law directly, it used it indirectly in determining the protection afforded by U.S. statutory law.

The second case, mentioned above in the discussion of self-executing treaties, is *In re Alien Children Education Litigation*. In addition to arguing that article 47(a) of the Protocol of Buenos Aires was self-executing, plaintiffs asserted that this and similar provisions in other international human rights instruments reflected an emerging rule of customary international law guaranteeing children free elementary school education. Although acknowledging that "[t]hese human rights instruments recognize the right of all persons to literacy or to a free primary education"[61] the district court concluded "that the right to education, while it represents an important international goal, has not acquired the status of [customary] international law."[62]

Admittedly, the right to education is not nearly as crystallized as the prohibitions of torture and arbitrary detention. Yet the provisions in the human rights instruments invoked by the plaintiffs, especially article 26(1) of the Universal Declaration, certainly are clear, precise, and easily distinguishable from other provisions in these same instruments that are aspira-

tional in nature. The district court's failure to articulate and apply a
conceptualistic framework for determining whether the right to education
has been received into customary international law[63] and its confusion
about the nature and enforceability of international law in general (and
international human rights law in particular)[64] also come as a distinct dis-
appointment in contrast to the sophisticated approach displayed by the
Filartiga court. While reasonable men may differ about whether customary international law now recognizes a right to free elementary school
education, few persons reading the court's opinion are likely to regard it
as a jurisprudential contribution to the development of international human rights law.

Using International Human Rights Law to Infuse U.S. Constitutional and Statutory Standards

Far more likely than a court's holding that the human rights clauses of
the UN Charter are self-executing or a particular article of the Universal
Declaration reflects customary international law is the possibility that a
court will regard them as infusing U.S. constitutional and statutory standards with their normative content. This "indirect incorporation" of the
Charter and Declaration—and other international human rights instruments as well—warrants greater attention than it has received to date.[65]
Professor Schachter astutely observed over thirty years ago that "it would
be unrealistic to ignore the influence . . . of the Charter as a factor in
resolving constitutional issues which have hitherto been in doubt."[66] His
recommendation has been followed in a growing number of federal and
state cases which, with increasing frequency in recent years, have referred
explicitly to the Charter, the Declaration, or other international human
rights instruments to determine the content and reach of rights guaranteed
by U.S. law.[67]

In *Oyama* v. *California*, a case decided as far back as 1948, two justices
of the U.S. Supreme Court, in a concurring opinion in a case striking
down a portion of the California Alien Land Law as contrary to the fourteenth amendment, remarked that the statute's "inconsistency with [article
55(3) of] the Charter, which has been duly ratified and adopted by the
United States, is but one more reason why the statute must be condemned."[68] How could the United States "be faithful to [its] international

pledge," two other concurring justices inquired, "if state laws which bar land ownership and occupancy by aliens on account of race are permitted to be enforced?"[69] While none of the four justices asserted that an inconsistency between a provision of the Charter and a state law automatically invalidated the latter, they believed, as a district court judge later concluded, that "the fact that an article of the United Nations Charter is incongruent with a state law is an argument against the validity of such law."[70] In a similar case decided in 1949, the Supreme Court of Oregon, in *Namba* v. *McCourt*, held the Oregon Alien Land Law violative of the equal protection clause of the fourteenth amendment. In so holding, the court pointed out that "significant changes . . . in our relationship with other nations and other people,"[71] specifically alluding to article 55 of the UN Charter, was one of the factors it had taken into account in reaching its decision.

Over the years, various groups and scholars have stressed the important interpretative function the human rights clauses of the Charter could and should have. Thus the Commission to Study the Organization of Peace stated a dozen years ago that the clauses, even if not deemed to be self-executing, "can assist in more liberal interpretation of constitutional and legislative provisions, thus enlarging the sphere of the domestic protection of human rights."[72] From a slightly different perspective, a writer recently observed that, "since lawyers are widely reluctant to confess that the values established by the national constitutions fall below any requirement of the Charter, they will rarely explicitly rely on the Charter. This reluctance may eventually lead the courts to more liberal interpretation of the basic rights and freedoms embodied in the constitution."[73]

It is interesting to note that if the human rights clauses of the UN Charter are viewed as tools for the classification and expansion of constitutional rights rather than as norms capable of direct enforcement, the spectre of *Fujii* becomes considerably less haunting. There seems little doubt that the California Supreme Court's opinion in that case was an overreaction to the intermediary appellate court's unabashed reliance on the UN Charter. Had the lower court simply cited the Charter's human rights clauses as persuasive authority for a holding based upon the equal protection clause of the fourteenth amendment, rather than using them to establish an independent rule of decision for the case, the California Supreme Court never would have had to embark on its somewhat crabbed analysis of the purposes and meaning of the Charter provisions. If international human rights advocates today not only argue that the human rights clauses in the UN Charter are self-executing, but also continuously invoke them indirectly in a manner that gradually increases the judiciary's consciousness of the existence and, perhaps more importantly, the potential of this body of law, chances are that the result sought by the lower court in *Fujii* eventually will be achieved, albeit through an indirect route.

The same approach applies with respect to the Universal Declaration. Although it has been invoked twice recently in direct fashion to help establish rules of customary international human rights law—in *Filartiga* and *Fernandez v. Wilkinson*—the Declaration's principal usefulness has been and most likely will remain that of assisting U.S. courts in indirect fashion to determine the content of constitutional and statutory standards. Numerous litigants and judges already have invoked the Declaration for precisely this purpose.[74] Other cases have cited the Declaration as a reason for extending economic and social rights.[75] Thus it could be that, as with the human rights clauses of the UN Charter, the provisions of the Declaration will have their greatest impact on U.S. law by influencing the courts' approach to constitutional and statutory standards.[76]

Finally, numerous other international human rights instruments afford the same opportunities for infusing human rights norms into such standards that the UN Charter and the Universal Declaration provide. As mentioned above, no U.S. court explicitly has held the Refugees Protocol to be self-executing, yet, as the U.S. Court of Appeals for the Fifth Circuit recently wrote, "[t]he obligations of the United States as set forth in the Protocol have informed the asylum policy of the United States as expressed in 8 U.S.C. § 1253(h)."[77] So, too, have the UN Standard Minimum Rules for the Treatment of Prisoners helped the U.S. District Court for the District of Connecticut to define what constituted overcrowded prison conditions for eighth amendment purposes.[78]

As suggested at the outset of this section, international human rights law, at least until the United States ratifies more self-executing human rights treaties or more norms in the Universal Declaration ripen into customary international law, may serve an important function shaping the content and reach of constitutional and statutory standards. At the very least, through the invocation of the established principles of statutory interpretation that "an Act of Congress ought never to be construed to violate the law of nations, if any other possible construction remains,"[79] it should have substantial impact in many cases involving statutory construction. Thus, while the infusion process may offend some international law purists, to the human rights advocate anxious to achieve results it offers significant as well as virtually limitless possibilities for achieving the goals of the international human rights movement.

Conclusion

Using domestic courts to enforce international human rights law, whether directly or indirectly, is a new and challenging area of human rights advocacy. In addition to the substantive problems addressed in this chapter, many procedural difficulties—carrying such labels as standing,[80] sovereign immunity,[81] act of state,[82] and the political-question doctrine[83]—face the party anxious to invoke international human rights law in the domestic context. While words of caution may be in order, however, counsels of despair should be ignored. Considerable progress in enforcing international human rights law in domestic courts has been made during the last decade and, with imaginative ideas, thorough research, sound judgment, and skillful advocacy, substantial new gains await the making.

Notes

1. *See, e.g.*, Asakura v. Seattle, 265 U.S. 332, 341 (1924); Ware v. Hylton, 3 U.S. (3 Dall.) 199, 236–37 (1796).

2. The Paquete Habana, 175 U.S. 677, 700 (1900).

3. RESTATEMENT OF THE FOREIGN RELATIONS LAW OF THE UNITED STATES (REVISED) § 135(1), Reporters' Note 1 at 68 (Tent. Draft No. 1, 1980) [hereinafter cited as RESTATEMENT]. *But see* Murphy, *Customary International Law in U.S. Jurisprudence—A Comment on Draft Restatement II*, INT'L PRACTITIONER'S NOTEBOOK No. 20, at 17 (Oct. 1982).

4. *See, e.g.*, The Over the Top, 5 F.2d 838, 842 (D. Conn. 1925). *See* RESTATEMENT § 135(2).

5. Diggs v. Shultz, 470 F.2d 461, 465–67 *passim* (D.C. Cir. 1972), *cert. denied*, 411 U.S. 931 (1973). *See* RESTATEMENT § 135(3).

6. 27 U.S. (2 Pet.) 253, 314 (U.S. 1829).

7. Dreyfus v. von Finck, 534 F.2d 24, 30 (2d Cir.), *cert. denied*, 429 U.S. 835 (1976). While there is general agreement about the *effects* of a self-executing treaty, there is considerable confusion about the *criteria* to be used in determining whether a treaty is self-executing in the first place. The best discussion of the problems involved may be found in Riesenfeld, *The Doctrine of Self-Executing Treaties and* U.S. v. Postal: *Win at Any Price?*, 74 AM. J. INT'L L. 892 (1980).

8. Schulter, *The Domestic Status of the Human Rights Clauses of the United Nations Charter*, 61 CALIF. L. REV. 130 (1973). *See generally* Houston, *Human Rights Enforcement Issues of the United Nations Conference on International Organization*, 53 IOWA L. REV. 272 (1967).

9. Among them are Argentina, Austria, Belgium, Cyprus, Egypt, France, Federal Republic of Germany, Greece, Italy, Japan, Luxembourg, Malta, Mexico, the Netherlands, Spain, Switzerland, Turkey, and the European Communities. Memorandum Submitted by Dean Norman Redlich on Behalf of Freedom House, *reprinted in Human Rights Treaties, Hearings before the Senate Comm. on Foreign Relations*, 96th Cong. 1st Sess. 291, 293 n.23 (1979).

10. RESTATEMENT § 131(4) comment h at 46 (emphasis added).

11. 97 A.C.A. 154, 217 P.2d 481 (1950), *aff'd*, 38 Cal.2d 718, 242 P.2d 617 (1952).

12. 38 Cal.2d at 722–25, 242 P.2d at 621–22. The Supreme Court of Michigan had used similar reasoning in an earlier case involving the enforceability of the UN Charter provisions. Sipes v. McGhee, 316 Mich. 614, 25 N.W.2d 638 (1947), *rev'd*, 334 U.S. 1 (1948). There it noted that the "pronouncements [of the Charter] are merely indicative of a desirable social trend and an objective devoutly to be desired by all well-thinking peoples." *Id.* at 628, 25 N.W.2d at 644.

13. Civil No. 74–1292 (D.D.C. 14 May 1975), *reprinted in* 14 I.L.M. 797, 804 (1975), *aff'd sub nom.* Diggs v. Richardson, 555 F.2d 848 (D.C. Cir. 1976). For an excellent critique of the district court's decision, see Note, 24 KAN. L. REV. 395 (1976).

14. 555 F.2d at 850. For commentary on the *Diggs* case, see Newman & Burke, *Diggs v. Richardson: International Human Rights in U.S. Courts*, 34 NAT'L LAW. GUILD PRAC. 52 (1977); Comment, *Public Interest Litigation and United States Foreign Policy*, 18 HARV. INT'L L.J. 375 (1977).

15. 265 U.S. 332, 342 (1924). *See also* Kolovrat v. Oregon, 336 U.S. 187, 193 (1961): "This Court has many times set its face against treaty interpretations that unduly restrict rights a treaty is adopted to protect."

16. Sarosdy, *Jurisdiction Following Illegal Extraterritorial Seizure: International Human Rights Obligations as an Alternative to Constitutional Stalemate*, 54 TEX. L. REV. 1464 (1976).

17. *See* Comment, *Self-Executing Treaties and the Human Rights Provisions of the United Nations Charter: A Separation of Powers Problem*, 25 BUFFALO L. REV. 773, 783–84 (1976). *Cf.* Sarosdy, *supra* note 16, at 1465; Schulter, *supra* note 8, at 144–49.

18. Schachter, *The Charter and the Constitution: The Human Rights Provisions in American Law,*, 4 VAND. L. REV. 643, 655 (1951).

19. *See* I. BROWNLIE, PRINCIPLES OF PUBLIC INTERNATIONAL LAW 596–98

(3d ed. 1979); M MCDOUGAL, H. LASSWELL & L. CHEN, HUMAN RIGHTS AND WORLD PUBLIC ORDER 581–611 *passim* (1980).

20. Advisory Opinion on the Continued Presence of South Africa in Namiba (South West Africa), [1971] I.C.J. 16, 57.

21. During the Ford and Carter Administrations, the United States consistently took the position that the human rights clauses of the UN Charter had legal effect and thus must be complied with by all countries, including the United States. Thus Acting Legal Adviser of the Department of State, George Aldrich, observed in 1974 that "members of the United Nations have a legal duty to promote respect for and protection of human rights around the world. . . . The Charter of the United Nations and the Universal Declaration of Human Rights are the basic texts in their field. I would point, in particular, to Articles 55 and 56 of the United Nations Charter. . . . The United States recognizes these obligations and is determined to live up to them." [1974] DIGEST OF UNITED STATES PRACTICE IN INTERNATIONAL LAW 125 (1975).

President Carter reaffirmed this position in his March 1977 address to the United Nations, declaring that "[t]he solemn commitments of the United Nations Charter, of the United Nations Universal Declaration for Human Rights, of the Helsinki Accords, and of many other international instruments must be taken just as seriously as commercial or security agreements." [1977] PUB. PAPERS OF THE PRES. 449–50.

22. Letter from Secretary of State Livingston to Mr. Serurier, 3 June 1833, *reprinted in* 2 F. WHARTON, DIGEST OF THE INTERNATIONAL LAW OF THE UNITED STATES 67 (1866) (emphasis added).

23. 502 F.2d 90 (9th Cir. 1974), *cert. denied*, 420 U.S. 1003 (1975). Significantly, the court of appeals noted that "the substantive rights guaranteed through the Trusteeship Agreement are not precisely defined. However, we do not believe that the agreement is too vague for judicial enforcement. Its language is no more general than such terms as 'due process of law,' 'seaworthiness,' 'equal protection of the law,' 'good faith,' or 'restraint of trade,' which courts interpret every day." *Id.* at 113–14.

24. Even the most liberal and enlightened judges continue to hold the Charter's human rights clauses to be non-self-executing. *See, e.g.*, Lareau v. Manson, 507 F. Supp. 1177, 1187–88 n.9 (D. Conn. 1980), *aff'd*, 651 F.2d 96 (2d. Cir. 1981).

25. Immigration and Nationality Act of 1952, § 243(h), 8 U.S.C. § 1235(h) (1976). *See* Carliner, *The Implementation of Human Rights Under the U.S. Immigration Law*, in INTERNATIONAL HUMAN RIGHTS LAW AND PRACTICE 133, 139 (J. Tuttle ed. 1978).

26. *Id.* at 140.

27. The issues raised in these cases are set out in Kramer, *Due Process Rights*

for Excludable Aliens Under United States Immigration Law and the United Nations Protocol Relating to the Statutes of Refugees—Haitian Aliens, a Case in Point, 10 N.Y.U. J. INT'L.L. & POL'Y 203 (1977), and Lieberman & Krinsky, *Political Asylum and Due Process of Law: The Case of the Haitian Refugees*, 33 NAT'L LAW. GUILD PRAC. 102 (1976).

28. 427 F. Supp. 1270 (S.D.Fla.), *vacated mem.*, 566 F.2d 104 (5th Cir. 1977). *See also* Sannon v. United States, 460 F. Supp. 458 (S.D. Fla. 1978) (same case on remand).

29. 427 F. Supp. at 1276, 1274.

30. 525 F.2d 933, 935 (5th Cir. 1976). *Cf.* Pierre v. United States, 547 F.2d 1281, 1287–89 (5th Cir.), *vacated and remanded*, 434 U.S. 962 (1977) (statutory provision consistent with protocol).

31. *See, e.g.*, Coriolan v. Immigration & Naturalization Serv., 559 F.2d 933, 996–97 (5th Cir. 1977); Kashani v. Immigration & Naturalization Serv., 547 F.2d 376, 379 (7th Cir. 1977); *In re* Sindona, 450 F. Supp. 672, 694 (S.D.N.Y. 1978); Chim Ming v. Marks, 367 F. Supp. 673, 676–81 (S.D.N.Y. 1973), *aff'd on opinion below*, 505 F.2d 1170, 1171–72 (2d Cir. 1974) (per curiam), *cert. denied*, 421 U.S. 911 (1975); and Kan Kam Lin v. Rinaldi, 361 F. Supp. 117, 179 n.1 & 183–86 (D.N.J. 1973), *aff'd*, 493 F.2d 1229 (3d Cir.), *cert. denied*, 419 U.S. 974 (1974).

32. Refugee Act of 1980, Pub. L. No. 96–212, § 201(a) & 203(3), 94 Stat. 102, 107 (codified as amended at 8 U.S.C. §§ 1101(a) (42) (A) & 1253 (h) (1) (Supp. V 1981)). *See* chapter 14.

33. Protocol of Amendment to the Charter of the Organization of American States ("Protocol of Buenos Aires"), *signed* 27 Feb. 1967, *entered into force* 27 Feb. 1970, 21 U.S.T. 607, T.I.A.S. No. 6847.

34. 458 F. Supp. 569 (E.D. Tex. 1978), *aff'd*, 628 F.2d 448 (5th Cir. 1980), *aff'd,*—U.S.—, 102 S.Ct. 2382 (1982).

35. 458 F. Supp. at 592.

36. 628 F.2d at 453. Nor, of course, had it ever been held to be non-self-executing, save in the related case of In re Alien Children Education Litigation, note 38 *infra*, which the court of appeals footnotes only in connection with the equal protection issue. *Id.* at 450 n.5.

37. *Id.* at 454.

38. 501 F. Supp. 544 (S.D. Tex. 1980), *aff'd,*—F.2d—(5th Cir. 1981), *aff'd,*—U.S.—, 102 S.Ct. 2382 (1982).

39. *Id.* at 590.

40. Actually, in addition to article 47(a) the district court examined only the preambulatory part of article 47, which requires states to "exert the greatest efforts, in accordance with their constitutional processes, to ensure the effective

exercise of the right to education." It neglected to consider articles 47(b) and 47(c), both of which are less concrete and specific than article 47(a) and hence, by contrast, serve to underscore the mandatory character of the latter's requirement that elementary education *shall be* free and compulsory for all children of school age.

41. In the interest of full disclosure, it should be noted that the writer testified for the plaintiffs as an expert witness on international law and argued, inter alia, that article 47(a) was self-executing. Expert witness for Texas was Prof. Covey T. Oliver, whose contrary views may be found in Oliver, *The Treaty Power and National Foreign Policy as Vehicles for the Enforcement of Human Rights in the United States*, 9 HOFSTRA L. REV. 411 (1981).

42. Message of the President Transmitting Four Treaties Pertaining to Human Rights, S. Exec. Doc. No. 95-C, D, E & F, 95th Cong., 2d Sess. (1978). *See* U.S. RATIFICATION OF THE HUMAN RIGHTS TREATIES: WITH OR WITHOUT RESERVATIONS? (R. Lillich ed. 1981).

43. *See* 3 UN GAOR 934, UN Doc. A/177 (1948).

44. Humphrey, *The International Bill of Rights: Scope and Implementation*, 17 WM. & MARY L. REV. 527 (1976). Humphrey himself now believes that the Declaration "is part of the customary law of nations and therefore is binding on all states. The Declaration has become what some nations wished it to be in 1948: the universally-accepted interpretation and definition of the human rights left undefined by the Charter." *Id.*

45. *See, e.g.*, statements by members of the U.S. Executive Branch suggesting that the Declaration sets forth internationally recognized human rights in R. LILLICH, THE USE OF INTERNATIONAL HUMAN RIGHTS NORMS IN U.S. COURTS 18–19 (1980). Of prime importance is former President Carter's assertion that "[t]he Declaration is the cornerstone of a developing international consensus on human rights. It is also the authoritative statement of the meaning of the United Nations Charter, through which member nations undertake to promote respect for and observe human rights and fundamental freedoms for all, without discrimination." [1978] PUB. PAPERS OF THE PRES. 2090

46. Case Concerning United States Diplomatic and Consular Staff in Tehran (U.S. v. Iran), [1980] I.C.J. 3.

47. Memorial of the United States at 71, Case Concerning United States Diplomatic and Consular Staff in Tehran (U.S. v. Iran) (International Court of Justice, Jan. 1980) (emphasis added).

48. 630 F.2d 876 (2d Cir. 1980). There have been many articles on this seminal case; *see generally* Schneebaum, *The Enforceability of Customary Norms of Public International Law*, 8 BROOKLYN J. INT'L L. 289 (1982).

49. Judiciary Act, ch. 20, § 9, 1 Stat. 73 (1789) (current version at 28 U.S.C.

§ 1350 (1976)). Plaintiffs also invoked general federal question jurisdiction under 28 U.S.C. § 1331 (1976). The court of appeals recognized that "our reasoning might also sustain jurisdiction under the general federal question provision. 28 U.S.C. § 1331. We prefer, however, to rest our decision upon the Alien Tort Statute, in light of that provision's close coincidence with the jurisdictional facts presented in this case." 630 F.2d at 887 n.22. Since plaintiffs were aliens, the basis of jurisdiction was unimportant in *Filartiga*, but the court's dictum about federal question jurisdiction would become important in future actions brought by U.S. citizens.

50. *Id.* at 880. At the time of the alleged act the defendant was Inspector-General of Police in Asunción, Paraguay. *Id.* at 878.

51. *Id.* at 881 (emphasis added).

52. 630 F.2d at 883.

53. *Id.* at 884.

54. Kaufman, *A Legal Remedy for International Torture?*, N.Y. Times, 9 Nov. 1980, § 6 (Magazine), at 44. For a misguided attempt to establish that acts of "international terrorism" violate customary international law and hence are actionable under the Alien Tort Claims Act, see Hanoch Tel-Oren v. Libyan Arab Republic, 517 F. Supp. 542 (D.D.C. 1981). The district court's *obiter dictum* in that case is criticized strongly by Schneebaum, *International Law as Guarantor of Judicially-Enforceable Rights: A Reply to Professor Oliver*, 4 Hous. J. Int'l L. 65, 71–74 (1981). *Compare* Note, *Terrorism as a Tort in Violation of the Law of Nations*, 6 Fordham Int'l L.J. 236 (1982).

55. 505 F. Supp. 787 (D. Kan. 1980), *aff'd on other grounds sub nom.* Rodriguez-Fernandez v Wilkinson, 654 F.2d 1382 (10th Cir. 1981). Both opinions are thoroughly evaluated in Hassan, *The Doctrine of Incorporation: New Vistas for the Enforcement of International Human Rights?* 5 Human Rights Q. 68 (1983). *See also* Note, *Fernandez v. Wilkinson: Making the United States Accountable Under Customary International Law*, 10 Denver J. Int'l L. & Pol'y 360 (1981) (discussion of lower court opinion).

56. 505 F. Supp. at 795.

57. *Id.*

58. *Id.* at 798 (emphasis added).

59. 654 F.2d at 1388.

60. *Id.* at 1390.

61. 501 F. Supp. at 544.

62. *Id.* at 596.

63. One explanation for this brevity may be that the court thought its treatment of the self-executing character of article 47(a) of the Protocol of Buenos Aires dispositive of this issue too. If so, then the point needs making that, assuming

arguendo a treaty provision like article 47(a) is non-self-executing, it does not necessarily follow that the right set out in the treaty provision, read in conjunction with similar provisions found in numerous other international human rights instruments, does not reflect customary international law.

64. The district court supports its conclusion that the right to education has not acquired the status of customary international law for purposes of enforcement in U.S. courts by reference to "the nature of international law," which it intimates should be enforced on a state-to-state basis through diplomatic channels. *Id.* Why the possibility of diplomatic remedies (available, of course, only when aliens are involved) should bar domestic courts from enforcing customary international law rights the court does not explain. Its misunderstanding of the role of domestic courts in the enforcement, much less the development, of customary international law is profound, harking back to Banco Nacional de Cuba v. Sabbatino, 376 U.S. 398 (1964), which it quotes approvingly. 501 F. Supp. at 596.

65. For recent scholarly support of the writer's views in this regard, see Bilder, *Integrating International Human Rights Law into Domestic Law—U.S. Experience*, 4 Hous. J. Int'l L. 1 (1981); Christenson, *The Use of Human Rights Norms to Inform Constitutional Interpretation*, 4 *id.* 39 (1981); Christenson, *Using Human Rights Law to Inform Due Process and Equal Protection Analyses*, 52 U. Cin. L. Rev. 3 (1983); Louden, *The Domestic Application of International Human Rights Law: Evolving the Species*, 5 Hastings Int'l & Comp. L. Rev. 161 (1981); Martineau, *Interpreting the Constitution: The Use of International Human Rights Norms*, 4 Human Rights Q. 87 (1983); and Paust, *Human Rights: From Jurisprudential Inquiry to Effective Litigation* (Book Review), 56 N.Y.U.L. Rev. 227 (1981). *Cf.* Oliver, *Problems of Cognition and Interpretation in Applying Norms of Customary International Law of Human Rights in United States Courts*, 4 Hous. J. Int'l L. 59 (1981).

66. Schachter, *supra* note 18, at 658.

67. Courts in other countries also have used the Charter as a guide to public policy. *See, e.g., re* Drummond, 1943–45 Ann Dig. 178, 179 (High Ct., Ont., Canada, 1945).

68. 332 U.S. 633, 673 (1948) (Murphy, J. & Rutledge, J., concurring).

69. *Id.* at 650 (Black, J. & Douglas, J., concurring).

70. United States v. Vargas, 370 F. Supp. 908, 914–15 (D.P.R. 1974), *vacated and remanded*, 558 F.2d 631 (1st Cir. 1977).

71. 185 Ore. 579, 604, 204 P.2d 569, 579 (1949).

72. Commission to Study the Organization of Peace, 18th Report, the United Nations and Human Rights 4 (1968).

73. Schulter, *supra* note 8, at 157 n.268.

74. The cases are collected in R. Lillich, International Human Rights

INSTRUMENTS at 440.6–440.7 (1983). This looseleaf service lists all U.S. federal and state court cases discussing or citing the forty-nine principal international human rights instruments.

75. *See, e.g.*, Pauley v. Kelley, 255 S.E.2d 859, 864 (W. Va. 1979); Copeland v. Secretary of State, 226 F. Supp. 20, 31 n.16 (S.D.N.Y.), *vacated and remanded*, 378 U.S. 588 (1964).

76. *See* Schwelb, *The Influence of the Universal Declaration of Human Rights on International and National Law*, 53 AM. SOC'Y INT'L L. PROC. 217, 219 (1959). This conclusion is supported by the fact that courts in other countries have relied upon the Declaration in civil and political rights cases. *See, e.g., In re* Pietras, 1951 Y.B. ON HUMAN RIGHTS 14, 15 (United Nations)(Belgium); Public Prosecutor v. F.A.v.A., 1951 *id.* 252 (United Nations) (Netherlands); and *In re* Bukowicz, 1953 Y.B. ON HUMAN RIGHTS 21 (United Nations) (Netherlands).

77. Haitian Refugee Center v. Smith, 676 F.2d 1023, 1029 n.8 (5th Cir. 1982). *See also* the cases cited in note 31 *supra*.

78. *See* chapter 12.

79. Murray v. Schooner Charming Betsy, 6 U.S. (2 Cranch) 64, 118 (1804). *Accord*, Lauritzen v. Larsen, 345 U.S. 571, 578 (1953). *See* RESTATEMENT § 134. British courts follow the same rule of interpretation, with the results recommended in the text. "[S]ince there is a presumption that Parliament does not intend to break the international obligations of the United Kingdom, ambigious provisions in Acts of Parliament will be construed by the courts to conform so far as possible with the Convention." McBride & Brown, *The United Kingdom, The European Community and the European Convention on Human Rights*, 1981 Y.B. EUR. L. 167, 177. *See also* Duffy, *English Law and the European Convention on Human Rights*, 29 INT'L & COMP. L.Q. 585 (1980).

80. The leading standing case is Diggs v. Shultz, note 5 *supra*, where Congressman Diggs and other plaintiffs sued for injunctive relief and a declaratory judgment that the Byrd Amendment, permitting the United States to resume the importation of chrome from Southern Rhodesia, in violation of UN Security Council Resolution 232, was null and void. The U.S. Court of Appeals for the District of Columbia reversed the district court's determination that plaintiffs lacked standing to bring the action, holding that they were "unquestionably within the reach of [the] purpose [of Security council Resolution 232] and among its intended beneficiaries"; that they were injured "in fact"; and that there was a "logical nexus" between their alleged injuries and the "challenged [congressional] action." 470 F.2d at 464. This decision so troubled the Ford Administration that the U.S. subsequently argued, fortunately in vain, that on this point Diggs v. Shultz "was wrongly decided." Diggs v. Richardson, *supra* note 13, at 850. The two cases are

discussed in Lillich, *The Role of Domestic Courts in Promoting International Human Rights Norms*, 24 N.Y.L.S.L. REV. 153, 165–68, 172–76 (1978).

81. The leading sovereign immunity case is Letelier v. Republic of Chile, 488 F. Supp. 665 (D.D.C. 1980), a suit in the U.S. District Court for the District of Columbia arising out of the assassination in Washington, D.C., of the former Chilean foreign minister, Orlando Letelier. The Chilean government, who the plaintiffs alleged had ordered the assassination because Letelier outspokenly opposed the ruling junta, claimed that the Foreign Sovereign Immunities Act, 28 U.S.C. § 1602–11 (1976), deprived the court of jurisdiction. The court, correctly, disagreed. 488 F. Supp. at 673. *See* Note, 21 VA. J. INT'L L. 291 (1981). Certainly the FSIA was not designed to thwart adjudication of cases arising out of human rights violations and should not be so construed. *Cf.* Youngblood, *1980 Survey of International Law in the Second Circuit*, 8 SYR. J. INT'L L. & COM. 159, 203–4 (1980).

82. In *Filartiga*, the defendant argued on appeal that "[i]f the conduct complained of is alleged to be the act of the Paraguayan government, the suit is barred by the Act of State doctrine." 630 F.2d at 889. The court of appeals found it unnecessary to decide the question, but in *dictum* expressed doubt "whether action by a state official in violation of the Constitution and laws of the Republic of Paraguay, and wholly unratified by that nation's government, could properly be characterized as an act of state." *Id.*

This approach clearly is consistent with the nature and purpose of the act of state doctrine as formulated in Banco Nacional de Cuba v. Sabbatino, note 64 *supra*, which, contrary to the New York Court of Appeals in New York Times Co. v. City of New York, Commission on Human Rights, 41 N.Y.2d 345, 352, 361 N.E.2d 963, 972, 393 N.Y.S.2d 312, 317 (1977), assuredly does not preclude U.S. courts from adjudicating cases involving human rights violations by foreign government officials. *See* Lillich, *supra* note 80, at 159–62.

83. The political question doctrine remains the most serious obstacle in many cases to persons seeking to litigate international human rights law issues in U.S. courts. *Cf.* Diggs v. Richardson, *supra* note 13, at 851. *See* Gordon, *American Courts, International Law and Political Questions Which Touch Foreign Relations*, 14 INT'L LAW. 297, 312 (1980), who rightly criticizes this blind adherence to traditional—and outmoded—dogma.

14

Domestic and International Protection of Refugees

DAVID CARLINER

Historical Background

Exodus tells us that God "will appoint a place whither [one unjustly accused of murder] may flee." Moses, obedient to God's will, commanded Israel to "separate three cities whence [innocent] manslayers may flee." The Egyptians, Greeks, and Romans designated temples of worship as places of refuge and extended the right to fugitive slaves, defeated soldiers, and accused criminals.[1] Constantine made all Christian churches places of asylum,[2] and the concept of general asylum emerged from the Benedictine Order of Cluny in the tenth century when the "Peace of God" was invoked during combat for church environs and their inhabitants.[3]

By the time Grotius wrote the treatise in 1625 that was to become the basis of international law, the grant of sanctuary and asylum was an established practice for individuals seeking refuge.

Asylum in instances of mass flight, so familiar today, also has long-standing precedents. The thirteenth, fourteenth, and fifteenth centuries saw the expulsion of thousands of Jews from England, France, Spain, and Portugal and their dispersal throughout other European countries, North Africa, and, subsequently, to the Dutch, Spanish, and Portuguese possessions in America.[4] A century later, Geneva became perhaps the first major city created by refugees when it became a center for French, English, and

Italian Protestant refugees after Calvin's flight from France in 1541. When the Edict of Nantes was repealed in 1685, ending all semblance of legal protection for Protestants in France, more than 400,000 were granted asylum in various North European countries.[5] The political and economic upheavals in the eighteenth and nineteenth centuries accelerated the movement of exiles and refugees in Europe and Asia and in the settlement of North and South America.

But it has been the twentieth century that has become known as the "century of refugees and prisoners"[6] and of the "homeless man,"[7] as more than 100 million people have been displaced from their native countries by war, revolution, and repression. In 1981, it was estimated that more than 12.6 million remained unsettled either by repatriation or by resettlement elsewhere.[8]

It is in this historical context that domestic and international law has evolved for determining the right of asylum and the status of refugees.

The first such municipal law may have been the Edict of Potsdam, which granted asylum in Prussia to the French Huguenots ten days after the repeal of the Edict of Nantes, followed in 1708 by the English "Act for Naturalizing Foreign Protestants." In 1832, France adopted the *Loi Relative Aux Etrangers Refugiés Qui Resideront en France*. In a related area, Belgium forbade the extradition of persons for political offenses in 1833, incorporating this prohibition for the first time in any international agreement in the Franco-Belgian Extradition Treaty of 1834. The Belgian precedent, followed by Switzerland in 1848 and the Netherlands in 1849, has since become universal.[9]

Although the violation of fundamental human rights engaged international attention during the nineteenth century, no international agreements or domestic laws assisting refugees were adopted until the aftermath of World War 1. The initial action was taken in 1921 by the League of Nations "as an obligation of international justice" to deal with the plight of 800,000 Russian refugees. The Office of High Commissioner for Refugees was created and its functions eventually extended to include the exchange of Greek and Turkish populations; the resettlement of Bulgarian, Armenian, Assyrian, and Assyro-Chaldean refugees; and, with the coming to power of Hilter, assistance of refugees from Germany, Austria, and Czechoslovakia.[10]

In 1933, the League of Nations adopted a comprehensive Convention Relating to the International Status of Refugees, which assured refugees civil rights, including access to the courts; the right to employment; admission to schools and universities; and freedom of movement. A notable achievement of the Office of the High Commissioner during this period was the creation of the so-called "Nansen passport," accepted as a certificate of identity for stateless persons permitting them to travel and to return to their host countries.

With the dissolution of the League of Nations and the termination of the mandate of its Office of High Commissioner for Refugees, a succession of agencies assumed responsibility for these matters: the Inter-Governmental Committee on Refugees, the United Nations Relief and Rehabilitation Agency (UNRRA), and the International Refugee Organization (IRO). In January 1951, the UN General Assembly established the UN Office of High Commissioner for Refugees (UNHCR), and on 28 July 1951, a specially convened conference adopted the Convention Relating to the Status of Refugees as an international code establishing basic rights of refugees.[11] A 1967 Protocol to the Convention, which expanded the definition of refugee, has now been ratified by eighty-nine nations, including the United States.[12]

The Convention and Protocol Relating to the Status of Refugees

The Convention applies to any person who

[o]wing to well-founded fear of being persecuted for reasons of race, religion, nationality, membership of a particular social group, or political opinion, is outside the country of his nationality and is unable or, owing to such fear, is unwilling to avail himself of the protection of that country; or who, not having a nationality and being outside of the country of his former habitual residence as a result of such events, is unable or, owing to such fear, is unwilling to return to it.[13]

"Well-founded fear"

This phrase has been interpreted to require a showing of objective facts that demonstrate the likelihood of such persecution through past experiences endured by the applicant or other comparable persons.[14]

Persecution

The term "persecution" includes threats to life; bodily harm; torture; detention for prolonged periods; repeated arrests or interrogations; internal exile; prosecution for offenses other than those "genuinely arising from non-political crimes"; discriminatory treatment in obtaining employment, education, or other basic rights; or a combination of factors that singly do not establish persecution but cumulatively portray an "atmosphere of insecurity." Persecution typically arises from governmental conduct, including non-action by authorities who fail to provide protection to persons victimized by groups within the population.

Reasons for Persecution

1. "Race" is defined broadly to include any ethnic, tribal, or social group having a common descent.
2. "Religion" embraces identification with a denomination, sect, order, or community of persons sharing a common faith. Persecution may arise from interference with the practice of religious beliefs or refusal to permit conduct that is religiously motivated, such as (some decisions have held) refusal to perform military service.
3. "Nationality" includes ethnic and linguistic groups and statelessness, as well as formal country citizenship.
4. "Social group" encompasses any kind of status not otherwise defined and has been applied to former capitalists and to past members of the Foreign Service.
5. "Political opinion" includes the expression of views and disagreement with the policies of the government and has been held also to include reliance upon those views as a motive for committing nonpolitical offenses (other than heinous crimes), such as refusal to perform military service, desertion, civil disobedience, and departing from a country illegally.

Outside of the Country of Nationality or Former Habitual Residence

In order to invoke the international protection afforded by the Convention, a person claiming to be a refugee must be "outside of the country of his nationality" or, if stateless, outside the country of former habitual residence. The term excludes not only persons still residing in such countries but also those who have obtained temporary refuge in foreign embassies which, although outside the host country's jurisdiction, are nevertheless within its territory.

It is sufficient that the refugee *be* outside his or her former country, there being no requirement of having left the country of origin in order to escape persecution. A person may be a refugee if there has been a change in circumstances within the country of origin since the refugee's departure.

Unable or Unwilling to Return to the Former Country

Inability to return to the country of origin is established if the country refuses to accept the refugee, denies passport facilities, or if a state of war or armed hostilities or the absence of diplomatic relations between the country of origin and the country of refuge prevent return.

Unwillingness to return to the country of origin is accepted if based, as defined above, upon a "well-founded fear of persecution" and is a valid reason for refusal to return to the country of origin even if the fear of persecution exists only as to certain areas within the country rather than as to the entire country.

Persons Excluded from the Convention

Excluded from the protection of the Convention are:
1. Refugees receiving assistance from other UN agencies, such as the United Nations Relief and Works Agency for Palestine Refugees in the Near East (UNRWA);
2. Persons who have acquired the "rights and obligations" of nationals in the country in which they have taken up residence, e.g., the "connational" ethnic German Refugees (*Volksdeutsche*) who resettled in the Federal Republic of Germany; and
3. Any person as to whom there are "serious reasons for considering" that he or she (a) has committed a crime against peace, a war crime, or a crime against humanity; (b) has committed a serious nonpolitical crime outside the country of refuge prior to his admission to that country as a refugee; or (c) has been "guilty of acts contrary to the purposes and principles of the United Nations."

The definitions of a crime against peace, a war crime, or a crime against humanity are derived from international agreements adopted at the close of World War II and include the conduct of wars of aggression and those in violation of international treaties; mistreatment of civilians and prisoners of war; plunder and "wanton destruction . . . not justified by military necessity"; the enslavement and murder of civilian populations; and political, racial, and religious persecution.

The term "serious nonpolitical crime" is not defined but has been interpreted to refer to major offenses punishable by death or by "the deprivation of liberty for several years." The determination is made in accordance with the law of the country of refuge rather than the law of the country in which the crime has been committed.

The phrase "acts contrary to the purposes and principles of the United Nations" has rarely been invoked, but one commentator states that it is directed against leading government officials guilty of persecutory measures and conduct in defiance of human rights or acts of state contrary to the maintenance of a just peace, as well as to private individuals who "are guilty of especially flagrant violations of human rights," such as the ownership of slaves, slave trading, torture, and the deprivation of the right to vote.[15]

Cessation of Refugee Status

A person who has been recognized as a refugee under the terms of the Convention loses such status if he or she
1. has voluntarily reaccepted the protection of the country of nationality or resettled in the country originally left due to fear of persecution;
2. has voluntarily reacquired his or her nationality;
3. has acquired a new nationality and enjoys the protection of the country of the new nationality; or
4. the circumstances that led to recognition as a refugee have ceased to exist, unless there are compelling reasons arising out of the previous presecution for refusing to return to the country in which he or she was persecuted.

Reavailing oneself of the protection of the country of nationality (e.g., by obtaining a passport), the reacquisition of nationality, or the acquisition of naturalization in another country must be voluntary. Where citizenship has been conferred by operation of law without affirmative action on the part of the recipient or protection is sought because of constraining circumstances beyond the refugee's control, it will not lead to the cessation of refugee status.

The change in circumstances referred to in the Convention must be fundamental, not merely transitory or events such as a grant of amnesty or expiration of a statute of limitations on any offense with which the refugee may be charged. The change of circumstances contemplated is the replacement of an oppressive regime with a democratic government.

Procedures for Determining Refugee Status

The determination of refugee status is made by each of the state parties to the Convention rather than by the Office of the High Commissioners, and thirty-two countries have enacted domestic legislation prescribing procedures for determining refugee status.[16] However, in order to assure that an applicant for refugee status is guaranteed minimal standards of fairness in the consideration of his application, the Executive Committee of the High Commissioner's Programme has recommended that the domestic procedures of each of the contracting countries provide the following basic requirements:

a. The competent official (*e.g.*, immigration officer or border police officer) to whom the applicant addresses himself at the border or in the territory of a Contracting State should have clear instructions for dealing with cases which might come within the purview of the relevant international instruments. He should be required to act in accordance with the principle of *nonrefoulement* and to refer such cases to a high authority.

b. The applicant should receive the necessary guidance as to the procedure to be followed.

c. There should be a clearly identified authority—wherever possible a single central authority—with responsibility for examining requests for refugee status and taking decisions in the first instance.

d. The applicant should be given the necessary facilities, including the services of a competent interpreter, for submitting his case to the authorities concerned. Applicants should also be given the opportunity, of which they should be duly informed, to contact a representative of UNHCR.

e. If the applicant is recognized as a refugee, he should be informed accordingly and issued with documentation certifying his refugee status.

f. If the applicant is not recognized, he should be given a reasonable time to appeal for a formal reconsideration of the decision, either to the same or to a different authority, whether administrative or judicial, according to the prevailing system.

g. The applicant should be permitted to remain in the country pending a decision on his initial request by the competent authority referred to in paragraph *c* above, unless it has been established by that authority that his request is clearly abusive. He should also be permitted to remain in the country while an appeal to a higher administrative authority or to the courts is pending.[17]

Rights of Refugees

Although the Convention refers to individuals and does not directly include family members, the Final Act of the conference that adopted the
1951 Convention recommended that the "unity of the refugee's family be
maintained particularly in cases where the head of the family has fulfilled
the necessary conditions for admission to a particular country." The principle applies both to immediately accompanying members of the refugee's
family and to family members who follow later.

The Convention contains no express provision requiring that a state
admit refugees to its territory, although the Final Act recommends that
governments "continue to receive refugees in their territories and that they
. . . cooperate . . . in order that . . . refugees may find asylum and the
possibility of resettlement." However, three provisions of the Convention
do offer substantial protection to persons who have entered a country for
refuge.

Article 31 excepts refugees from normal immigration procedures and
provides that states "shall not impose penalties, on account of their illegal
entry or presence, on refugees, who come in directly from a territory where
their life or freedom was threatened . . . ; enter or are present in their
territory without authorization, provided they present themselves without
delay to the authorities and show good cause for their illegal entry or
presence."

Article 32 provides that the contracting states "shall not expel a refugee
lawfully in their territory save on grounds of national security or public
order."

Article 33 is perhaps the most important article in the Convention and
establishes the fundamental principle of *nonrefoulement*. This provides
that no state "shall expel or return a refugee in any manner whatsoever to
the frontiers of territories where his life or freedom would be threatened
on account of his race, religion, nationality, membership of a particular
social group or political opinion," except a refugee for whom "there are
reasonable grounds for regarding as a danger to the security of the country
in which he is, or who, having been convicted by a final judgment of a
particularly serious crime, constitutes a danger to the community of that
country."

These three provisions have given effective protection to millions of
refugees who have crossed frontiers, legally and illegally, and, to the extent they are observed by the parties, they have prevented the return of
refugees to countries in which they fear persecution.

Once refugee status has been granted by a receiving country, the Convention requires certain substantive rights for all refugess. These rights fall under four different standards of equality in treatment.

1. *The same treatment as is accorded to nationals of the host country.* These rights include freedom of religion and religious education; free access to the courts, including legal assistance and exemption from any requirement that foreigners deposit court costs in advance; protection of industrial property, such as inventions and trade names, and rights in literary, artistic, and scientific works; and equal treatment in rationing, public relief and assistance, elementary education, labor legislation, social security, and taxation. Refugees with three years' residence or a spouse or child who is a national of the country are to have the same rights to wage-earning employment as nationals.

2. *The most favorable treatment accorded to nationals of a foreign country.* These rights include employment for wage earners with less than three years' residence and the right to belong to trade unions and to nonpolitical and non-profit-making associations.

3. *Treatment as favorable as possible and, in any event, not less favorable than that accorded aliens generally in the same circumstances.* These rights include ownership of movable and immovable property; self-employment in agriculture, industry, handicrafts, and commerce, including the right to establish commercial and industrial companies; to practice a liberal profession; to obtain housing; and access to higher education, including remission of fees and the award of scholarships.

4. *The same treatment as is accorded to aliens generally.* These rights include freedom of residence and movement within the country and any other rights not specifically set forth in the convention.

In addition, refugees are to be given identity papers and travel documents to permit them to travel outside the country, except for compelling reasons of national security or public order.

Other International Agreements

In addition to the 1951 Convention Relating to the Status of Refugees and the 1967 Protocol, regional agreements have been adopted that have served to reinforce the rights of refugees.

The most significant has been the Convention Governing the Specific Aspects of Refugee Problems in Africa, adopted by the Organization of

African Unity (OAU) in 1969.[19] The Convention reiterates the principle of *nonrefoulement* and, for the first time in any international agreement, it imposes upon states the obligation to

. . .use their best endeavors consistent with their respective legislations to receive refugees and to secure the settlement of those refugees who, for well-founded reasons, are unable or unwilling to return to their country of origin or nationality.

If a state

. . .finds difficulty in continuing to grant asylum to refugees, such Member State may appeal directly to the other Member States and through the OAU and such other Member States shall in the spirit of African Solidarity and International Cooperation take appropriate measures to lighten a burden of the Member State granting asylum.[20]

The OAU Convention also expands the definition of refugee, which reflects recent African experience and includes

. . .every person who, owing to external aggression, occupation, foreign domination or other events seriously disturbing public order in either part or the whole of his country of origin and nationality, is compelled to leave his place of habitual residence in order to seek refuge in another place outside of his country of origin or nationality.[21]

In order both to give protection to the refugee and to minimize problems with the country of origin, the Convention underscores that "the grant of asylum to refugees is a peaceful and humanitarian act and shall not be regarded as an unfriendly act by any Member State," and it obligates signatory states to "prohibit refugees residing in their respective territories from attacking any Member State of the OAU, by any activity likely to cause tension between Member States and in particular by use of arms, through the press, or by radio."[22] To reinforce these provisions, the Convention provides that "for reasons of security, countries of asylum shall, as far as possible, settle refugees at a reasonable distance from the frontier of their country of origin."[23]

Several conventions dealing with asylum have been adopted in the Americas, but there is no comprehensive agreement regarding the status of refugees. The American Convention on Human Rights includes provisions comparable to those of the 1951 Convention providing that:

Every person has the right to seek and be granted asylum in a foreign territory, in accordance with the legislation of the State and International Conventions, in the event he is being pursued for political offenses or related common crimes; . . . In no case may an alien be deported or returned to a country regardless of whether or not it is his country of origin, if in that country his right to life or personal freedom is in danger of being violated because of his race, nationality, religion, social status, or political opinions.[24]

Despite serious refugee problems, no regional convention has been adopted in Asia. In 1966, the Asian-African Legal Consultative Committee (an intergovernmental advisory body) adopted the "Bangkok Principles Concerning the Treatment of Refugees," which expand the definition of "refugee" set forth in the 1951 Convention. However, there has been no further definitive action toward the adoption of a convention, despite subsequent meetings.

Domestic Laws Relating to Refugee Status

Those countries that have adopted domestic laws for the determination of refugee status have implemented the recommendations of the UNHCR unevenly.[25]

Each of the laws designates a "competent authority": eleven countries vest the authority in security agencies (the Ministry of the Interior or Justice or police authorities); five in the Ministry of Foreign Affairs; six in independent immigrant or refugee agencies; six in governmental authorities such as the Head of State, Prime Minister, or Minister of State; and in five countries the function is shared jointly by designated agencies (the Ministries of Foreign Affairs and Justice/Interior).

Twenty-five countries permit the UNHCR to participate in the proceedings to determine refugee status. This participation may be as a member of the "competent authority," as an observer or adviser, or through the provision of direct assistance to the refugee applicant. Seven countries make no provision for UNHCR assistance.

Appeal is allowed by seventeen countries; seven countries permit requests for reconsideration upon the basis of new facts or, occasionally, for error. Eight countries allow neither appeal nor reconsideration.

All thirty-two countries issue an identification document to refugees. This document ranges from a formal refugee identification card to a letter notifying the applicant that he has been granted refugee status; certain countries issue only a travel document.

Countries that have no domestic legislation to implement the Convention, or which are not parties to the Convention itself, have accepted refugees, nonetheless, some in substantial numbers. For example, Burundi, Cameroon, Nigeria, and Sudan had more than one million refugees in their populations in 1981; Pakistan shelters approximately two million Afghans; Thailand has nearly 400,000 refugees from Kampuchea, Laos, and Vietnam; approximately one and a half million Palestinian refugees live in Jordan, Lebanon, Syria, and the Gaza Strip; and at least 200,000 refugees are scattered in various countries of Central and South America.[26]

The substantive rights granted refugees also vary widely, from the grant of permanent residence and rights virtually equal to those accorded to citizens, to the provision only of safe facilities in refugee camps. Most nations have enacted laws that limit the employment of aliens, although many European countries have granted refugees the right to work, including the practice of a profession. This right has not yet been assured in most African countries, with the exception of Senegal, which has adopted provisions more favorable than those in the 1951 Convention in assuring employment rights, education, and social benefits.

United States Practice

Although the general standards defining a "refugee" are international, the practitioner is much more likely to be concerned with domestic legislation, regulations, and political considerations that influence implementation of the international norms. This section on U.S. practice is offered as an example of the kinds of procedures which may have to be utilized in individual cases.

Following a succession of ad hoc statutory and executive measures after World War II, Congress enacted the Refugee Act of 1980 "to provide a permanent and systematic procedure for the admission . . . of refugees of special humanitarian concern to the United States, and to provide comprehensive and uniform provisions for the effective resettlement and absorption of those refugees who are admitted."[27]

The rights provided by the statute and its implementing regulations, with important variations, conform generally with the provisions of the Convention and the recommendations of the UNHCR.

The statutory definition of "refugee" duplicates the language of the Convention but also includes persons who are still within the geographical territory of their home country, "in such special circumstances as the President after appropriate consultation . . . may specify."[28] This modification reflects the admission to the United States of Cuban and Vietnamese refugees directly from their country of origin and authorizes the admission to the United States of persons who have obtained temporary refuge in embassies or who are being detained by the government in their home country.

The statute also specifies a wider range of persons excluded from refugee status than is found in the Convention. Specifically excluded are persons who traffic in narcotics; "who ordered, incited, assisted, or otherwise participated in the persecution of any person on account of race, religion, nationality, membership in a particular special group or political opinion";[29] and those who are believed to be entering the United States "to engage in activities which will be prejudicial to the public interest, or endanger the welfare, safety, or security of the United States."[30]

The Act fixes the number of refugee admissions for the first three years at 50,000 per year, the number to be determined annually thereafter by the President after consultation with Congress. If an "unforeseen emergency refugee situation exists," additional refugees may be admitted under special allocations if justified by "grave humanitarian concerns" or if in the "national interest," subject also to prior consultation with Congress.[31]

Procedures[32]

These few pages cannot consider all the complexities of refugee and asylum procedures in the United States, and they should be considered only as a broad outline of the kinds of practical and procedural issues that may face an applicant for refugee status. In addition, current congressional and administration concern over perceived refugee problems may result in substantial modifications to present refugee procedures.

A person who seeks admission to the United States as a refugee, is in a foreign country, and has not been firmly resettled, may apply to an Immigration and Naturalization Service (INS) office overseas, or, if remote from such an office, to the nearest designated U.S. consulate. Every applicant must appear personally before an INS officer to establish eligibility for admission. In addition to meeting the definitional requirement, the applicant must fall within the category of refugees for whom the President has made an annual allocation and must present an "acceptable sponsorship agreement and guaranty of transportation" from a "responsible person or organization."³³ The governing regulation does not provide for assistance to an applicant for refugee 'status, but numerous voluntary organizations help refugees in submitting applications and in obtaining the required sponsorship agreements and guaranty of transportation.³⁴

Each applicant whose application is accepted for filing by INS is registered as of the date of filing. Although the date of filing is the "priority date for case control," refugees or groups of refugees may be selected for processing regardless of their filing dates, upon the basis of criteria "that will best support the policies and interests of the United States," such as "reuniting families, close association with the United States, compelling humanitarian concerns, and public interest factors."³⁵ Guidelines issued by the INS and the State Department have authorized the processing of "immediate action cases" for foreign diplomats facing serious threat of repatriation or any national of the Soviet Union or of one of fourteen other communist countries who is on an official visit or is part of a cultural or athletic exchange program.³⁶

The decision on the application for admission to the United States as a refugee is made by the officer in charge at the overseas INS installation. If approved, the applicant is authorized to travel to the United States, where an INS District Director is empowered to grant admission as a "conditional entrant." No appeal is permitted from a denial of refugee status, but motions for reconsideration may be entertained by the INS officer who had denied the application. In appropriate cases involving a substantial question of law or a possible precedential determination, the decision may be certified to the Central Office of the INS.

An applicant who has been granted conditional entry to the United States is issued an arrival-departure record (Form I-94), and a notation is entered on any passport to record the entry. In addition, the refugee may obtain an international refugee travel document.

Different procedures are prescribed for aliens physically present in the United States or for those who present themselves at a port of entry without having obtained approval of refugee status overseas. They may be granted asylum in the United States, provided that they meet the definition for being a refugee.

An application for asylum must be filed with the INS District Director, except for aliens who have been placed under proceedings to exclude or to deport them from the United States. Aliens who are under such proceedings must file their applications for asylum with the docket clerk of the immigration court in which their proceedings are pending.

All applicants are required to appear before the appropriate officer to establish eligibility to obtain asylum. No formal assistance is given to the applicant in submitting his request for asylum; however, the applicant may bring his own interpreter and attorney or obtain the assistance, if available, of a voluntary organization.

Persons whose applications for asylum are submitted in exclusion or deportation proceedings to be adjudicated by an immigration judge similarly may be represented by counsel obtained individually or through the assistance of voluntary social agencies. Interpreters, however, are provided in these proceedings by the INS.

In all cases, the District Directors and the immigration judges are required to request an "advisory opinion" from the Bureau of Human Rights and Humanitarian Affairs (BHRHA) of the Department of State regarding the country of origin of each applicant for asylum and the likelihood that the applicant would be subject to persecution in that country.

If the decision of the District Director or judge is based upon the BHRHA opinion, the opinion must be made a part of the record, unless classified as secret. If the BHRHA opinion is included in the record, the asylum applicant has an opportunity to examine, explain, or rebut it.

The District Director is empowered to decide applications for asylum in the "exercise of discretion." Asylum shall be denied if any of the statutory grounds for denial is present or if there is an outstanding offer of resettlement by a third nation where the applicant will not be subject to persecution, and resettlement is in the public interest.

If the application is approved, asylum is granted for a period of one year. No appeal is allowed from the denial of an application by the District Director, but the application may be renewed before an immigration judge in exclusion proceedings (by an alien who submitted his application upon arrival at a U.S. port of entry and is technically considered to be "outside" the United States) and in deportation proceedings (by an applicant who is present within the United States). The decisions rendered by such judges may be appealed to the Board of Immigration Appeals and to a Circuit Court of Appeals (in deportation cases) or to a District Court through habeas corpus proceedings (in exclusion cases).

Refugee status may be revoked if the District Director subsequently finds that the person was not, in fact, a refugee as defined by the statute at the time of admission. The refugee is given the opportunity to present evidence to show why the status should not be terminated, and, if the status is revoked, exclusion proceedings may be initiated (with the same opportunities to reassert refugee status and to appeal as noted above).

A person who has been admitted into the United States as a refugee under the procedures described above for "conditional entry" is required to appear before an immigration office one year after the date of entry to determine admissibility to the United States as a permanent resident. If found to be admissible, the refugee will be granted status as a lawful permanent resident as of the date of original arrival in the United States. Admissibility requires, among other factors, that the refugee has been physically present in the United States for at least one year and that he or she continues to be a refugee within the meaning of the statute. If the applicant is found to be inadmissible, a request for admission to the United States as an immigrant may be made in exclusion proceedings, with possible appeals as already noted.

An alien who has applied for asylum, unlike an alien who has been admitted as a refugee under conditional entrant status, is subject to termination of permission to remain in the United States if the Attorney General determines that there has been a "change of circumstances" in the alien's country of origin. Otherwise, the alien who has been granted asylum, like the conditional entrant, may be granted permanent residence upon application to the District Director or an immigration judge, within an annual quota limitation of 5,000 such "adjustments of status."

Substantive Rights of Refugees and Asylees

Insofar as they fall within U.S. constitutional protections, refugees in the United States generally enjoy greater substantive rights than those set forth in the Convention.

Freedom of religion, including religious education, and the right of association in labor unions and political and other associations, are assured to all persons by the First Amendment to the Constitution.[37]

Refugees, asylees, and lawful permanent residents have the same right as citizens to choose their place of residence and to travel freely within the United States, the sole requirement being that notice be given to the INS.[38] Equality before the law is guaranteed under the equal protection clause of the Fourteenth Amendment and the due process clause of the Fifth Amendment.[39]

Refugees and asylees have the right to acquire and to own movable property, including intangible property, and real property, subject to limitations in a few states as to the amount of real property that can be owned by aliens. The right of alien inventors to obtain patents is subject to a limitation that a patent for an invention "made" in a territory hostile to the United States may not be issued to a national of the country unless permited by the Attorney General.[40]

Persons who have been admitted to the United States as refugees under conditional entrant status or as asylees are authorized to be employed immediately upon approval of their status. For most occupations, such authorization suffices to enable the refugee/asylee to seek employment. However, eligibility varies as to occupations for which local, state, or federal licensing or permission are required.

An Executive Order by the President forbids the employment of aliens, including refugees, in the competitive Civil Service of the federal government.[41] State prohibitions on the employment of aliens, including refugees, as public schoolteachers and as police officers have been upheld by the Supreme Court.[42] Many states prohibit the employment of aliens in various occupations ranging from that of an accountant to that of a veterinarian.[43] However, such statutory prohibitions are of doubtful constitutionality as applied to aliens who have been granted permanent residence, since a 1973 Supreme Court decision invalidating a state law that required attorneys to be U.S. citizens.[44]

Government benefits, including public education, protective labor legislation, social security, housing assistance, public relief, and welfare are generally available to refugees and asylees as they are to citizens. There are limits and exceptions,[45] but there are also special refugee programs. These programs provide reimbursement to state and local governments for all cash welfare and medical costs for refugees who have been in the United States for less than three years; for grants to voluntary social service agencies to assist them in resettling refugees in the United States; and for funding English language programs, vocational training, and employment counseling and job placement programs for refugees.[46]

Observations

While the laws and regulations described above provide a legal framework for the rights of persons seeking refuge and asylum in the United States, the determination of who is entitled to refugee and asylee status is conspicuously inconsistent. For example, a high-income ballerina with no previous evidence of the likelihood of persecution in the Soviet Union is granted immediate refugee status; a poverty-stricken Haitian who has been punished capriciously by the *ton-ton macoutes* is not. An ethnic, irreligious Jew from the USSR may be accepted without the need to show that he, individually, has a reasonable fear of persecution; a religious Jew from Ayatollah Khomeini's Iran is found not to have established a reasonable fear of persecution because the Iranian constitution provides freedom of worship to minority religions, including Judaism.[47] While the State Department has held, with regard to Haitians, that one does not qualify for asylum merely by showing that serious human rights abuses exist in the home country and that an applicant must instead show "that he is likely to be singled out as a victim of such abuses," boatloads of escapees from Vietnam are permitted to enter the United States as refugees without the need for such individualized evidence.

As this chapter is written, the rights of refugees are in flux. The President of the United States has authorized the "interdiction" of vessels carrying Haitians who intend to apply for asylum in the United States, providing for shipboard interviews to determine whether the fleeing Haitian nationals may have a well-founded fear of persecution. Those whose claims are not accepted by INS officers will be returned forthwith to Haiti. Such a procedure, of course, precludes the assistance of voluntary social service agencies, the UNHCR, or of counsel, as well as the right of appeal for those persons whose claims are rejected.

Legislation is also pending to revise the procedures now available to applicants for asylum within the U.S. The proposed legislation would provide for summary exclusion of persons seeking asylum and sharply limited judicial review of such decisions.[49]

Conclusion

The office of the UN High Commissioner for Refugees was awarded the Nobel Prize for Peace in 1981, the second time the UNHCR has been so honored. The award highlights not only the UNHCR's excellent work, but also the fact that refugees and/or displaced persons constitute a major problem facing many members of the world community—many of them ill-equipped to assume the additional technical and financial burdens of large numbers of refugees.

The protection of the rights of refugees is a curious combination of broad international norms and often extremely detailed domestic legislation. At both levels, political considerations loom paramount in individual cases (a Soviet ballerina or Czech tennis player in the United States) as well as in situations of mass exodus (Afghanistan, the Middle East, Southeast Asia, the "freedom flotilla" of Cubans into the United States).

It should be well noted that neither international nor domestic law provides a right of *entry* into any particular country to a refugee. Rather, the norm is a negative one, only prohibiting the return of a refugee to a country in which he or she may face persecution. Where the country of origin and the country of refuge share a common border, the difference may be negligible; in other cases—for example, Salvadoran refugees attempting to enter the United States at the Mexican border—the distinction may have a significant effect on the legal obligations of the countries concerned.

As the focus shifts from individuals fleeing political or religious persecution to great numbers of persons fleeing war, poverty, and instability, the human rights principles upon which the 1951 Convention and other instruments are based become less important than political and economic considerations. At the domestic level, pleas for equality of treatment among different refugee groups founder on fundamental political disagreements, which often masquerade as legal or procedural issues.

These and other considerations distinguish refugee questions from most of the other "human rights" issues and procedures discussed in this book, although the rights concerned are certainly no less important. Because of the well-developed refugee law in the United States and many other countries, actual refugee cases can be brought by specialized lawyers who generally are not available to assist in the other procedures described herein. The average human rights practitioner and NGO will generally be more concerned with documenting the causes and facts of repression and persecution that have created refugees in, for example, El Salvador, Haiti, Iran, Afghanistan, and the Soviet Union.

The Biblical injunction which opens this chapter reflects a concern that is thousands of years old. In a sense, the existence of refugees is unfortunate testimony to the violation of human rights around the world. By addressing those volations, we may eventually avoid the need for separate discussion of how to treat victims seeking to escape persecution.

Notes

1. *Asylum, Right of,* in RELIGIOUS ENCYCLOPEDIA 337 (1945).

2. Wright, *Asylum,* in 1 ENCYCLOPEDIA OF SOC. SCI. 595–97 (1949).

3. *Asylum,* in 2 ENCYCLOPAEDIA BRITANNICA 82 (11th ed. 1911).

4. M. MARGOLIS and A. MERT, A HISTORY OF THE JEWISH PEOPLE 384 *et*

seq., 501 *et seq.* (1977); C.D. DARLINGTON, THE EVOLUTION OF MAN AND SO-CIETY 456–71 (1969).

5. DARLINGTON, *supra* note 4, at 488–90.

6. Heinrich Böll, quoted in W. S. MOONEYMAN, SEA OF HEARTBREAK 207 (1980).

7. Beyer, *The Political Refugee: 35 Years Later*, 15 INT'L MIGRATION REV. 26 (1981).

8. UNITED STATES COMMITTEE FOR REFUGEES, 1981 WORLD REFUGEE SURVEY 32–33 (1981) (hereinafter cited as 1981 SURVEY).

9. This brief historical survey is from A. GRAHL-MADSEN, 1 THE STATUS OF REFUGEES IN INTERNATIONAL LAW 10–11(1966) (hereinafter cited as STATUS OF REFUGEES). *See also* Harvard Law School, Research in International Law, *Extradition, Jurisdiction with respect to Crime, Law of Treaties*, 26 AM. J. INT'L L. (Supp. 1935); Evans, *The New Extradition Treaty of the United States*, 59 AM. J. INT'L L. 351 (1965).

10. These League of Nations actions are discussed in L. HOLBORN, REFUGEES: A PROBLEM OF OUR TIME 6–43 (1975).

11. Convention relating to the Status of Refugees, 189 U.N.T.S. 137, *reprinted in* HUMAN RIGHTS, A COMPILATION OF INTERNATIONAL INSTRUMENTS, UN Doc. ST/HR/1/Rev. 1, UN sales no. E.78.XIV.2, at 86 (1978) (hereinafter cited as 1951 Convention).

12. Protocol relating to the Status of Refugees, 606 U.N.T.S. 267, *reprinted in* UN COMPILATION, *supra* note 11 at 93.

13. 1951 Convention, art. 1.

14. This and the following interpretations are drawn largely from OFFICE OF THE UN HIGH COMMISSIONER FOR REFUGEES, HANDBOOK ON PROCEDURES AND CRITERIA FOR DETERMINING REFUGEE STATUS (1979) (hereinafter cited as HANDBOOK) and STATUS OF REFUGEES, note 9 *supra*.

15. STATUS OF REFUGEES at 286.

16. Executive Committee of the High Commissioner's Programme, *Report on the 31st Session, Note on Procedures for the Determination of Refugee Status under International Instruments*, UN Doc. A/AC.96/INF.152/Rev.2 (1980).

17. Executive Committee of the High Commissioner's Programme, *Report on the 28th Session, Conclusions on International Protection*, UN Doc. A/32/12/Add. 1 (1977) at 12–16.

18. 1951 Convention, arts. 31, 32, 33.

19. OAU Doc. CM/267/Rev.1, *reprinted in* 8 INT'L LEGAL MATERIALS 1288 (1969). See also S. AMAIZE AIBONI, PROTECTION OF REFUGEES IN AFRICA (1978).

20. OAU Convention, *supra* note 19, arts. II(1) and II(3).

21. *Id.*, art. I(2).

22. *Id.*, arts. II(2) and III(2).

23. *Id.*, art. II(6).

24. OAS Treaty Series No. 36, at 1, *reprinted in* OAS HANDBOOK OF EXISTING RULES PERTAINING TO HUMAN RIGHTS, OAS Doc. OEA/SER.L/VII.50, doc. 6 (1980).

25. Much of the following material is taken from *Note on Procedures*, note 16 *supra*.

26. 1981 SURVEY.

27. Pub. L. No. 96–212, 94 Stat. 109 (1980), codified at 8 U.S.C. § 1157 (Supp. 1981) (hereinafter cited as Refugee Act of 1980).

28. *Id.*, sec. 201.

29. *Id.*, sec. 207(C)(3).

30. *Id.* See also 8 U.S.C. § 1182 (a) (27) and (29).

31. 140,000 refugee admissions were proposed for fiscal year 1982, allocated as follows: Asia, 100,000 (of which all but 200 are Indochinese); Soviet Union and Eastern Europe, 29,000; Near East, 5,000; Africa, 3,000; Latin American and the Caribbean, 3,000. 46 Fed. Reg. 55233 (1981).

32. In addition to the Refugee Act of 1980, the basic texts are contained in INS regulations set forth in 8 C.F.R. Parts 207–09 (1981).

33. 8 C.F.R. Parts 207, 209 (1981). One might query whether these additional sponsorship requirements are consistent with the spirit of the Refugee Act of 1980 or international standards. [Ed. note]

34. The major voluntary social service organizations that assist refugees include the American Council for Nationalities Services, Church World Service, Hebrew Immigrant Aid Society, International Rescue Committee, Lutheran Immigration and Refugee Service, and the U.S. Catholic Conference. *See* J.V, TAFT *et al.* REFUGEE RESETTLEMENT IN THE UNITED STATES 39–42 (1979).

35. 8 C.F.R. § 207.5 (1981).

36. Department of State, *Interim Guidelines for Processing of Refugee Applications by Consular Officers*, 81 State [Telegram] 11652 (27 Mar. 1981). Again, one might query whether this anticommunist bias is consistent with the spirit of either the Convention or the Refugee Act. [Ed. note]

37. Bridges v. California, 314 U.S. 252 (1941).

38. Mathews v. Diaz, 426 U.S. 67 (1935).

39. D. CARLINER, THE RIGHTS OF ALIENS (1979).

40. *Id.*

41. 29 Fed. Reg. 37 (1976).

42. Ambach v. Norwick, 441 U.S. 68 (1979); Foley v. Connelie, 435 U.S. 291 (1978).

43. RIGHTS OF ALIENS, *supra* note 39 at 205–55, App. D.

44. *In re* Griffiths, 413 U.S. 717 (1973).

45. *E.g.*, hospital costs for certain persons over sixty-five and others over seventy-two who have not had the required social security insurance coverage are not available to refugees or asylees. 42 U.S.C. § 426(a) (4) (1974, Supp. 1981), § 428(a) (3) (1974).

46. Refugee Act of 1980, Title III.

47. Letter by P. Peter Sarros, Acting Assistant Deputy Secretary of State of Human Rights and Humanitarian Affairs, to Wallace Gray, District Director, Immigration and Naturalization Service, 16 Sept. 1981.

48. *Hearings Before the Subcomm. on Immigration of the House Comm. on the Judiciary*, 96th Cong., 2d Sess. (17 June 1980) (statement of Stephen E. Palmer, Jr., Deputy Assistant Secretary of State for Human Rights and Humanitarian Affairs). *See* Dept. of State, Current Policy No. 191, *Haitian Migration to the U.S.*, at 4.

49. The Immigration Reform and Control Act of 1983, Title I, part C, S.529, H.R. 1810, 98th Cong. 1st Sess.

15

Domestic Human Rights Advocacy: Strategies for Influencing Governmental Policy

JOSEPH T. ELDRIDGE

Under articles 55 and 56 of the UN charter, all states have an international obligation to promote and protect human rights and fundamental freedoms. In a few countries, such as the United States and the Netherlands, domestic legislation also may require the promotion of human rights to be part of foreign policy.[1] More often than not, however, governments will ignore the human rights practices of another state in favor of political, economic, or national security considerations when formulating foreign policy. The introduction of human rights concerns into the conduct of foreign affairs is a relatively recent development, as promotion of the rights of citizens of another country was traditionally considered to be beyond the legitimate interests of a foreign government. In any event, it usually falls to the private or nongovernmental sector to pressure the government to express concern over human rights in other countries.

Influencing the government's foreign policy to reflect concern for human rights can be undertaken in a variety of political, economic, or social contexts; in addition, access to the government's decision-making process varies greatly from country to country. The present chapter considers techniques for promoting human rights through influencing foreign policy. The United States provides a good example of many of these techniques, and they may be applicable, perhaps with variations, to other countries in which active participation in the political process is possible.

The Political Context and Nongovernmental Organizations

"Human rights" are, by definition, international and universal, but strategies for their promotion in the United States must be firmly grounded in an understanding of the domestic political context of decision making within the U.S. government. The system of "checks and balances" among the executive, legislative, and judicial branches of government established by the U.S. Constitution has resulted in an enormously complex, often competing, network of governmental departments, committees, and agencies. Each branch of the government reflects its own internal institutional dynamics and responds to its own external constituencies (which include the sometimes conflicting demands of one or both of the other two branches). The result is often a puzzling array of procedures and possibilities, which human rights advocates need to understand.

Reflecting the complexity of the federal government and American society, a vast and diverse collection of nongovernmental interest groups (NGOs) will intervene whenever their interests are considered by governmental bodies. These NGOs are as varied as their constituencies, and they range from well-financed business and trade organizations to labor unions, religious bodies, "public interest" consumer groups, and diverse human rights organizations. Some influence government through their financial strength, others through grass-roots organizations that can muster voter support or opposition; many persuade primarily by technical and substantive education of their governmental targets, emphasizing the merits of their own position.

The primary focus of the NGO's work is to establish contacts with information gatherers and policy makers at all levels and in all three branches of government, impart well-documented evidence, and present persuasive arguments that concern for human rights serves the immediate political, economic, or strategic goals with which the person approached is concerned.

The Administration

Conduct of foreign affairs within the U.S. system of government is traditionally a function of the executive branch. The primary policy makers in this area are the President (and the White House staff) and the Department of State, but others are involved with important aspects of foreign policy and should not be ignored. These secondary or more specialized bodies whose foreign affairs activities may affect human rights include the Departments of Treasury, Commerce, Justice, and Defense, the White House's National Security Council, and the various components of the intelligence community (including the Central Intelligence Agency and the Defense Intelligence Agency).

It is important to contact these secondary (in human rights terms) institutions with respect to particular issues relevant to them—for example, refugee policies are largely decided by the Immigration and Naturalization Service within the Justice Department; many decisions on international loans or the granting of preferred trading status are made within the Treasury and Commerce Departments; and the provision of military assistance and weapons is obviously a function of the Defense Department. However, the most accessible and directly relevant institutions to the human rights advocate are the Department of State and, to a lesser extent, the White House.

Policy deliberations in the White House are conducted primarily by the National Security Council (NSC), whose members are all political appointees. They are assigned either functional or geographical responsibilities and, as a rule, tend to be more influenced by the purely political implications of decisions than is the Department of State. Not surprisingly, "security" concerns are paramount, and effective human rights advocacy (which most often will take the form of informal communications with the NSC staff member responsible for either global issues or a particular region) requires that discussions be oriented toward the compatibility of the promotion of human rights with long-term U.S. strategic considerations.

The State Department is headed by several dozen political appointees, in addition to those designated as U.S. ambassadors abroad, supported by assistants and deputy assistants. The great majority of those within the Department, however, are career civil servants or foreign service officers who generally provide continuity and support for whatever broad policies are decided at the top, even if their duties may shift with changing administrations. It is these career professionals who are most often the focus of NGO lobbying efforts and to whom most information is directed.

The Department is divided along both functional and geographic lines. The bureaus of European, African, East Asian and Pacific, Inter-American, and Near Eastern and South Asian Affairs are each headed by an Assistant Secretary of State, and each country is usually assigned a specific "desk officer" who follows its affairs. Knowing these desk officers is essential for those NGOs with a relatively narrow country or regional focus.

Functionally, the most important interdepartmental bureau is the Bureau of Human Rights and Humanitarian Affairs, which is discussed below. In addition, there is an attorney with specific human rights responsibilities within the Legal Adviser's Office, and human rights concerns often arise in the Office of Refugee Affairs and the Bureau of International Organization Affairs. Finally, a "human rights officer" (who usually has other responsibilities, as well) may be designated in each U.S. embassy.

Policy directives flow from the top down, and "policy" as such is not made below the Assistant Secretary level. If human rights are not in favor at the top, concern with human rights among those charged with implementing policy at the bottom will likely cease.

But while the professional foreign service staff primarily implement policy, they also are responsbile for providing the information and analyses upon which ultimate policy decisions are based. Information gathering is never a neutral activity, and influencing and contributing to this process should be one of the primary goals of human rights advocates. Access to information is often a source of power in Washington, and the area of human rights is no exception. Personal contacts with embassy personnel abroad or foreign service officers in Washington may indicate the kind of information being received in Washington or result in requests to NGOs by the Department for information to supplement or confirm that which has been received from other sources. Once information is channeled by a NGO to the State Department, follow-up contacts are often possible that may lead to a continuing dialogue.

The obvious focus of human rights activity in the State Department is the Bureau of Human Rights and Humanitarian Affairs. This formalization of human rights functions within the Department was due to congressional initiatives, which resulted in designation of a Coordinator for Human Rights and Humanitarian Affairs in 1977 and subsequent upgrading of the position to that of an Assistant Secretary in 1978. The Assistant Secretary is responsible for maintaining "continuous observation and review of all matters pertaining to human rights," including the gathering of "detailed information . . . regarding the observance of and respect for internationally recognized human rights" relevant to human rights restrictions on U.S. security and economic assistance.[2] Among the Bureau's most important specific responsibilities is preparation of the annual "country reports" on human rights conditions in all UN member states, which include consideration of "the relevant findings of appropriate international organizations, including nongovernmental organizations, . . . and the extent of cooperation by such government in permitting an unimpeded investigation by any such organization of alleged violations of internationally recognized human rights."[3]

This legislatively mandated responsibility of the Bureau is an excellent focus for human rights NGOs, as both public and private attention can be appropriately focused on the Bureau no matter what the human rights views of a given administration. The Bureau also engages in less public activities that require the active participation and cooperation of NGOs in providing information and prodding the Bureau to take action where U.S. involvement appears to be useful.

All presidential nominees for Assistant Secretary and above must be confirmed by the Senate, and the confirmation process can be utilized as a useful educational tool to stress the importance of human rights. As demonstrated by the defeat of President Reagan's first nominee for Assistant Secretary of State for Human Rights and Humanitarian Affairs in 1981, human rights NGOs also can contribute substantively to the maintenance of human rights as a legitimate component of U.S. foreign policy.

Supplying information and developing personal contacts with the administration are thus essential, even if there are limits on the pressure that can be brought to bear on an administration which desires to downplay or essentially to eliminate human rights issues as major foreign policy concerns.

The Congress

Congressional participation in shaping U.S. foreign policy has increased greatly in the past decade, as the Vietnam War and Watergate ended what acquiescence remained in the legislative branch. In the field of human rights, a series of hearings and reports by a House Subcommittee chaired by then-Congressman Donald Fraser of Minnesota in 1973–74 heralded a new congressional interest and assertion of authority.[4]

One of the most important attributes of Congress is its diversity. In contrast to the executive branch, where priorities are set at the top and administered by a hierarchical bureaucracy, each member of Congress sets his or her own priorities. Among the 535 members, it is not difficult to find a few who will sympathize with or have a particular interest in human rights. Over time, personal relationships can be established, and the political longevity of many members of Congress can become a valuable asset irrespective of changes in the administration.

All members of Congress are attentive to the needs and demands of contituents, and the surest way to instill a concern for human rights issues is to develop grass-roots support for human rights in a congressional district. Where that is not possible (and many NGOs do not have the financial base or organizational skills to create such support), one should attempt to link a specific human rights concern to a constituent or a home district organization, such as a trade union or university. Where such linkage is possible, the "personalization" of human rights may lead to further investigation and greater support for human rights in general.

The Subcommittee on Human Rights and International Organizations of the House Foreign Affairs Committee provides the institutional focus for human rights activity in Congress, parallel to the Human Rights Bureau in the State Department. Most members work extremely diligently; however, an overall state of "issue fatigue" may hamper the human rights activist in capturing a Representative's or Senator's attention. Other lobbyists and constituents are vying for attention, and it is essential that issues be presented to congressional offices in as clear and concise a manner as possible. Once interest is aroused, there will usually be plenty of time for more detailed discussion and information.

The personal and committee staffs do much of the actual work of the Congress and are the main focus of much NGO activity. Rather than viewing the staff as another hurdle to overcome, NGOs should approach staff members as potential allies whose advice and guidance will be sought by the Congressperson. The staff generally write the letters, make the phone calls, and relay the inquiries, and it is not unusual to find a staff person who is initially much more receptive to human rights issues than is the Congressperson.

The most direct congressional impact on human rights has been exercised through the appropriation process. In the past several years Congress has approved several laws that impose various conditions on the expenditure of U.S. foreign assistance funds, and virtually every dollar of U.S. bilateral and multilateral assistance is linked in some way to human rights concerns. While no country has formally been found guilty of a "consistent pattern of gross violations of internationally recognized human rights,"[5] various forms of aid have been denied to countries with egregious human rights conditions. In addition, specific legislation has been adopted (although not all remains in force) concerning Angola, Argentina, Chile,

Cuba, El Salvador, Kampuchea, Laos, Mozambique, South Africa, South Korea, Uganda, Vietnam, and Zaire.[6]

Congressional hearings are the most important forum in which human rights concerns can be raised publicly. They may be held in connection with specific legislation (e.g., the foreign aid authorization bill or a bill to grant most-favored-nation trade status), or they may be informational hearings in which specific countries, regions, or issues may be explored as a prelude to possible future legislation. Both public and government (administration) witnesses often are invited to testify, and such testimony can be an important avenue for NGOs to raise formal and public concerns with respect to human rights. Hearings are also important tools with which to educate members of Congress and their staffs.

While Congress is naturally most accessible to those NGOs based in Washington or New York, concerns can be usefully expressed to home offices as well. A telephone call will often suffice to identify the staff person responsible for human rights in a congressional district office, and letters addressed to him or her (or copies of letters addressed to the Congressperson) will at least be read—even if the answer is received from a computerized typewriter. Ultimately, human rights will become a truly integral issue in the legislative process only if such constituent interest can be developed.

Communications Media

The news media are often considered to constitute a kind of "fourth estate" of influence and power in the United States. Given the evident importance of the federal government internationally and domestically and the desire of most politicians for publicity, it is not surprising that Washington is an extremely media-conscious city. It is a primary communications center that is home to offices of all the major newspapers, radio and television networks, wire services, and foreign media representatives.

The potential for publicity about human rights issues is enormous, but so is the competition for the attention of reporters and editors. Although it is perhaps obvious, it is important to remember that journalists prefer to write about issues which interest them; some will be more sympathetic to human rights generally, or to stories involving particular countries, than others.

While politicians or government officials may become involved in an issue because it is relevant to their job, a journalist will only report a story that is in some sense "news." The mere description of a human rights violation is usually not sufficient to create press interest, although such information may be worth sending to a journalist as background material connected to a past or potential story. What is required is a newsworthy angle or peg on which to hang a story, such as a pending appropriation bill, the visit of a foreign head of state, the report of a mission of inquiry (particularly if the mission included a prominent personality), or truly new information on a major and unique human rights violation (imprisonment of an important political figure, massacres, mass arrests).

A very useful technique is to rally sympathetic leaders to one's cause through the vehicle of an open letter or public declaration—although, again, the more specific and timely the cause, the better. On the other hand, the mere filing of an international complaint before the Inter-American Commission of Human Rights, for example, is unlikely to create much press interest unless the situation is a compelling one. As in other areas of human rights work, one should not underestimate the value of personal relationships, and providing a journalist with reliable information without the expectation of an immediate return is generally worth the effort.

Even if a human rights story is written, publication requires the approval of an editor, and education of editorial staffs is a difficult and gradual process. Contacting editors about the possibility of a short opinion article or letter to the editor is a good idea, even if the article or letter is not published. Reacting to a published piece is somewhat easier than originating an idea, and it reinforces the impression that the subject—human rights—is important and of interest. While critical responses are probably more common, one should also not hesitate to praise a well-written article or support an editorial with which one agrees.

Although press statements may be issued at little cost to the issuing NGO and do serve the purpose of formalizing a NGO's position, calling a press conference should not be undertaken without sufficient advance work and personal contact with journalists to gauge potential interest.

Concluding Observations

The motives and credentials of human rights organizations in the United States are constantly under review, and credibility remains the most important asset of any human rights NGO. Critics from both sides of the political spectrum will attack human rights groups for political bias, whether or not such bias (perhaps attributable to NGO focus on a particular geographical region or kind of right) exists in fact. The only defense to such charges is the accuracy of the information presented, although questions as to why one country is being attacked as a human rights violator rather than another with allegedly more serious problems is an issue that is certainly not confined to the United States.

Domestic human rights work must be viewed against a backdrop of competing interests and conflicting priorities, and it should be remembered that neither foreign affairs in general nor human rights issues in particular are major public concerns. Nevertheless, occasional events do interest the public at large—Jacobo Timmerman's story, the treatment of major Soviet dissidents such as Andrei Sakharov, the trial of Kim Dae Jung, the continuing conflict in El Salvador—and government officials outside the traditional channels of foreign policy-making may become involved in such issues in response to constituent interest and public pressure.

Nevertheless, human rights must compete for an official's time with what may seem to be much more pressing domestic issues, and the "payoff" of human rights activism is seldom immediate or tangible. Even where human rights are accepted as an appropriate concern of the individual or agency approached, problems and requests for governmental action should be formulated as carefully as possible in order to present the decision maker with a relatively simple issue.

Human rights advocacy is not conducted in a vacuum, and human rights issues are perceived as being inherently political by most Washington observers. Indeed, human rights *is* "political" insofar as it addresses the relationship between the government and the governed, but it is important that human rights advocates not be identified as partisans in the domestic political context. This is not always easy, as the extent to which human rights is a component of foreign policy decision-making has been questioned by the Republican Reagan administration and contrasted to the strong human rights rhetoric of the Democratic Carter administration. It would not be helpful if human rights policies became a partisan political issue.

Human rights advocacy occurs within a particular context, and this chapter can only offer general guidelines as to forms of possible activity within the U.S. political system. The goals and politics of the NGO, and even legal considerations that limit the "lobbying" of tax-exempt organizations, also play a role in determining strategies for approaching governments.

Effective advocacy requires commitment, imagination, and perseverance, and the creative aspects of human rights work are perhaps more evident in attempting to influence governments than in successfully negotiating the procedures described elsewhere in this book. The suggestions contained in this chapter are only an introduction, and experimentation and innovation are essential to translate concerns into action.

Notes

1. *See, e.g.* U.S. LEGISLATION RELATING HUMAN RIGHTS TO U.S. FOREIGN POLICY (International Human Rights Law Group ed., 3d ed. 1982) for a compilation of such statutes. *See also* Cohen, *Conditioning U.S. Security Assistance on Human Rights Practices*, 75 AM. J. INT'L. L. 246 (1982).

2. Sec. 624(f) of the Foreign Assistance Act of 1961, as amended by Pub. L. No. 95–105, 91 Stat. 846 (1978) and Pub. L. No. 94–329, 90 Stat. 750 (1976), codified at 22 U.S.C. sec. 2384(f)(1979). *Cf.* Weissbrodt, *Human Rights Legislation and U.S. Foreign Policy*, 7 GA. J. INT'L & COMP. L. 231 (1977).

3. Secs. 116(d) and 502B(b) of the Foreign Assistance Act of 1961, as amended, 22 U.S.C. secs. 2151n, 2304 (1974, Supp. 1981).

4. *See, e.g., Human Rights in the World Community: A Call for U.S. Leadership: Report of the Subcomm. on International Organizations and Movements of the House Comm. on Foreign Affairs*, 93d Cong., 2d Sess. 1 (1974); *cf.* Weissbrodt, *supra* note 2 at 232–40.

5. Sec. 116 of the Foreign Assistance Act, note 3 *supra*.

6. U.S. LEGISLATION, note 1 *supra*.

APPENDIXES

Appendix A
Bibliographic Note

An extensive annotated bibliography is not only beyond the scope of the present guide, but it is likely to be of only limited value to most practitioners directly concerned with alleviating human rights abuses. This brief note therefore focuses only on the essential, largely official documents of which the practitioner should be aware.

For a more exhaustive survey of the literature available on particular aspects of human rights law, two excellent bibliographic essays are available:

Diana Vincent-Davis, *Human Rights Law: A Research Guide to the Literature: Part I, International Law and the United Nations*, 14 N.Y.U. JOURNAL OF INTERNATIONAL LAW & POLITICS 209 (1981), and *Part II: International Protection of Refugees, and Humanitarian Law*, 14 N.Y.U. J. INT'L L. & POL. 487 (1982) (*Part III* to follow); and

Thomas H. Reynolds, *Highest Aspirations or Barbarous Acts . . . The Explosion in Human Rights Documentation: A Bibliographic Survey*, 71 LAW LIBRARY JOURNAL 1 (No. 1, 1978).

Two recent publications that focus specifically on international procedures for the protection of human rights are:

MAX TARDU, HUMAN RIGHTS: THE INTERNATIONAL PETITION SYSTEM (3 vols., 1979–); and

Symposium: International Human Rights, 20 SANTA CLARA LAW REVIEW (No. 3, 1980).

Among the professional journals that regularly devote space to human rights issues, mention should be made of:

The editor expresses his appreciation to Kevin Boyle, Richard Greenfield, and Robert Norris for some of the material included in this note.

BULLETIN OF HUMAN RIGHTS (Geneva; published irregularly by the UN Human Rights Centre);

HUMAN RIGHTS JOURNAL (Paris; published irregularly);

HUMAN RIGHTS LAW JOURNAL (Kehl/Rhein, Federal Republic of Germany; Strasbourg, France; and Arlington, Virginia; began publication in 1980);

HUMAN RIGHTS QUARTERLY (edited by the Urban Morgan Institute for Human Rights at the University of Cincinnati; formerly UNIVERSAL HUMAN RIGHTS);

HUMAN RIGHTS REVIEW (London; primarily European materials); and

REVIEW OF THE INTERNATIONAL COMMISSION OF JURISTS (Geneva; useful summaries of major UN meetings).

Many collections of human rights documents have been published, although none includes the entire range of conventions, declarations, and resolutions discussed in this guide. Such a compilation, in photocopied form, may be obtained from the International Human Rights Law Group in Washington, D.C. The best commercially available collections are:

RICHARD B. LILLICH, INTERNATIONAL HUMAN RIGHTS INSTRUMENTS (William S. Hein, 1983);

IAN BROWNLIE, BASIC DOCUMENTS ON HUMAN RIGHTS (Oxford, 2d ed. 1981); and

HUMAN RIGHTS: A COMPILATION OF INTERNATIONAL INSTRUMENTS, UN Sales No. E..78.XIV.2 (1978).

The notes following deal primarily with official documents issued by intergovernmental organizations and include the major collections of human rights texts, procedural rules, and relevant official reports.

United Nations

UN documents are organized by a system of code numbers and letters, with a different code assigned to each organ and suborgan within the UN system. In addition to identifying the body in which the document was issued, the code also identifies the kind of documents, e.g., resolution, summary record, NGO statement, etc. While the entire system appears complex, a knowledge of the basic codes that may be relevant to human rights is essential to an easy understanding of the human rights material available within the UN system.

Following is a partial list of UN codes that are likely to be of use in human rights work:

General Assembly

A/	Document for plenary
A/INF	Information paper for the General Assembly
A/RES	General Assembly Resolution
A/C.1 through C.6, A/SEC, A/BLR	These are the main committees of the General Assembly. The Third Committee (A/C.3) considers social, humanitarian, and cultural matters, including human rights; the Sixth Committee deals with legal matters. These documents are issued only during Assembly sessions.
A/AC.109	Special Committee on Colonialism
A/AC.115	Special Committee on Apartheid
A/AC.131	Council for Namibia
A/AC.160	Committee on International Terrorism

Economic and Social Council

E/	Document for ECOSOC plenary
E/INF	Information papers for ECOSOC
E/RES	Economic and Social Council Resolution
E/C.2	Committee on Non-Governmental Organizations
E/CN.4	Commission on Human Rights
E/CN.4/Sub.2	Sub-Commission on Prevention of Discrimination and Protection of Minorities
E/CN.5	Commission for Social Development
E/CN.6	Commission on Status of Women

Other Major Organs

DC/	Disarmament Commission
S/	Security Council
ST/	Secretariat
T/	Trusteeship Council

Covenant on Civil and Political Rights

CCPR/C	Human Rights Committee
CCPR/SP	Meetings of the states parties

International Covenant on Economic, Social and Economic Rights

E/   Sessional Working Group of ECOSOC

International Convention on the Elimination of All Forms of Racial Discrimination

CERD/C   Committee on the Elimination of Racial Dis-
                                      crimination

Functional codes

——/Add.	Addendum
——/CONF.	Conference
——/Corr.	Corrigendum
——/L.	Document with limited distribution (often draft resolutions or reports, generally available only at the time of issue)
——/NGO	Document submitted by a nongovernmental organization
——PR.	Press release
——/R.	Document with restricted distribution (not generally available to NGOs or individuals)
——/Rev.	Revision
——/SR.	Summary records
——/WG.	Working group

Each of the major UN bodies concerned with human rights publishes an ANNUAL REPORT of its activities. The reports of the *Human Rights Committee* and the *Committee on the Elimination of Racial Discrimination* are issued as supplements to the official records of the General Assembly; the report of the *Commission on Human Rights* is issued as a supplement to the official records of ECOSOC; and the report of the *Sub-Commission on Prevention of Discrimination and Protection of Minorities* is issued as both a Sub-Commission (E/CN.4/Sub.2/—) and Commission (E/CN.4/—) document.

One of the best and least expensive collections of human rights texts (although it excludes regional conventions) is HUMAN RIGHTS: A COMPILATION OF INTERNATIONAL INSTRUMENTS, cited above. UNITED NATIONS ACTION IN THE FIELD OF HUMAN RIGHTS, UN Sales No. E.79.XIV.6

(1980), is a somewhat turgid but fairly extensive survey of UN activities since 1945. The UN's YEARBOOK ON HUMAN RIGHTS (published annually from 1946 until 1972, and biennially thereafter) tends to be badly out of date when it appears and is not of great value to the human rights practitioner.

The Inter-American System

The essential document for those filing human rights complaints within the structure of the Organization of American States is the HANDBOOK OF EXISTING RULES PERTAINING TO HUMAN RIGHTS (1980), OAS Doc. OEA/ Ser.L/V/II.50, doc. 6. The Handbook contains the texts of the American Convention on Human Rights, the Statute and Regulations of the Inter-American Commission on Human Rights, and the Statute of the Inter-American Court, and it is updated periodically.

In addition to the Handbook, the basic documents are the Commission's ANNUAL REPORT TO THE GENERAL ASSEMBLY, individual country reports, and the INTER-AMERICAN YEARBOOK ON HUMAN RIGHTS. The Annual Report (published since 1971) contains examples of resolutions taken in individual cases and short reports on the situation of human rights in member states that have previously come under the Commission's scrutiny. The country reports contain a more detailed analysis of the state of human rights in a particular country, but not all of the members of the OAS have been the subject of a special report. The most recent (1974–81) country reports include Argentina, Bolivia, Chile, Columbia, Cuba, El Salvador, Guatemala, Haiti, Nicaragua, Panama, Paraguay, and Uruguay. The Inter-American Yearbook presently consists of only four volumes, covering the years 1960–67, 1968, 1969–70, and 1971–81.

The minutes and most of the relevant documents of the Conference of San Jose (at which the Convention was drafted) are available in Spanish only in *Conferencia Especializada Interamericana sobre Derechos Humanos, Actas y Documentos*, OAS Off. Rec. OEA/Ser.K/XVI/1.2. The history of the draft Convention is summarized in English in the 1968 volume of the Yearbook referred to above.

HUMAN RIGHTS: THE INTER-AMERICAN SYSTEM (Oceana, 1982–83), edited by Judge Thomas Buergenthal of the Inter-American Court of Human Rights, and Robert Norris, consists of three looseleaf binders, which contain, respectively, basic documents, documents relating to the legislative history of the American Convention, and a collection of cases and decisions of the Inter-American Commission.

All of the official OAS documents are available through the Department of Publications of the OAS in Washington, D.C.

The European System

The texts of the European Convention and its Protocols, the Rules of Procedure of the European Commission and Court, the current status of ratifications, and other information are contained in the Council of Europe publication COLLECTED TEXTS, which is updated periodically and is an essential reference tool. Commission decisions (on admissibility and on the merits) are first published separately in soft-cover format, and most are also collected in DECISIONS AND REPORTS (which replaces the previous COLLECTION OF DECISIONS), which appears several times a year. Court decisions are published separately; Series A contains the Court's judgments and decisions, and Series B contains pleadings, oral arguments, and documents. Selections of both Commission and Court materials are published in the YEARBOOK OF THE EUROPEAN CONVENTION ON HUMAN RIGHTS, which also contains information on other Council of Europe activities in the field of human rights and references to the Convention in national parliaments and courts.

The Commission publishes an ANNUAL REVIEW, which summarizes the activities of each session, a very helpful bi-annual analysis of developing jurisprudence entitled STOCK-TAKING ON THE EUROPEAN CONVENTION ON HUMAN RIGHTS, and occasional brief surveys entitled CASE-LAW TOPICS. The Council of Europe publishes a series of occasional booklets on specific topics or rights entitled HUMAN RIGHTS FILES. These have thus far included *Human Rights in Prison* (1971); *Family Life* (1972); *Bringing an Application before the European Commission of Human Rights* (1972); *The Right to Liberty and the Rights of Persons Deprived of Their Liberty as Guaranteed by Article 5 of the European Convention on Human Rights* (1981); and *Conditions of Detention and the European Convention on Human Rights and Fundamental Freedoms* (1981). Finally, the Council of Europe has published a BIBLIOGRAPHY ON THE EUROPEAN CONVENTION ON HUMAN RIGHTS (1978).

All of the above publications are available in English and French from the Council of Europe, Strasbourg, France.

Appendix B

Checklist to Help Select the Most Appropriate Forum

The following series of questions is designed to elicit the basic information that one needs in order to decide what courses of action might be most appropriate to redress a particular human rights violation. Used in conjunction with the similar issues raised in the Model Communication which immediately follows the Checklist, an individual or NGO should be able to make a preliminary assessment of what forums might be available to address the human rights concern; reference should then be made to the detailed substantive chapters in parts II and III.

I. In *which country* did the violations occur?
   A. Is it a *party to* any human rights or other relevant *treaties*?
     1. Universal—International Convenant on Civil and Political Rights and Optional Protocol? International Covenant on Economic, Social and Cultural Rights? International Labor Organization conventions? Convention on the Elimination of All Forms of Racial Discrimination? Apartheid Convention? Convention and Protocol on the Status of Refugees?
     2. Regional—European Convention on Human Rights (including acceptance of the right of individual petition under article 25)? American Convention on Human Rights?
   B. Is it a country of *special interest to international bodies*?
     1. South Africa?
     2. Israel-occupied territories?
     3. Bolivia?
     4. Chile?
     5. El Salvador?
     6. Guatemala?
     7. Subject of a current study by the Inter-American Commission on Human Rights?
   C. To which *international organizations* does the country belong?
     1. United Nations?

      2. UNESCO?

      3. International Labor Organization?

      4. Organization of American States?

      5. European Economic Community?

  D. If not a party to any relevant conventions, a state may still be held responsible under such procedures as ECOSOC Resolution 1503 for violations of rights set forth in the Universal Declaration of Human Rights or other widely accepted norms such as prohibitions against torture, genocide, slavery, apartheid, or discrimination.

II. *What rights* have been violated? Are they the subjects of specialized conventions, agencies, or procedures?

  A. Trade union rights or freedom of association? (ILO)

  B. Cultural, educational, social, or scientific freedom? (UNESCO)

  C. Racial discrimination? (Committee on Racial Discrimination)

  D. Disappearance of the victim? (Human Rights Commission Working Group)

  E. Slaverylike practices? (Sub-Commission Working Group)

  F. Prison conditions? (Standard Minimum Rules)

III. Is the victim a victim of an *individual violation* or of a widespread *pattern of violations*?

  A. If an *individual* violation, who is complaining?

    1. Victim himself or herself?

    2. Relative or legal representative?

    3. nongovernmental organization or person unconnected to the victim?

    4. If not connected to the victim, what is the basis for the complaint on his or her behalf?

    5. Does the NGO have direct and/or reliable knowledge of the alleged violations?

  B. If a *widespread* violation, there may be no requirement to exhaust domestic remedies (see below), but communications which seek to raise broad issues rather than to redress individual complaints can be raised by individuals or NGOs (as opposed to governments) only under ECOSOC Resolution 1503 ("consistent pattern of gross violations"), the relevant ILO conventions (available only to recognized employers' or employees' groups), the procedures of the Inter-American Commission on Human Rights, or submitted to specialized UN bodies such as the working group on disappearances of the Human Rights Commission, the working group on slavery of the Sub-Commission on Prevention of Discrimination and Protection of Minorities, and the special rapporteurs or committees concerned with Bolivia, Chili, El Salvador, Guatemala, the Israeli-occupied territories, and southern Africa.

IV. What steps have been taken to obtain *redress at the domestic* (national) *level*?

  A. Are there effective administrative or judicial procedures available?

  B. If so, have they been fully exhausted?

    1. As noted (question III), those procedures which address country sit-

uations involving large-scale violations, as well as noncomplaint procedures such as UN rapporteurs or working groups, do *not* generally require prior exhaustion of domestic remedies.

    2.Individual complaint procedures—e.g., under the European Convention on Human Rights—*do* generally require exhaustion.

V. What *remedy* is sought?

    A. Publicity only?

    B. Investigation?

    C. Changes in national legislation?

    D. Individual remedies?

        1. Protection, release from detention?

        2. Specific redress—e.g., compensation, granting of exit permit or visa, change in civil status?

    E. Even confidential procedures may create diplomatic pressure on a responsive government, and they may have a greater chance of resolving individual cases than more public procedures. In the case of widespread violations, however, maximum publicity may be more important than the quiet or partial resolution of only a few individual cases.

VI. Can *more than one procedure* be utilized at the same time? Is the same situation appropriate for treatment as both an individual complaint and an investigation into a pattern or practice of violations?

VII. What *resources* are available to the complainant?

    A. Are the procedures so complex or the violations so massive that the assistance of a lawyer, NGO, or even a government is essential?

    B. What actual costs (research, photocopying, travel, etc.) are involved?

    C. What political (in a broad sense) resources are available—e.g., help from a friendly government, sympathetic trade union, church group, domestic political groups, journalists, parallel interest groups?

Appendix C
Model Communication

Each procedure discussed in the present book should be examined carefully to ensure that a communication or complaint meets the technical and substantive requirements imposed by that particular system. Several procedures offer a sample form for all complaints, although none (except UNESCO) requires use of any specific form. The relevant forms may be requested from the Organization of American States (contained in the *Handbook of Existing Rules Pertaining to Human Rights*), the Council of Europe *(Bringing an Application before the European Commission on Human Rights)*, UNESCO *(Form for Communications concerning Human Rights to be Submitted to UNESCO)*, and the Human Rights Committee (in care of the UN Human Rights Centre in Geneva, for communications under the Optional Protocol of the Covenant on Civil and Political Rights). No special forms have been developed for other procedures, such as a communication under ECOSOC Resolution 1503 or the various ILO procedures.

The following composite or sample form can be utilized for any of the procedures discussed in this book, with the caveat that attention must be paid to the specific scope of each. For example, some procedures permit any person or NGO to raise questions of human rights violations; others permit only the alleged victim or a direct representative to file a complaint. The requirement to exhaust domestic remedies is common to nearly every procedure, but its interpretation varies considerably.

This form should be used in conjunction with the immediately preceding Checklist of questions as a guide to the proper forum for complaints or communications.

I. *Name of the country* considered responsible for the alleged violation ____

II. *Information concerning the alleged victim(s) of the violations*

Name (in full) _____

Nationality _____

Date and place of birth _____

Occupation _____

Present address _____

_____

Address to be used in correspondance (if different from the above)

_____

_____

_____

[If known, other means of identification such as passport or other identification number should also be included.]

III. If the author of the communication is *not* the same person as the victim
described in II, *the same information should also be provided for the author*

Name (in full) _____

Nationality _____

Date and place of birth _____

Occupation _____

Present address _____

_____

Address to be used in correspondence (if different)

_____

_____

Relationship (if any) to the alleged victim _____

[Any supporting documents which establish a relationship between the victim and the author should be included, e.g., birth certificate, power of
attorney, personal letter authorizing the representative to work on the victim's behalf, etc.

If the author is a nongovernmental organization, a *brief* description of
the organization should be included along with an explanation of why the
NGO is submitting the communication.]

IV. *Human rights allegedly violated*

[Particularly if the communication/complaint is based on a specific international instrument—e.g., the American Convention on Human Rights—
a summary list of the specific articles relevant to the violations is often
helpful. If there is no relevant convention or treaty to which the state is a
party, reference can be made to the Universal Declaration of Human Rights,

the two International Covenants or (in the Americas) the American Declaration of the Rights and Duties of Man.

If the procedure is specialized, e.g., UNESCO or ILO, this section should point out the connection between the alleged violation and the specific areas of interest and competence of the body to which the communication is addressed.]

V. *Statement of the facts*

[If the complaint concerns an *individual* or group of individuals who are the victims of specific violations, a detailed chronological narrative of the incidents that allegedly violated the victim's rights should be set forth. As much specific information as possible should be included, such as the date, time, and place of the incident(s); name, rank, or description of the government official responsible; authority under which the acts took place (laws, regulations, emergency decrees, etc.); place of detention; and the names and addressed of witnesses or others with special knowledge of the events.

If the communication concerns a *widespread practice* of human rights violations or a "consistent pattern of gross violations" of human rights, a brief historical summary of the situation in the country might be set forth as an introduction. If many rights have allegedly been violated (as opposed to focus on a single right or rights, such as the right to form trade unions or freedom of expression) it may be a good idea to include a separate narrative for each right violated (already mentioned in part IV). Again, the information should be as specific as possible and should include the laws or regulations involved; the dates, times, and places of specific incidents; the names of both victims and witnesses; and the type of government involvement (or reasons for holding the government responsible, if it is not evident that government officials were involved).

In either case, the source(s) of the information should be given, and documentation may be included as appendixes or annexes to the communication itself. Such documentation might include press reports, findings or reports of NGOs, texts of laws and regulations, affidavits from victims and witnesses, medical reports, and any other information that supports the allegations. It is best *not* to include general political analyses or materials, unless this is directly relevant to the alleged violations (e.g., the texts of seized documents might be included to demonstrate that they were within the limits of normal political activity and not subversive or a threat to state security).]

VI. *Means of redress attempted*

Domestic: [Any steps taken to obtain redress from domestic authorities should be described in detail, including formal or informal complaints or reports to the police or others; administrative appeals; requests for information about a detainee and the response of the authorities; and judicial remedies, including details as to any actions commenced, type of writ filed (e.g., habeas corpus, amparo), dates and texts of any decisions reached, and the results of any appeal if an appeal is possible.

If no domestic remedies have been attempted or remedies have been only partially exhausted, explain why there are no adequate or effective remedies. This may be due to many factors, e.g., nonexistence of remedies to challenge the law or regulation under which the acts complained of were authorized, existence of a pattern of acts which indicates that any attempt at remedies would be useless, long delays in any redress theoretically available, lack of independence of the judiciary, failure of similar attempts in the past, fear of reprisals, etc.]

International: [Has this complaint or communication been submitted to any other international body for investigation? If so, what is the status of that communication?]

VII. *Purpose of the communication*

[If appropriate, a specific request or prayer for relief may be stated, e.g., permission for access to a detainee by relatives, lawyer, or doctor; release from detention; return of seized materials; investigation by an international body; declaration of violation and request for cessation of a practice or repeal of a law or regulation; or request for appropriate compensation to the victim.]

VIII. *Confidentiality of the communication*

[The author should declare whether he or she wishes any part of the communication to remain confidential, such as the identity of the author, victim, or witnesses. Some procedures, e.g., under UNESCO Decision 104 EX/3.3, require that the author's name be divulged to the government concerned.]

IX. *Signature and date*

[If someone other than the victim is submitting the complaint, the formal representative or NGO officer identified in part III should sign the communication.]

Appendix D

Addresses of Intergovernmental Organizations to Which Human Rights Complaints or Communications Should Be Sent

Communications under ECOSOC Resolution 1503:
    Secretary-General of the United Nations
    Human Rights Centre
    United Nations Office
    Palais des Nations
    1211 Geneva 10
    SWITZERLAND

Communications under the Optional Protocol to the International Covenant on Civil and Political Rights:
    Human Rights Committee
    c/o Human Rights Centre
    United Nations Office
    Palais des Nations
    1211 Geneva 10
    SWITZERLAND

Communications to UNESCO:
    Secretary-General of the United Nations Educational, Scientific and Cultural Organization (UNESCO)
    c/o Division of Human Rights and Peace
    7, place de Fontenoy
    75700 Paris
    FRANCE

Complaints, representations, or other communications to the ILO:
Director-General
International Labor Office
1211 Geneva 22
SWITZERLAND

Individual complaints under article 25 of the European Convention on Human Rights:
Secretary-General of the Council of Europe
c/o European Commission of Human Rights
67006 Strasbourg
FRANCE

Communications concerning members of the Organization of American States:
Inter-American Commission on Human Rights
General Secretariat
Organization of American States
Washington, D.C. 20006
UNITED STATES OF AMERICA

Information concerning human rights directed to the Committee on the Elimination of Racial Discrimination, the Human Rights Committee (with respect to state reports under the Covenant on Civil and Political Rights), the Group of Three established by the Human Rights Commission under the Apartheid Convention, or addressing general matters with in the UN's competence:
Human Rights Centre
United Nations Office
Palais des Nations
1211 Geneva 10
SWITZERLAND

Appendix E
Ratifications of Selected Human Rights Instruments

Adopted under UN Auspices

International Covenant on Civil and Political Rights: Ratifications (as of 31 Dec. 1982)

Australia, Austria[a], Barbados[b], Bolivia[b], Bulgaria, Byelorussian S.S.R., Canada[a,b], Central African Republic[b], Chile, Colombia[b], Costa Rica[b], Cyprus, Czechoslovakia, Denmark[a,b], Dominican Republic[b], Ecuador[b], Egypt, El Salvador, Finland[a,b], France, Gambia, German Democratic Republic, Federal Republic of Germany[a], Guinea, Guyana, Hungary, Iceland[a,b], India, Iran, Iraq, Italy[a,b], Jamaica[b], Japan, Jordan, Kenya, Democratic People's Republic of Korea, Lebanon, Libya, Madagascar[b], Mali, Mauritius[b], Mexico, Mongolia, Morocco, Netherlands[a,b], New Zealand[a], Nicaragua[b], Norway[a,b], Panama[b], Peru[b], Poland, Portugal, Romania, Rwanda, Saint Vincent and the Grenadines[b], Senegal[a,b], Spain, Sri Lanka[a], Suriname[b], Sweden[a,b], Syria, Tanzania, Trinidad and Tobago[b], Tunisia, Ukrainian S.S.R., Union of Soviet Socialist Republics, United Kingdom[a], Uruguay[b], Venezuela[b], Vietnam, Yugoslavia, Zaire[b]

[a] Also has recognized the competence of the Human Rights Committee to hear interstate complaints under article 41.
[b] Also has ratified the Optional Protocol.

International Covenant on Economic, Social and Cultural Rights: Ratifications (as of 31 Dec. 1982)

Australia, Austria, Barbados, Bolivia, Bulgaria, Byelorussian S.S.R., Canada, Central African Republic, Chile, Colombia, Costa Rica, Cyprus, Czechoslovakia, Denmark, Dominican Republic, Ecuador, Egypt, El Salvador, Finland, France, Gambia, German Democratic Republic, Federal Republic of Germany, Guinea, Guyana, Honduras, Hungary, Iceland, India, Iran, Iraq, Italy, Jamaica, Japan,

Jordan, Kenya, Democratic People's Republic of Korea, Lebanon, Libya, Madagascar, Mali, Mauritius, Mexico, Mongolia, Morocco, Netherlands, New Zealand, Nicaragua, Norway, Panama, Peru, Philippines, Poland, Portugal, Romania, Rwanda, Saint Vincent and the Grenadines, Senegal, Solomon Islands, Spain, Sri Lanka, Suriname, Sweden, Syria, Tanzania, Trinidad and Tobago, Tunisia, Ukrainian S.S.R., Union of Soviet Socialist Republics, United Kingdom, Uruguay, Venezuela, Vietnam, Yugoslavia, Zaire

International Convention on the Elimination of All Forms of Racial Discrimination: Ratifications (as of 1 July 1982)

Algeria, Argentina, Australia, Austria, Bahamas, Bangladesh, Barbados, Belgium, Bolivia, Botswana, Brazil, Bulgaria, Burundi, Byelorussian S.S.R., Cameroon, Canada, Cape Verde, Central African Republic, Chad, Chile, China, Colombia, Costa Rica[a], Cuba, Cyprus, Czechoslovakia, Denmark, Ecuador[a], Egypt, El Salvador, Ethiopia, Fiji, Finland, France[a], Gabon, Gambia, German Democratic Republic, Federal Republic of Germany, Ghana, Greece, Guinea, Guyana, Haiti, Holy See, Hungary, Iceland[a], India, Iran, Iraq, Israel, Italy[a], Ivory Coast, Jamaica, Jordan, Republic of Korea, Kuwait, Laos, Lebanon, Lesotho, Liberia, Libya, Luxembourg, Madagascar, Mali, Malta, Mauritius, Mexico, Mongolia, Morocco, Nepal, Netherlands[a], New Zealand, Nicaragua, Niger, Nigeria, Norway[a], Pakistan, Panama, Papua New Guinea, Peru, Philippines, Poland, Qatar, Romania, Rwanda, Saint Vincent and the Grenadines, Senegal[a], Seychelles, Sierra Leone, Solomon Islands, Somalia, Spain, Sri Lanka, Sudan, Swaziland, Sweden[a], Syria, Tanzania, Togo, Tonga, Trinidad and Tobago, Tunisia, Uganda, Ukrainian S.S.R., Union of Soviet Socialist Republics, United Arab Emirates, United Kingdom, Upper Volta, Uruguay[a], Venezuela, Vietnam, Democratic Yemen, Yugoslavia, Zaire, Zambia

[a] Has recognized the right of the Committee to receive individual complaints under article 14.

Convention on the Prevention and Punishment of the Crime of Genocide: Ratifications (as of 1 July 1982)

Afghanistan, Albania, Algeria, Argentina, Australia, Austria, Bahamas, Barbados, Belgium, Brazil, Bulgaria, Burma, Byelorussian S.S.R., Canada, Chile, Colombia, Costa Rica, Cuba, Cyprus, Czechoslovakia, Denmark, Ecuador, Egypt, El Salvador, Ethiopia, Fiji, Finland, France, Gambia, German Democratic Republic, Federal Republic of Germany, Ghana, Greece, Guatemala, Haiti, Honduras, Hungary, Iceland, India, Iran, Iraq, Ireland, Israel, Italy, Jamaica, Jordan, Democratic Kampuchea, Republic of Korea, Laos, Lebanon, Lesotho, Liberia,

Luxembourg, Mali, Mexico, Monaco, Mongolia, Morocco, Nepal, Netherlands, New Zealand, Nicaragua, Norway, Pakistan, Panama, Papua New Guinea, Peru, Philippines, Poland, Romania, Rwanda, Saint Vincent and the Grenadines, Saudi Arabia, Spain, Sri Lanka, Sweden, Syria, Tonga, Tunisia, Turkey, Ukrainian S.S.R., Union of Soviet Socialist Republics, United Kingdom, Upper Volta, Uruguay, Venezuela, Vietnam, Yugoslavia, Zaire

International Convention on the Suppression and Punishment of the Crime of Apartheid: Ratifications (as of 1 July 1982)

Algeria, Bahamas, Barbados, Benin, Bulgaria, Burundi, Byelorussian S.S.R., Cameroon, Cape Verde, Central African Republic, Chad, Cuba, Czechoslovakia, Ecuador, Egypt, El Salvador, Ethiopia, Gabon, Gambia, German Democratic Republic, Ghana, Guinea, Guyana, Haiti, Hungary, India, Iraq, Jamaica, Democratic Kampuchea, Kuwait, Laos, Liberia, Libya, Madagascar, Mali, Mexico, Mongolia, Nepal, Nicaragua, Niger, Nigeria, Panama, Peru, Philippines, Poland, Qatar, Romania, Rwanda, Saint Vincent and the Grenadines, São Tomé and Príncipe, Senegal, Seychelles, Somalia, Sri Lanka, Sudan, Suriname, Syria, Tanzania, Trinidad and Tobago, Tunisia, Ukranian S.S.R., Union of Soviet Socialist Republics, United Arab Emirates, Upper Volta, Vietnam, Yugoslavia, Zaire

Convention on the Elimination of All Forms of Discrimination against Women: Ratifications (as of 1 July 1982[a])

Austria, Barbados, Bhutan, Bulgaria, Byelorussian S.S.R., Canada, Cape Verde, China, Colombia, Cuba, Czechoslovakia, Dominica, Ecuador, Egypt, El Salvador, Ethiopia, German Democratic Republic, Guyana, Haiti, Hungary, Laos, Mexico, Mongolia, Nicaragua, Norway, Panama, Philippines, Poland, Portugal, Romania, Rwanda, Saint Vincent and the Grenadines, Sri Lanka, Sweden, Ukrainian S.S.R., Union of Soviet Socialist Republics, Uruguay, Vietnam, Yugoslavia

[a]The Convention was adopted only in 1979 and entered into force in 1981; fifty-one additional states have signed but not yet ratified it.

Convention and Protocol Relating to the Status of Refugees: Ratifications (as of 1 July 1982)

Algeria, Angola, Argentina, Australia, Austria, Belgium, Benin, Bolivia, Botswana, Brazil, Burundi, Cameroon, Canada, Central African Republic, Chad, Chile, Colombia, Congo, Costa Rica, Cyprus, Denmark, Djibouti, Dominican

Republic, Ecuador, Egypt, Ethiopia, Fiji, Finland, France, Gabon, Gambia, Federal Republic of Germany, Ghana, Greece, Guinea, Guinea-Bissau, Holy See, Iceland, Iran, Ireland, Israel, Italy, Ivory Coast, Jamaica, Japan[b], Jordan[a], Kenya, Lesotho, Liberia, Liechtenstein, Luxembourg, Madagascar[a], Mali, Malta, Monaco[a], Morocco, Netherlands, New Zealand, Nicaragua, Niger, Nigeria, Norway, Panama, Paraguay, Peru[a], Philippines, Portugal, Rwanda, São Tomé and Príncipe, Senegal, Seychelles, Sierra Leone, Somalia, Spain, Sudan, Suriname, Swaziland[b], Sweden, Switzerland, Tanzania, Togo, Tunisia, Turkey, Uganda, United Kingdom, United States of America[b], Upper Volta, Uruguay, Yemen, Yugoslavia, Zaire, Zambia, Zimbabwe

[a] Ratified the Convention only.
[b] Ratified the Protocol only, which incorporates the Convention by reference.

Convention for the Suppression of the Traffic in Persons and of the Exploitation of the Prostitution of Others: Ratifications (as of 1 July 1982)

Albania, Algeria, Argentina, Belgium, Brazil, Bulgaria, Byelorussian S.S.R., Cameroon, Central African Republic, Congo, Cuba, Czechoslovakia, Djibouti, Ecuador, Egypt, Ethiopia, Finland, France, German Democratic Republic, Guinea, Haiti, Hungary, India, Iraq, Israel, Italy, Japan, Jordan, Republic of Korea, Kuwait, Laos, Libya, Malawi, Mali, Mexico, Morocco, Niger, Norway, Pakistan, Philippines, Poland, Romania, Senegal, Singapore, South Africa, Spain, Sri Lanka, Syria, Ukranian S.S.R., Union of Soviet Socialist Republics, Upper Volta, Venezuela, Yugoslavia

Adopted under the Auspices of the Organization of American States: Ratifications (as of Jan. 1983)

American Convention on Human Rights

Barbados[c], Bolivia, Colombia, Costa Rica[a,b], Dominican Republic[c], Ecuador[c], El Salvador[c], Grenada[c], Guatemala[c], Haiti, Honduras[b], Jamaica[a,c], Mexico[c], Nicaragua, Panama, Peru[b], Venezuela[a,b,c]

[a] Filed declaration accepting interstate complaints.
[b] Filed declaration accepting jurisdiction of Inter-American Court.
[c] With a declaration or reservation.

OAS Charter

Antigua and Barbuda, Argentina, Bahamas, Barbados, Bolivia, Brazil, Chile, Colombia, Costa Rica, Cuba, Dominica, Dominican Republic, Ecuador, El Salvador, Grenada, Guatemala, Haiti, Honduras, Jamaica, Mexico, Nicaragua, Panama, Paraguay, Peru, Saint Lucia, Saint Vincent and the Grenadines, Suriname, Trinidad and Tobago, United States of America, Uruguay, Venezuela

Adopted under the Auspices of the Council of Europe: Ratifications (as of 31 Dec. 1982)

The European Convention on Human Rights

Austria[a], Belgium[a], Cyprus, Denmark[a], France[a], Federal Republic of Germany[a], Greece, Iceland[a], Ireland[a], Italy[a], Liechtenstein[a], Luxembourg[a], Malta, Netherlands[a], Norway[a], Portugal[a], Spain[a], Sweden[a], Switzerland[a], Turkey, United Kingdom[a]

[a] Accepted right of individual petition under article 25.

Protocol No. 1

Austria, Belgium, Cyprus, Denmark, Federal Republic of Germany, Greece, Iceland, Ireland, Italy, Luxembourg, Malta, Netherlands, Norway, Portugal, Sweden, Switzerland, Turkey, United Kingdom

Protocol No. 4

Austria, Belgium, Denmark, France, Federal Republic of Germany, Iceland, Ireland, Italy, Luxembourg, Malta, Netherlands, Norway, Portugal, Sweden, Switzerland, United Kingdom

European Agreement Relating to Persons Participating in Proceedings of the European Commission and Court of Human Rights

Belgium, Cyprus, Federal Republic of Germany, Ireland, Italy, Luxembourg, Malta, Netherlands, Norway, Portugal, Sweden, Switzerland, United Kingdom

Appendix F
Membership of Individual Expert Bodies

Members of the Sub-Commission on Prevention of Discrimination and Protection of Minorities (terms expire in 1984)

Name of Member	*Country of Nationality*
Mr. Antonio Martinez Baez	Mexico
Ms. Elizabeth Odio Benito	Costa Rica
Mr. Marc Bossuyt	Belgium
Mr. John Carey	United States
Mr. Dumitru Ceausu	Romania
Mr. Abu Sayeed Chowdhury	Bangladesh
Ms. Erica-Irene Daes	Greece
Mr. Asbjørn Eide	Norway
Mr. Raul Ferrero	Peru
Mr. Jonas K. D. Foli	Ghana
Mr. Riyadh Aziz Hadi	Iraq
Mr. Ibrahim Jimeta	Nigeria
Mr. Louis Joinet	France
Mr. Nasser Kaddour	Syria
Mr. Ahmed Khalifa	Egypt
Mr. Syed S. A. Masud	India
Mr. L. C. Mubanga-Chipoya	Zambia
Mr. Mohamed Yousif Mudawi	Sudan
Mr. Julio Oyhanarte	Argentina
Mr. S. Shariffudin Pirzada	Pakistan
Mr. Jorge Eduardo Ritter	Panama
Mr. Vsevolod N. Sofinsky	USSR
Mr. Ivan Toševski	Yugoslavia
Ms. Halima Warzazi	Morocco
Mr. Benjamin Whitaker	United Kingdom
Mr. Fisseha Yimer	Ethiopia

Members of the Human Rights Committee

Name of Member[c]	Country of Nationality
Mr. Andrés Aguilar[a]	Venezuela
Mr. Mohammed Al Douri[a]	Iraq
Mr. Néjib Bouziri[b]	Tunisia
Mr. Joseph A. L. Cooray[b]	Sri Lanka
Mr. Vojin Dimitrijecic[b]	Yugoslavia
Mr. Felix Ermacora[a]	Austria
Mr. Roger Errera[b]	France
Sir Vincent Evans[a]	United Kingdom
Mr. Bernhard Graefrath[b]	German Democratic Republic
Mr. Vladimir Hanga[a]	Romania
Mr. Leonte Herdocia Ortega[a]	Nicaragua
Mr. Andreas V. Mavrommatis[a]	Cyprus
Mr. Anatoly Petrovich Movchan[a]	USSR
Mr. Torkel Opsahl[b]	Norway
Mr. Julio Prado Vallejo[b]	Ecuador
Mr. Walter Tarnopolsky[a]	Canada
Mr. Christian Tomuschat[b]	Federal Republic of Germany

[a] Term expires 31 December 1984.
[b] Term expires 31 December 1986.
[c] One vacancy as of mid-1983.

Members of the Committee on the Elimination of Racial Discrimination

Name of Member	Country of Nationality
Mr. Jean-Marie Apiou[b]	Upper Volta
Mr. Yuli Bahnev[a]	Bulgaria
Mr. Stanislav A. Bessonov[a]	USSR
Mr. Pedro Brin Martinez[a]	Panama
Mr. Andre Dechezelles[a]	France
Mr. Silvo Devetak[a]	Yugoslavia
Mr. Demitrois J. Evrigenis[b]	Greece
Mr. Abdel Moneim M. Ghoneim[b]	Egypt
Mr. José D. Inglés[a]	Philippines
Mr. George O. Lamptey[b]	Ghana
Mr. Erik Nettel[a]	Austria
Mr. Manuel V. Ordoñez[a]	Argentina

Mr. Karl Joseph Partsch[b]	Federal Republic of Germany
Mrs. Shanti Sadig Ali[a]	India
Mr. Agha Shahi[b]	Pakistan
Mr. Michael E. Sherifis[b]	Cyprus
Mr. Luis Valencia Rodriguez[b]	Ecuador
Mr. Shuaib Uthman Yolah[b]	Nigeria

[a] Term expires 19 January 1984.
[b] Term expires 19 January 1986.

Members of the Inter-American Commission on Human Rights

Name of Member[c]	Country of Nationality
Mr. Andrés Aguilar[b]	Venezuela
Mr. Marco Gerardo Monroy Cabra[a]	Colombia
Mr. Luis Demetrio Tinoco Castro[b]	Costa Rica
Mr. Tom J. Farer[a]	United States
Mr. Francisco Bertrand Galindo[a]	El Salvador
Mr. Cesar Sepulveda[b]	Mexico

[a] Term expires in 1983.
[b] Term expires in 1985.
[c] One vacancy as of mid-1983.

Members of the European Commission of Human Rights (in order of precedence)

Name of Member	Country of Nationality
Mr. C. A. Nørgaard[a]	Denmark
Mr. G. Sperduti[b]	Italy
Mr. J. A. Frowein[a]	Federal Republic of Germany
Mr. J. E. S. Fawcett[a]	United Kingdom
Mr. F. Ermacora[a]	Austria
Mr. M. A. Triantafyllides[c]	Cyprus
Mr. E. Busuttil[a]	Malta
Mr. T. Opsahl[a]	Norway
Mr. G. Jörundsson[b]	Iceland
Mr. G. Tenekides[b]	Greece

Mr. S. Trechsel[b]	Switzerland
Mr. B. Kiernan[b]	Ireland
Mr. M. Melchior[a]	Belgium
Mr. J. E. Branco de Sampaio[a]	Portugal
Mr. J. A. Carillo[a]	Spain
Mr. J. C. Soyer[b]	France
Mr. A. Weitzel[b]	Luxembourg
Mr. A. Seref Gözübüyük[b]	Turkey
Mr. H. Schermers[a]	Netherlands
Mr. H. Danelius[b]	Sweden
[To be elected]	Liechtenstein

[a] Term expires 17 May 1984.
[b] Term expires 17 May 1987.
[c] In accordance with article 22(6) of the Convention, Mr. Triantafyllides still sits as a member of the Commission, although his term of office has formally expired.

Members of the Committee on the Elimination of All Forms of Discrimination against Women (terms expire in 1986)

Name of Member	*Country of Nationality*
Ms. Aleksandra Pavlona Biryukova	USSR
Ms. Marie Caron	Canada
Ms. Irene R. Cortes	Philippines
Ms. Graciela Escudero Moscoso	Ecuador
Ms. Shirley Field	Guyana
Ms. Aida Gonzales Martinez	Mexico
Ms. Luvsandanzangyn Ider	Mongolia
Ms. Zagorka Ilic	Yugoslavia
Ms. Vinitha Jayasinghe	Sri Lanka
Ms. Vanda Lamm	Hungary
Ms. Raquel Maledo de Sheppart	Uruguay
Ms. Lia Patino de Martines	Panama
Ms. Gian Minquian	China
Ms. Maria Margarida de Rego da Costa Salema Moura Ribeiro	Portugal
Ms. Landrada Mukayiranga	Rwanda
Ms. Nguyen Ngoc Dung	Vietnam
Mr. Johan Nordenfeldt	Sweden
Ms. Edith Oeser	German Democratic Republic
Ms. Vesselina V. Peytcheva	Bulgaria

Ms. Maria Regent-Lechowicz   Poland
Ms. Rakel Surlien   Norway
Ms. Mervat Tallawy   Egypt
Ms. Esther Veliz Diaz de Villal-   Cuba
villa

Contributors

Richard B. Bilder is Professor of Law at the University of Wisconsin, where he teaches courses in public and private international law. He is the author of *Managing the Risks of International Agreement* (1981) and of numerous articles in the field of international and foreign relations law. Professor Bilder was an attorney for a number of years in the Office of the Legal Adviser of the U.S. State Department; served as Senior Rapporteur at the 1968 Montreal Assembly for Human Rights; and was Carnegie Lecturer at the Hague Academy of International Law in 1975. He is currently Vice-President of the American Society of International Law, a member (since 1972) of the Board of Editors of the American Journal of International Law, and a member of the Advisory Council of the International Human Rights Law Group.

Theo C. van Boven was Director of the UN's Division of Human Rights from 1977 to 1982 and is currently on the Faculty of Law at the University of Limburg. Prior to assuming that position, he worked with the Department of International Organizations of the Netherlands Ministry of Foreign Affairs, serving as a member of the UN Human Rights Commission and ECOSOC and, in his personal capacity, as a member of the Sub-Commission on Prevention of Discrimination and Protection of Minorities. Mr. van Boven received an M.A. in Comparative Law from Southern Methodist University and Master and Doctor of Law degrees from the University of Leiden.

Kevin Boyle is Professor of Law at University College, Galway, Ireland, where he is in the process of establishing a Centre for the Study of Human Rights. Formerly Senior Lecturer in Law at Queen's University, Belfast, Professor Boyle is coauthor of two books on the effect of emergency legislation on the criminal justice system in Northern Ireland. He has represented several clients in proceedings before the European Commission of Human Rights, on issues that have included state responsibility for torture, the rights of homosexuals, and prison conditons.

David Carliner is Chairman of the International Human Rights Law Group and an attorney with the firm of Carliner & Gordon, Washington, D.C. A member of the Board of Directors of the International League for Human Rights and the National Advisory Council of Amnesty International–U.S.A., Chairman of the

Immigration and Nationality Committee of the Administrative Law Section of the American Bar Association, and former General Counsel to the American Civil Liberties Union, Mr. Carliner is the author of *The Rights of Aliens*.

Joseph T. Eldridge has been Director of the Washington Office on Latin America since its founding in 1974 by a coalition of church and other nongovernmental groups. The Reverend Mr. Eldridge is a minister of the United Methodist Church and served as a missionary in Chile from 1970 to 1973. He received his M.A. degree in Latin American Studies from American University and a Master of Theology degree from the Perkins School of Theology of Southern Methodist University.

Dana D. Fischer has recently edited a book on the International Covenants and written another on the Human Rights Committee, both under the auspices of the American Society of International Law. She has written several articles and books on human rights and the International Court of Justice and is presently an Associate of the Inter-American Institute of Human Rights in San Jose, Costa Rica. Formerly Assistant Professor of Political Science at George Washington University, Ms. Fischer received her M.A. and Ph.D degrees in Political Science from the University of Washington.

Richard Gittleman served in the Peace Corps for two years in Zaire and attended the 1981 Organization of African Unity summit in Nairobi, Kenya, at which the African Charter on Human and Peoples' Rights was adopted. He received his J.D. degree from Washington College of Law, American University, in 1982 and was an intern with the International Human Rights Law Group in 1981–82.

Hurst Hannum is Executive Director of the Procedural Aspects of International Law Institute and a consultant in the areas of public international and human rights law. He has written numerous articles on international human rights and has acted as counsel in cases filed before the United Nations, European Commission of Human Rights, and Inter-American Commission on Human Rights. Mr. Hannum received his A.B. and J.D. degrees from the University of California, Berkeley, and serves on the Board of Directors of the International Human Rights Law Group and Amnesty International–U.S.A.

Menno Kamminga, Assistant Legal Adviser of Amnesty International, has represented Amnesty International at the UN Commission on Human Rights and at its Sub-Commission on Prevention of Discrimination and Protection of Minorities since 1979.

Richard B. Lillich is Howard W. Smith Professor of Law at the University of Virginia and President of the Procedural Aspects of International Law Institute. He has written widely in the fields of human rights, international claims, and other areas of public and private international law, and is co-author of the leading coursebook in human rights, *International Human Rights: Problems of Law and Policy* (1979). Professor Lillich served as the first Chairman of the International Human Rights Law Group and presently is Chairman of the Committee on Human Rights of the International Law Association.

Stephen Marks is a staff member of the Division of Human Rights and Peace of UNESCO and was formerly with the International Institute of Human Rights in Strasbourg. He received his B.A. degree from Stanford University, is a graduate of the Institut des Hautes Etudes Internationales of the University of Paris, and holds a French State doctorate in law. Mr. Marks has written numerous articles on human rights, development, disarmament, and related topics.

Robert E. Norris received his Ph.D. In Ibero-American Studies from the University of New Mexico and his J.D. from the University of Texas Law School. He served for several years as Senior Specialist in Human Rights with the Inter-American Commission on Human Rights, has been a consultant with the UN Division of Human Rights in Geneva, and is co-author of *Human Rights: The Inter-American System*.

Nigel S. Rodley, the Legal Adviser of Amnesty International, is also part-time lecturer in law at the London School of Economics and Political Science. A former law professor and UN official, he has written widely on international law and organizations, particularly in the field of international protection of human rights.

Dinah L. Shelton is Associate Professor of Law at the University of Santa Clara (California) and received her J.D. degree from the University of California, Berkeley. Among other activities, she is a member of the Executive Council of the American Society of International Law and of the International Institute of Human Rights in Strasbourg. She is currently preparing a major project on the effectiveness of international human rights procedures.

Lee Swepston is a graduate of the University of North Carolina and Columbia University Law School. After a period with the International Commission of Jurists, he joined the International Labor Office, where he is an official in the International Labor Standards Department and Regional Adviser for International Labor Standards for the English-Speaking Countries of Africa.

Jiri Toman is Deputy Director of the Henry Dunant Institute in Geneva, a research and study center affiliated with the International Red Cross, and Lecturer at the Geneva University. He holds the degrees of JUDr. (Prague) and Dr. ès sciences politiques (Geneva) and was formerly Assistant Professor of Law at the Charles University in Prague.

David Weissbrodt is Professor of Law at the University of Minnesota, where he teaches a seminar on international human rights law and supervises law students in various clinical projects on human rights. Professor Weissbrodt received his law degree from the University of California at Berkeley. After graduation he received a Robbins Fellowship from the University of California Law School for work at the International Commission of Jurists in Geneva. Professor Weissbrodt has represented, and/or served as an officer of, a number of international nongovernmental human rights organizations. His scholarship has included articles on the work of these human rights organizations, on human rights treaties, international fact finding, and international trial observers.

Amy Young-Anawaty has been Executive Director of the International Human Rights Law Group since its establishment in 1978 and also has served as Vice-Chairman of the Human Rights Committee of the International Law Section of the American Bar Association. She has taught human rights seminars as Lecturer at the University of Virginia School of Law and Adjunct Professor at American University's Washington College of Law. Ms. Young-Anawaty received her J.D. degree from American University and LL.M from the University of Virginia.